Sleeping Island

Sleeping Island

A Journey to the Edge of the Barrens

P.G. Downes

Foreword, notes and revised
photo section by R.H. Cockburn

HERON DANCE PRESS

HERON DANCE PRESS
Hummingbird Lane
179 Rotax Road
N. Ferrisburg, VT 05473
www.herondance.org

First published by Coward-McCann Inc., New York and Longman, Green
and Company, Toronto in 1943. A later edition was published in 1988.
This *Heron Dance* Edition was published in 2006.

Cover art by Roderick MacIver
Interior photographs courtesy R.H. Cockburn.

This book printed on Rolland Cascade New Life recycled paper.
Printed and bound in the United States.

For information about special discounts for bulk purchases,
please contact Ingram Publisher Services at 1-800-961-7698

Downes, P.G. (Prentice Gilbert), 1909–1959

ISBN: 1-933937-03-3

Sleeping Island

	Foreword to the *Heron Dance* Edition	ix
1	*North, Where?*	1
2	*Pelican*	17
3	*Reindeer Lake*	47
4	*Brochet*	61
5	*The Cochrane*	73
6	*The Little Lakes*	105
7	*Fort Hall Lake and the Kasmere*	127
8	*Nueltin Lake*	155
9	*Windy*	181
10	*Days in the Barrens*	213
11	*South Flight*	235
	Notes to the *Heron Dance* Edition	255

Foreword to the Heron Dance *Edition*

Prentice G. Downes was born in New Haven, Connecticut, in 1909 and was educated at the Kent School and Harvard, where he graduated *cum laude* in psychology in 1933. That year he accepted a teaching position with Belmont Hill School, a private boys' school on the outskirts of Boston, beginning an association that would end only with his death. He taught Latin, French, and English, but earned special acclaim from generations of students for his courses in history, geography, geology, and physiography. By 1936-37, when he did postgraduate work in cartography and geologic illustration at Harvard, the pattern of his prewar life was established.

Downes, an avid outdoorsman, had long been susceptible to northward yearnings, and in 1935 he made the first of the summer trips that were to mean so much to him and would lead to his becoming a northern figure and author of considerable stature. That summer he collected Montagnais and Naskapi lore on the North Shore of the lower St. Lawrence, an activity he resumed in 1936 before making an Eastern Arctic voyage in the Hudson's Bay Company ship *Nascopie* from Montreal to Churchill, after which he canoed, with a Cree companion, from Pelican Narrows, Saskatchewan, to Reindeer Lake. He returned to both these latter places in

1937, primarily to gather Cree and Chipewyan lore; then, once more aboard *Nascopie*, sponsored by the New England Museum of Natural History, he traveled to Baffin and Ellesmere islands and the Boothia Peninsula, where he collected geologic specimens and Eskimo artifacts. Nineteen thirty-eight found him paddling with Indians from He a la Crosse to Waterways, then on alone, in a 13'4" canoe, to Fort Fitzgerald; continuing by boat to Eldorado on Great Bear Lake, he eventually flew to the raw boomtown of Yellowknife before returning south by boat. But his most cherished trip was that of 1939, the one described in *Sleeping Island*.

The old North so irresistible to Downes—"the north," to use his words, "of no time, of game, of Indians, Eskimos, of unlimited space and freedom"—had dwindled and was in its final few years. The transformations that followed the Great War had been dramatic, had altered many seemingly timeless features of the northern way of life, and brought to a virtual end much that had been indigenous to the lives of both natives and whites. The bush plane was by now a fixture; outboard motors propelled freight canoes that only a few years earlier would have been paddled by men; great mining operations had been established, as had commercial fisheries; the Hudson's Bay Company's former far-reaching monopoly had been crippled by rivals and by a proliferation of free traders; and the tentacles of bureaucracy, both federal and provincial, had stretched to many a spot that hitherto had known only the authority of the Hudson's Bay Company, a missionary or two, and an infrequent Mounted Policeman.

Yet for all the changes the postwar years had brought in, there remained much that appeared everlasting. Indians, Christianized though nearly all of them were and despite the weakening of their cultures, held to their immemorial myths and skills. Among white trappers, traders, prospectors, missionaries, and policemen, feats of wilderness travel, by canoe in summer and with dogs in winter, were celebrated and remembered, and a man could still make his name by the distance he could run in thirty-below weather or by the weight of the load he could carry on a portage. The demands and hardships of climatic extremes, isolation, and tremendous physical challenges created among true northerners an attitude almost contemptuous toward those from "outside" who were strangers to such experience. These characteristics were still pronounced in the Reindeer Lake country and in the back-of-beyond reaching north and east from it, a region which in 1939 remained all but unmapped and would stay so until aerial mapping came fully into its own after 1945. Here lay Downes's destination, the Chipewyans' *Nu-thel-tin-tu-eh*, Sleeping Island Lake.

Downes always kept a journal while on the trail, and the narrative that unfolds in *Sleeping Island* derives directly from the four battered diaries and route book of sketch maps he kept during his 1939 journey. Compelling in themselves—the meticulously detailed entries are accompanied by cartoons, landscape drawings, and the remains of crushed mosquitoes—these small brown notebooks also serve to substantiate the regard in which *Sleeping Island* came to be held by northerners familiar with the settlements, the people, and the territory visited by Downes. What they most admired in the book were those of its qualities that were all too often missing from outsiders' accounts of the North: accuracy of knowledge, a close, sympathetic interest in both native and white inhabitants, and, above all, honesty; they found the absence of egotism and exaggeration particularly refreshing. A comparison of the diaries and the book proves the soundness of this judgment. Beginning with chapter 2, the narrative is faithful to the day by day experiences recorded in the journal. When quoting from his diaries, Downes improves upon his grammar and syntax, but otherwise reproduces exactly what he wrote at the time.

As a narrative of an arduous canoe trip, *Sleeping Island* has few equals. Downes was fortunate to have traveled when he did, into little-known, unmapped country where natives still lived on the land and there remained a tangible aura of wilderness mystery. Nowadays, more than sixty years on, the book kindles nostalgia. Here are vivid descriptions of trial and error on rivers and lakes, of poling and paddling, of sweat-drenched portaging; columns of smoke rise from bush fires on the horizon, across miles of water; deserted trading posts decay along abandoned trade routes; canoe loads of Chipewyans appear suddenly, down from the Barrens; foul weather and windbound camps are followed by days of surpassing beauty; depression and exhilaration, companionship and separation, are tellingly conveyed. It took Downes and his partner twenty-two days to canoe from Brochet, at the north end of Reindeer Lake, to their destination, the HBC's Nueltin Lake post on the Windy River, Northwest Territories. Canoe men today, armed with good maps, carrying freeze-dried food, skilled in white-water techniques, and paddling lighter, nearly indestructible synthetic canoes, have followed Downes's route in less time, but not, one supposes, with anything approximating his sensation of discovery and accomplishment.

Were *Sleeping Island* simply an account of a canoe trip, however, it would not have become the classic it is. By the time he set off for the Cote Nord in 1935, Downes had collected a library of books on northern exploration and travel; these excited his imagination, his wanderlust, and his romantic desire for adventure. But all of Downes's travels were invigorated also by his intellectual curiosity, by his consuming interests in fur trade history, geography, geology, and Indian cultures, interests that animate and enrich the book. The following occurrence illuminates this side of the man. While crossing Great Slave Lake in 1938, he became acquainted with George M. Douglas, who had canoed to the Coppermine in 1911, and who's superb narrative of that journey, *Lands Forlorn* (1914), he'd read. A few days later, at Fort Smith, they met Charles Camsell, himself a former hard traveler and famous northern figure, and Douglas introduced Downes with these words: "Dr. Camsell, I wish to introduce Mr. Downes: he knows more of the history of the north country than J.B. [Tyrrell] himself." It was this propensity in Downes—his unquenchable curiosity, his passion to learn all he could—that gives *Sleeping Island* so much of its flavor and appeal.

As fascinating as Downes found the history of exploration and the fur trade, and as committed as he was to enlarging his understanding of geography and geology, nothing mattered as much to him as the legends, myths, and ways of the Indians he encountered and with whom he traveled whenever possible. "I have never traveled with Indians and not found it a pleasure," he writes, and he was disappointed at having to make this, his most challenging trip, with a white man as his companion. Pages of his journals are filled with the lore and recollections he collected from venerable Indians, particularly those of the Peter Ballantyne Band of Crees at Pelican Narrows. He was always to regret that he did not devote more of *Sleeping Island* to such matters. Even so, there is much herein of native customs and beliefs, and it is impossible to read these pages without appreciating Downes's affinity for a people whose centuries-old heritage was so soon to be irretrievably lost.

It was this affinity that led Downes to return to Pelican Narrows following the events described in *Sleeping Island*; these anticlimactic weeks are referred to only glancingly in the book.

There, as summer waned, he joined a party of Cree canoe men freighting goods from Pelican to Amisk Lake and back. Returning in darkness on September 2, "we rounded the point and the nickering campfires of Pelican appeared. We were soon in." Stepping ashore, he learned that Germany had invaded Poland. "It is too incredible and insane," he wrote in his diary; "Better to be back in the Barrens among civilized people—Chips and Huskies."

Downes revisited the territory north of Brochet in 1940, his purpose being to retrace the route of J.B. Tyrrell's epic exploration of 1894 to Kasba Lake and the Kazan River. Again hoping to travel with an Indian partner, he had to settle for an elderly white one, and the result was that the enterprise failed on the boulder-choked Little Partridge River. Nevertheless, this proved a rewarding journey, for on their return, Downes encountered the southward migration of the Barren Land caribou and met the legendary recluse "Eskimo Charlie."

Downes's first marriage, in 1940, and the war brought his northern wanderings to a halt. *Sleeping Island* was written in 1941–42 and was published in 1943 by Coward–McCann of New York; a British edition, with differing pagination, was published in 1944. The misleading, but alluring, subtitle invented by his publisher, with its emphasis on "The Great

Barren Lands," angered Downes, whose trip had brought him only to the edge of the Barrens and who had no wish to misrepresent his accomplishment. His original, typically honest subtitle was "The Narrative of a summer's Travel in Northern Manitoba and the Northwest Territories." Nor was he altogether pleased with the choices made from the photographs he'd submitted or with the loss of definition some of them suffered when enlarged. The photographs selected for this fresh edition of the book are drawn from the hundreds of black-and-white pictures and color transparencies he took during his voyages north from Pelican Narrows. The best of the 1943 edition photographs have been kept; those new to this edition have been chosen with a view to depicting more evocatively than before the men and scenes of his travels.

It was unfortunate, of course, that *Sleeping Island* appeared when it did, at a time when there were such larger claims on the public's attention and when many of those who would have bought it were overseas. Although published to enthusiastic reviews, it was never reprinted.

From 1942 to 1945, Downes served as chief of the Target Research Department of the U.S. Army Map Service, compiling bombing charts for both the European and Pacific theatres, and was also seconded to Air Force Intelligence. In 1944 he was appointed to the National Research Council, Division of Cartographic Techniques. Throughout these years, he longed for the North, and he corresponded steadily with men he'd met on his journeys.

When, at war's end, Downes's first marriage broke up, he lived for five months as a hermit on a Vermont mountainside before being invited to work with the eminent cartographer Erwin Raisz at Harvard's Institute of Geographical Exploration. In 1947 he resumed his teaching career at Belmont Hill. That summer, after an absence of six years, he returned to northern Saskatchewan and made what was to be his final canoe trip, "a sort of dream trip, alone, just visiting Indians," from Amisk Lake to Lac la Ronge. Roads were being pushed northward, postwar modernity was in the air, and he was now thirty-eight. Still, the old hunger lingered, and his 1947 trip journal reveals that he hoped to reach remote parts of the North by canoe in the years ahead. But 1948 found him in the Aleutian Islands, drawing maps and investigating volcanoes for the Office of Naval Research; that summer was a miserable one for Downes, who came to so detest the man with whom he was teamed that he nearly murdered him.

Then, in 1949, Downes remarried. The responsibilities of an inspiriting marriage and two children, coupled with regret at the transformations that were occurring in the "new" North, marked the conclusion of his wilderness journeying. He made one last ethnological and nostalgic trip to The Pas and Amisk Lake by jeep in 1951. Otherwise, the final decade of his life was devoted to his family and to teaching, writing, and research into the life of the white Indian John Tanner. Vigorous and eager to the end, Downes died of a heart attack in 1959.

Early in that last year of his life, asked to contribute autobiographical notes for a school reunion, Downes wrote this of his wanderings in the Far North:

> *I liked that life and I liked the people there. I saw a lot of it just as the old north was vanishing; the north of no time, of game, of Indians, Eskimos, of unlimited space and freedom....I remember one time after a dreadful trip, camping on the edge of the tree line, again it was one of those indescribable smoky, bright-hazy days one sometimes gets in the high latitudes. I had hit the caribou migration and there was lots of meat; it was a curious spot, for all the horizon seemed to fall away from where I squatted, and I said to myself: Well, I suppose I shall never be so happy again.*

In the course of editing Prentice Downes's journals for publication and preparing this new edition of his book, I have heard from many persons who knew Downes and remember him well. As their letters offer vivid glimpses of his character and personality, a few such recollections can be allowed to further introduce him. A former colleague of his at Belmont Hill remarks that Downes "has always had the reputation from those who sat in his classes as 'the best teacher who ever came to Belmont Hill.' He had a dramatic flair in the classroom, knew an awful lot about everything, and kept the young men in front of him spellbound.... He certainly was an interesting man. He would disappear for the summer and usually get back late to school in the fall, with full beard and Eskimo jackets, chewing tobacco, and an odd assortment of paraphernalia.... He was a very democratic person; I was in awe of him because I was younger and he knew so much about life, books, and just about any topic you would want to bring up, but he was down-to-earth and never made you feel that he was any smarter than you were. I really respected him for that."

So did a young Anglican missionary and schoolteacher who knew Downes at Pelican Narrows: "P.G. helped me deal with my loneliness and my frustrations.... He was older and wiser than I was and he took time to encourage and befriend me. P.G. was the sort of person who saw the North and the Indians much in the same way that I did.... Probably we were both romantics with a keen sense of adventure who could not separate the Indians from the land and in a real sense had a great affection for both."

"My recollection of him," wrote a Hudson's Bay Company trader who met him at Brochet in 1937, "is of a short, compact man with tousled hair and a ready smile, a really likable chap. He was acutely interested in finding out all he could about the country, and I feel sure that anything he wrote of his travels would have been factual. So many people who visit the North for short periods and then write about it draw on their imaginations far more than on fact. P.G. was not one of them. I am sure everyone who met him accepted him as being génuinely interested in recording things accurately."

Those who met him north of 53° were impressed also by his toughness. As Downes explains in *Sleeping Island*, he had disciplined himself to travel light, and in the vernacular of his day he was known as a 'hard' traveler. That he deserved this tag is made clear in the following memory of him, from the pen of a Mounted Policeman with whom he descended the Reindeer River at summer's end in 1940 after returning from his failed attempt to canoe to Kasba Lake: "When I met Downes I found that he was on his way South, so we got together, rode in my [motorized] canoe and towed his. I must say I don't know how he managed the summer. His clothes were in tatters. His pack was very small and light, so he had to be tough. His food consisted of a dried bladder of barren land caribou which held about a half-pound of tea. He had another greasy bag which contained some jerky. Nothing else."

Finally, P.G. Downes in the flesh. Soft-spoken, blond-haired, with a sense of humor remarked among his northern friends, he stood 5' 7", weighed about 155 pounds, and was strongly built—he had "a short-set neck, great for the portage," says a man who knew him in those days. A ring of stars was tattooed around his left wrist, and he bore three other tattoos, one of them a dragon. His eyesight was wretched and he wore steel-framed spectacles always. Another friend, after recalling that "the only clothing he took into the bush was what he had on his back," goes on to say, "I remember asking him if he had a second pair of glasses, as he must have been quite blind without them. His reply was that he did not need a second pair, so did not carry them." In the pages that follow, nowhere does Downes so much as mention what would have been a persistent irritant and handicap: his lenses blurring over from rain, humidity, or the sluicing sweat of portaging under a tump-line. His ruggedness, while admirable, was not uncommon up north; it's being accompanied by a questing, tireless intelligence was what set him apart, made his reputation among northern men, and gave us this book.

✳   ✳   ✳

I wish to express my thanks to Mrs. E.G. Downes, whose invaluable help and unflagging encouragement made this new edition of Sleeping Island possible. I am also most appreciative of the timely and generous assistance provided me by the following institutions and individuals: the Hudson's Bay Company Archives; the Hudson's Bay Company Library; The University of New Brunswick's School of Graduate Studies and Research; W.E. Brown; William W. Buxton; the late Fr. A. Chamberiand, OMI; Bryan Clements; Mrs. G.M. Douglas; Roger F. Duncan; S.W. Horrall, RCMP historian; the late Archie Hunter; A. Wallace Laird; the late L.A. Learmonth; Kathy Lipsett; R.J. LeBlanc; George Luste; the late Dr. R.M. MacCharles; the late R. Glenn Madill; Allan Meadows; Alex Milliken; Phil Reader; Maurice Renard; Henry B. Sawyer, Jr.; Hugh Stewart; and C.E. Wenzel.

R.H. COCKBURN

ABOUT THE EDITOR

Robert Cockburn is a professor Emeritus of English at The University of New Brunswick in Fredericton. His writings on the North have appeared in *Appalachia*, *Arctic*, *The Beaver*, *Fram*, and *Northward Journal*. He is the contributing editor of *Toward Magnetic North: The Oberholtzer-Magee 1912 Canoe Journey to Hudson Bay* (2000).

"Tell me. Father, what is this white man's Heaven?"

"It is the most beautiful place in the world."

"Tell me, Father, is it like the land of the little trees when the ice has left the lakes? Are the great musk oxen there? Are the hills covered with flowers? There will I see the caribou everywhere I look? Are the lakes blue with the sky of summer? Is every net full of great, fat whitefish? Is there room for me in this land, like our land, the Barrens? Can I camp anywhere and not find that someone else has camped? Can I feel the wind and be like the wind? Father, if your Heaven is not all these, leave me alone in my land, the land of the little sticks."

—From the dialogue between a Dog-Rib Indian and a priest. Warburton Pike reported a slightly different version in his The Barren Ground of Northern Canada.

CHAPTER 1

North, Where?

I suppose it is pure heresy to open an account of a few months' wandering in the sub-Arctic of Canada with the statement that I was not particularly sure where I was going. Expeditions to the far North are, whether large or small, by convention prefaced with a staggering list of paraphernalia and minutiae, not to mention shy reference to weeks and months of painstaking plotting and planning to defeat the great empty spaces.

Unfortunately, I cannot in honesty offer any such foreword. I do know that, with the warm days of June, I became daily more restless and at last picked up my pack-sack, which had lain in the closet practically unpacked since the preceding summer when I had come down from the North, purchased a secondhand camera, some film, and set out.

The years I have spent roaming in various parts of Canada's vast northern empire have always prompted the question among my acquaintances of "why?" Why do you go back year after year to this forlorn world of rock and tundra, of millions of mosquitoes and no fresh vegetables, of Indians and caribou, of lakes and rivers?

Once again, in honesty, I find it very hard to give an answer, which is satisfying to the logical and kindly questioner. I am immediately embarrassed by the obvious fact that the

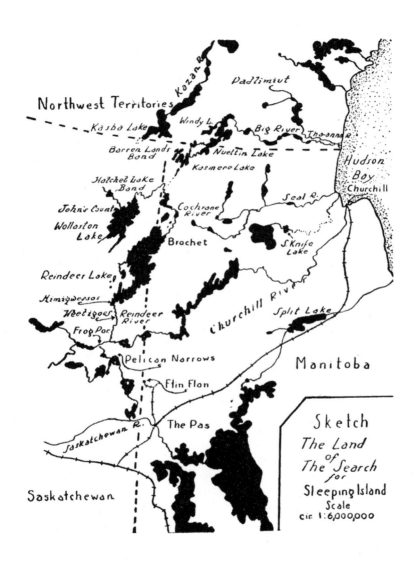

Northwest Territories

Kazan R.

Padlimiut

Kasba Lake   Windy L.   Big River   Thoenne R.

Barren Lands   Nueltin Lake   Hudson
Bond   Bay

Kasmere Lake   Churchill

Hatchet Lake
Bond   Seal R.

John's Count   Cochrane
Wollaston   River
Lake   S. Knife
Brochet   Lake

Reindeer Lake

Kimiqwessos

Keetigoes   Reindeer
River   Churchill River   Split Lake
Frog Por

Pelican Narrows   Manitoba

Flin Flon

Saskatchewan R.   The Pas   Sketch
                                  The Land
                                  of
                                  The Search
                                  for
Saskatchewan   Sleeping Island
                                  Scale
                                  cir. 1:6,000,000

questioner desires a reason, which, in his mind, is sufficiently worthwhile to justify the inconvenience of life in the world of the North, which he has imagined. There are innumerable answers one might give to this persistent and annoying "why." But it has always seemed to me that, whatever I might say, I was partially dishonest for I gave an incomplete answer and probably not the true one at all. The very apparent reason to myself is that I like it there in the land of the little trees, I like the people, I am happy there. But to any reasonable person this is very inadequate.

Sometimes I have collected folklore and legends, or have mapped routes and lakes. Always there has been the study of topography; once there was the collecting of data on various geological phenomena. There is even, in moments of profound introspection, the thought that among my ancestors were followers of Boone through Cumberland Gap and later a "forty-niner." There is a background of reading of almost all the historical northern accounts. There was a certain afternoon, in a certain living room, with pale winter sunlight faintly illuminating the dark cavernous interior of a brownstone house on Marlborough Street in Boston, where a very old man reminisced about his own lone wanderings thirty years before in the still unknown heart of Labrador.[1]

All these things, no doubt, are answers. But, obstinately, I am quite sure that without any or all of them this particular June would have found me once more leaving my classroom behind, bound North.

Just before leaving, I was given an unexpected opportunity to do some physiographic work in Mexico. In this attractive invitation I found my intention to go back again to the North considerably challenged. I decided to leave the decision to the days to come on the train. With no struggle at all the North triumphed, as in a few short days I found myself in Winnipeg.

A week before I started out, with the notion that I might be back in the Barrens I had wired an importing house in Montreal for a new rifle, which they were to send on to Winnipeg. It was thus necessary to go to Winnipeg; and once in Winnipeg, by force of long habit the only direction in which it seemed possible to continue was north.

The customs inspector who examined my belongings in their stout pack-sack did not have a very tiring search. There was my feather sleeping bag, a light eight-pound one; my ax, secured at Ile á la Crosse—it had been manufactured prior to the year 1811 and was very serviceable; a copper tea pail of unknown age; two shirts, one with the tail badly scorched; a medical kit consisting of a small bottle of iodine done up in adhesive tape, and surgical needles; a seven-by-nine piece of balloon silk, which I used as a tent and canoe sail; some twine, nails, trolling hooks, moccasins; a collapsible frying pan and spoon; a jack-knife; and, of infinite importance, a heavy soft leather strap with a broad head band called the "tump-line," by which all one's belongings are carried.

The outfit may appear boastfully small and inadequate, but it was the result of much hard discipline in previous years. The North is vast; distances are great. To travel at all, one must travel fast. To travel fast, one must travel light. To travel alone or with Indians one must travel like an Indian. And also, unless one is to advertise breakfast foods or tobacco or is representing a great foundation, a schoolteacher's salary does not encourage extravagance.

Obviously, there were a number of small addenda, which I was prepared to add en route. Ammunition and food would come later. Notebooks, leather-bound and of the best quality, and a small sewing kit I already had secured, as well as camera film and a fine pair of binoculars.

But to come back to my vague intentions and destination: The previous summer I had wandered deep in the northwestern part of Canada's Northwest Territories in the magnificent Mackenzie River and Great Bear Lake country, and had returned via Great Slave Lake and the furious and optimistic gold-strike camp of Yellowknife, making a last camp on the banks of the Slave River near Fort Smith in latitude sixty. From the moment I boiled my last pail of tea and climbed on the plane bound for the "outside" in late September, I had completely accepted the thought that next year I would be back in the North, and through the ensuing months it did not occur to me to work up any particular notion as to just where it would be. That definitive object was to me a matter of circumstance to be decided when the actual moment of departure should arrive.

The North is so huge—contrary to a common United States notion; Alaska and Greenland do not coalesce—and contains so many intriguing places that it is very hard to plan a particular objective. In the late night during the previous winter as I lay listening to the freight trains rumbling hollowly through the dark, headed west, my thoughts would swing about like the needle of a compass: northwest to Great Bear Lake, that great gloomy inland sea with its August ice, the radium mine, its flakes of leaf-like silver ore; the mighty Mackenzie and the dark towering Nahanni mountains, mountains-of-the-strangers, and the legend of the tropical valley which lay behind them; the muttering powerful Slave River, which grumbles with the deepest voice of any river I have known the Slave with its fragrance of the black poplar, the Bard of the voyageurs. Then the needle might swing a little east to Reindeer Lake with its thousands of islands—its islands which seem to march like a procession of "mistapeo" giants—and the time an Indian and I were starving and ate seagulls disagreeable entree! Swinging more north, my thoughts would turn to the silent great Eastern Arctic: the Northwest Passage, the great glaciers of Ellesmere Island, the crags and mighty turrets of the Baffin Island coastal range. With the instability and capriciousness of a compass nearing the magnetic pole, I would swerve then to thoughts of Hudson Bay and the pack ice in mid-August, the strange lava-topped islands of the east coast, or the low blue line of the west shore. Following a brief vision of the site of the magnetic pole, Boothia Peninsula, would come flashes of the Labrador coast—the mighty and grim home of the spirits, the Torn-gat range rearing fantastic brown peaks four thousand feet above the cold, gray, berg-infested waters of the Labrador Current—and a lesser host of small pictures: the Eskimo with the derby hat, the one with the wooden leg, and the old man who was disconsolate because the trading post had run out of candy. Then in my mind would be pictured again the thick, dense spruces of the North Shore of the Gulf; the great salmon leaping in the Ste. Marguerite; the Montagnais

Indians in their beehive-like *cabanes*, sitting about the tea pail with a few mighty hunters from the interior, Naskapis, and gravely discussing the predicament of one respected Indian who was annoyed at the presence of a pair of disembodied legs which he saw running around in his tent one evening.

But worst of all were the thoughts *not* of these places and incidents, not these recollections of familiar spots and friends, but thoughts of the other places, the other people yet to be seen before it was too late.

Is there really placer gold in the river above the big canyon on the South Nahanni? Are there trees like inverted carrots far out in the Barrens north of Kasba Lake? Does the ice actually stay all the year around on a lake so large no one knows its size—Hicoligjuak?[2] 'Is it true that musk oxen still are roaming in Boothia and maybe between the Dubawnt and the Kazan? What about the little band of "pagan" Indians on the Water Hen River. Do they still practice "Coosapitchigan," the shaking of the tent, calling in their ancient spirits to assist them? Why had the Eskimos at Sugluk claimed that they had seen the same three-toed great tracks, which had been so seriously reported by white men twenty years before at a spot six hundred miles away? Where did the platinum-bearing ore come from that the Bernier expedition picked up in Baffin Island in 1911? And the caribou—would I ever see the great migration, *la foule*, "the throng"?

Then under all of these and a thousand more was the constant, intangible, but powerful pull of friendship. How could I let another summer go by without chatting once again with my friend the Cree Indian, Solomon, or talking of "the old days long ago" with the medicine man, Adam? How could I bear to ignore the old Cree, Norman's, plea, "Come see me once more, my grandson, for all of these things are almost forgotten now and I shall die in two more winters."? How could I resist going back and hearing from his own lips the gusty tales of Magloire, the ancient relic of the once proud fur brigades? Could I ignore Joseph and Roslaine and the smell of the lard, and forget that when I was alone and hungry these had showed me the faded photograph of their dead child and given me something to eat and said: "You see we have nothing now, come into the forest with us." How could I not go back to the big lake, where one evening, with a sizzling moose heart on a stick, an old Chipewyan said, "Stay with us. It is strange for one so white, but you know some things that only old men should know. Maybe you are a born-twice and used to be here among us once?"

And always in these thoughts, and just before sleep, it seemed to me that there were so many faces: Indians—Crees, Naskapis, Montagnais, Caribou-Eaters, Bear-Lakers, Dog-Ribs; white men—prospectors, trappers, traders, Mounted Police—so many and so many and always a stiff brief handshake and, "You will come back?"

Even as I went west on the train, I postponed my final decision until my arrival in Winnipeg, where I might hear something of peculiar interest, which would determine my course. In this vagueness there was, however, one beacon, which was unwavering—the Barrens, back to the Barrens.

The Barrens, or as they are more properly called, the Barren Lands, is a name for the vast area above the sixtieth parallel crossing in a great arc northwest from Hudson Bay to the mouth of the Mackenzie. It is the North in which the endless spruce forest at last grudgingly gives way to dwarfed clumps and then to a vast land of rolling, treeless moss and sedge—the tundra. Just why this desolate frozen sea of emptiness, this desperate land of sullen, gray rock should call me so, I hesitate to analyze. Possibly the narrative may give some hint. But I knew that whatever my course, somehow I would get back to the Barrens.

I have never been particularly fond of Winnipeg. It is a fine, broad city. But in my mind it is associated with leaving the North or with frightfully hot weather—the great wide streets, the blinding sun of late June, and later the lonely feeling one has in coming down from the North into a large city and among people. This feeling an Indian who likewise had come to the city once aptly expressed to me. The thing that astonished him most was: "How can so many people live where there is nothing to hunt, and how can so many white men walk by each other without saying one word?" Winnipeg has one admirable feature, however—a multitude of cool beer parlors strategically placed so that one can just make one's way from one to the next and feel that each is a refuge in the nick of time from heat prostration. Then too, even in this thriving metropolis of agricultural man, there is a tiny park and the remnant of a gray gate, the relic of Fort Garry. Here one can sit in the shade and contemplate this hallowed spot of the North of long ago, all that is left of a mighty and historic past; through this portal once passed wayfarers from the North like oneself, the humble as well as the mighty titans whose resolution and energy created an empire of fur.

Certainly any mention of Winnipeg would be incomplete without reference to my abode of a few hours, one of the most extraordinary structures on the continent, the Empress Hotel. This remarkable accumulation of grim gray stone has served from time immemorial as a refuge for Northern men and in particular the servants of the Hudson's Bay Company. Legend has it that this hotel had the first elevator west of the Great Lakes. After one ride in it, one is inclined to move that boundary to the shores of the Atlantic. The groaning and erratic contraption is operated by an enormous brass wheel, which is cranked furiously both to start and stop it. In the interval between these operations, it has a life and pace apparently entirely of its own whim and fancy. Another oddity of the hotel is that room keys are strung on huge iron hoops. The device is certainly effective, if inconvenient. With an iron ring large enough to strangle a bullock attached to one's key one can neither forget it nor—and most particularly—put it in one's pocket.

Penciled on the walls of a vast coffin-like closet in my room, I discovered the names and dates of visit of many wanderers of the North. Several of them brought a pleasant thrill of recognition.

I soon had the spacious room knee-deep in excelsior, for a long brown box had arrived and in it my beautiful rifle, a Mannlicher-Schoenaur.

After a half-hour of caressing and complimenting my new rifle, I went down the street to see some friends at Hudson's Bay House, the large and industrious headquarters of the ancient Hudson's Bay Company. Despite the passage of years, the Hudson's Bay Company and the North are still inextricably bound together.* Chartered in 1670, this great and tradition-steeped organization still flourishes; without its help travel in the North over any extended period of time is still impossible. Though today in the larger cities of western Canada the "adventurers trading into Hudson's Bay" appear to have descended to the mundane function of large retail stores, their empire of trading posts is quite as extended and, though connected by radio, quite as distant as ever in their long and honorable history.[3]

One of the first men I saw was the district manager of Ungava and the Eastern Arctic. "Well, Downes," he greeted me, "you're just like the 'waves!' You show up from the South with the warm weather and show up from the North as freeze-up comes on. No one knows where you come from or where you go, but you're just as regular as the geese."

Soon I was closeted with a cordial friend and gentleman of deserved admiration and affection in the North, the manager of the Saskatchewan district.[4] After amenities and some reminiscence, he asked me what he could do for me and in particular where I was going this year. Now that the question was directly before me, a plan quickly took shape. I had already in my mind rejected a return to the Mackenzie region, though I still had a canoe cached there. The country was becoming too full of white people.

Years before, my Cree friends in northern Saskatchewan had often mentioned a huge lake far up on the edge of the Barrens called Nueltin Lake. A trip to Nueltin would not only mean meeting old friends in the Reindeer Lake Country, but to me it would be, north of Reindeer, all new territory, quite unmapped, the Barrens, and the possibility of running into the great caribou migration. The only written reference to Nueltin Lake, at least from direct observation, that I know of is its mention by Samuel Hearne, who crossed it in the winter of 1771 on his historic trip to the Arctic Sea. Having made

* There have been numerous books written about the company. The most recent and perhaps best informed is *The Honourable Company*, by Douglas Mackay. Indianapolis, New York, the Bobbs-Merrill Company, *1936*.

two trips to Reindeer Lake in the years before, I was anxious to see what lay beyond to the north. So to the district manager's question I promptly replied, "Nueltin Lake."

The Hudson's Bay Company for some years had had a post, very small and distant, called "Nueltin Lake Post," although it was not, properly speaking, on Nueltin Lake at all but lay somewhere off to the west of it out on the edge of the tree line. Since its establishment it had always been difficult to find, particularly from the air. In fact, several flights had been made at one time or another without any success at all, the plane being forced to come back without locating it. Though certain members of the staff had made flights to the post, they seemed to have little information as to just exactly where it was, and a diligent search through the files and records failed to produce any map showing its true location: The enormous region north of the Pas-Churchill railroad and to the north and east of Reindeer has never been really mapped. Of the interior there are a few scattered river traverses and one longer route map such as Tyrell's of 1894. The rivers on the coast are in some cases charted a short distance inland, and a very limited amount of geological reconnaissance has resulted in a scattering of small penetrations on the fringe of the area, but in the main the tremendous region is bare of other than the imagined lakes and rivers of Indian rumor. Somewhat to my surprise, I found among my effects a map of the region drafted by an ex-Hudson's Bay man who had a reputation as a good observer and traveler. As it turned out, however, I would have done much better to leave it at home.[6]

The huge fur-trade empire of the North is divided into certain districts by the Hudson's Bay Company, and each of these is under the personal direction and inspection of a district manager. These districts follow arbitrary lines, are geographical units rather than political and provincial, and I found that at this time the Nueltin Lake Post had been shifted from the Saskatchewan to the Nelson River district. I was referred to the manager of this latter district, and through him I reinforced my respectability with the usual letters of introduction and carte blanche to Hudson's Bay Company men in the two regions.

Briefly, the plan became this: I would go to the Pas and Flin Flon in northern Manitoba by train, fly from Channing —air base of the latter town—into Pelican Narrows, a trading post I knew well, and then by canoe via Frog Portage, Churchill River, and Reindeer River to Reindeer Lake. At the north end of Reindeer Lake was a trading post called Brochet, which I had visited in the past, and which had been my Ultima Thule in this particular section of the North. From here I would move on again north, up the Cochrane River, and leaving that river would somehow pick out the way through a series of lakes and rivers to Nueltin Lake and, I trusted, eventually, the post.

There was a plan under consideration to attempt freighting in goods to the post with Chipewyan Indians from Churchill. It was suggested that I might meet them somewhere on the way and return with them to Churchill. In any event, I could always return by the route I had come.

It was so long since any freighting had been done from Brochet by canoe that no one seemed to have any idea how long the canoe trip would take. In fact, no one seemed to have a very definite notion about anything—whether I could secure a canoe at Pelican, if there were any Indians at Brochet who might go with me, whether the small gasoline boat of the Brochet Post would be in at the south end of Reindeer Lake (a happy possibility for that would save a hundred and seventy miles of canoe work on the lake over a stretch which I had previously covered and examined).

In any event, I knew where I was going, and I now had a fairly serene feeling that I would get there somehow or other. I wonder whether my two conversant shared my confidence.

My plans and preparations made in a pleasant twenty minutes, I left the offices of the company, went down the street, and bought forty rounds of ammunition and a new pair of pants. I was ready to be off. At the last moment I decided to splurge and buy a new pair of long underwear pants. The pair I had in my pack I had worn all the previous summer and had somehow neglected to wash. Anyway, it was something of a last minute luxury to indulge in before "pulling out."

The next day I watched the beautiful green prairie; the endless horizon-bound wheat fields' verdant in abundant spring rains, slipping by the train window. There is nothing in the world quite like the prairie in June—the lush young wheat, the dark rich soil, and the great china-blue bowl of the sky. The train rolled endlessly on in the unbroken flatness of the world of wheat. It seems something of an anachronism in this land of tractors, grain elevators, and all that is agricultural that the names of the towns on the railroad line are all of a hunting and fur trade age—"Portage la Prairie," "Swan River," "Neepawa," "Dauphin."

It was largely the early "Canadian" traders who gave these names, the *coureurs de bois*, French traders from Montreal. Now they are all gone, with the buffalo, and squat blond immigrants from the Ukraine have taken their place. At one stop the largest building was an ornate mosque-like church.

At length to the west the hazy blue escarpment of the high plains began to appear. It is locally known as the "Riding Mountains," and the high, even ridge follows one nearly all the way to The Pas. By evening the topography had made a very abrupt change. The fertile, level prairie unexpectedly was broken by low sand hills. The country now was rolling and irregular, and a few trees began to appear. This is one of the shorelines of a tremendous extinct lake, Lake Agassiz, which once covered the great wheat belt east of the Riding Mountains. The remnants of this lake are Lake Winnipeg and Lake Manitoba.

I discovered, with the easy intimacy of train passengers, two agreeable companions, a young geologist bound for the country east of The Pas and a young Hudson's Bay Company man who was going back to the west coast of Hudson Bay after a brief respite in the city. He had spent a number of years trading in the Eskimo country at Padley Post. It was with regret that I said "good luck" to them on the following day. At The Pas our trails diverged. For here the railroad splits, one track extending over the lonely five-hundred-mile road to Churchill on Hudson Bay, and another making a short stab of seventy miles north to the mining town of Flin Flon.

The Pas basks indifferently in departed glory. It was once

the center of a booming and optimistic mining fever, the jumping-off place for the North, the trappers' haven, the prospectors' delight, scene of fabulous fur prices, dog races, high-stake poker games. Its citizens might awake in the morning to news of a new "strike" overnight or a man shot dead in a tree or a man kicked to death in a public latrine, or that a new fur buyer had bought a white cat skin for an arctic fox. But these heroic days exist now only in the garrulous reminiscence of the barflies. For the frontier moved on; enterprise, money, enthusiasm, youth went seventy miles north to the thriving, jostling, polyglot mining town of Flin Flon.

Flin Flon was brought into being by the eyes of an Indian, the fortitude and persistence of an Irishman and an Englishman, was nurtured by the wealth of a New York millionaire, administered with the canniness of a Yankee, and functions with the sinews of Welsh, Irish, Czechs, Poles, Russians, Finns, French, Norwegians, Swedes, Letts, and Chinese. From its beginnings it has had a touch of the fantastic.

The full story of Flin Flon is not for these pages; it awaits its place in the saga of the mighty mining stories of Canada's North. It dates back to 1914 when The Pas was still the end of the civilized world. An old-time, practical "bush" prospector, Tom Creighton, and his associates discovered the enormously rich body of copper-zinc ore and staked it under a name which legend has it they took from a paper-backed dime thriller they had been reading.* Its hero was a Professor Flintabbatey Flonatin. The great find—then but a few exposures of green, ice-smoothed rock—was staked as the Flin Flon claims after the eccentric professor. After the war, came capital and United States backing. The sanctity of the silent forest was ripped away with blasting and the labor of a thousand hands. The railroad, "steel," plunged forward over swamps and lakes. A great yawning pit, the "glory hole," soon gaped to the skies, and the yellow smoke of a smelter stood like a triumphant plume in the heart of the wilderness. Flin Flon was born.

For a few years it had the roaring vigor of a typical mining town. An army of stout adventurers burrowed into the

* *The Sunless City*, by J.E. Preston Muddock.

ground and came up again to the daylight or dark to form long queues outside the liquor stores or beer parlors. The ladies of the town maintained their aristocracy of beauty on a prominence known as "the Hill." In the chaos of solid rock and swamp, shacks replaced tents, and these in turn became houses. Like the shells of some extraordinary beetle, they took their form and contour from the solid rock exposures against which they were affixed. So close to the surface was the rock that the plumbing ran, and still runs, above ground in hay-insulated, wooden casings. But the ore-body was too rich for Flin Flon to exist more than temporarily in the full lustiness of a boom camp. A town and then a small city grew in the wilderness. Families came in; marriages were contracted, stores, hotels, and the inevitable Chinese restaurants migrated from the south. The high fever of a masculine frontier town abated, and the glitter of the Hill was dimmed. Today it is a wealthy to, but in the long twilight of the northern summer an occasional raucous shout sometimes cries feebly for the riotous days of the first boom.

The trip from The Pas to Flin Flon is an interesting one. The train scuttles over trestles; the interminable northern swamps called "muskegs," and bare rock at such a moderate pace that one can see everything there is to see.

The great muddy Saskatchewan with its broad hayfields is no sooner crossed than one plunges abruptly into the North and the forest. The flat plains that stretch from Winnipeg, some five hundred miles behind, give way to a more irregular terrain. Rock outcrops become abundant, crenulated, smoothed, gouged, and scarred by the great ice sheet of twenty thousand years ago. Lakes begin to appear. In a final, defiant gesture, thick yellow cliffs of limestone that have for hundreds of miles underlain the plains, fling themselves upward against the gray granite of the North. The train lurches on. Huge Lake Athapapascow opens out, and the rail stops take on curious little names like "Attik," "Athapap," "Payuk," and —a remembrance of the old fur brigade days—"Cranberry Portage." Occasionally the train stops, though there is no shack or station, to take on a passenger or to let one off at some milepost. There has always seemed to me a delightful and heart-warming informality in this type of railroading. The train is not an implacable monster of steel and determination sweeping you over the continent without the slightest regard for your timid wish to stop; for once it becomes an obliging servant to the individual. Sometimes, as the train rumbled over a trestle spanning a lake, a startled mother duck with her brood would paddle frantically out of the way.

The lethargy that always comes over me during a long train ride began to disappear. I began to feel faint stirrings of excitement at the first small landmarks of the homecoming stretch. Days of train travel and viewing of endless, impersonal prairie or the drab backyards and clotheslines of cities have such a numbing effect on me that I have no emotion more acute than irritation that the men's room is occupied. Then those first ducks on Lake Athapapascow! I peer out of the window, I find myself carrying on an almost audible and quite involuntary monologue: "Good place to camp... lots of dry wood there...nice bunch of dried tamarack for canoe poles... Bad place for net, too deep... . Ought to be some whitefish in that bay... . Tough place to make a canoe crossing with the wind like this... " The world has suddenly become a personal and live thing.

The ceaseless but now joyful ta-da-da-ta, ta-da-ta-ta of the train brought Schist Lake, narrow and cliff-hemmed, into view, then the white deserted buildings of the old Mandy Mine. At this moment without fail someone in the car will say: "I hear they're going to reopen the Mandy." In a short space the red-winged planes of the Arrow Airways were to be seen tethered to a small dock. The train slowed down.

I climbed off and some unseen hand flung my pack-sack out of the baggage car down onto the embankment. The train jiggled off to Flin Flon, the yellow smoke of whose smelter could be seen against the northern sky.

Around me was complete silence, a few shacks, and a false-fronted barn of a building with the dim legend, "The Empire," the thin, deserted railroad track, all encircled by the dark forest of spruce. I could not but think for a moment and, with a small, dark malevolence, say: "Give the wilderness a little more time, and it will take all this, too."

I found that the Empire had failed since my last visit some two years before. I went down to the airplane base and chatted with Bill the agent. By good fortune a plane was due to leave the following morning and it could be arranged to let me off at Pelican. This seemed to me an excellent start, a good omen.

CHAPTER 2

Pelican

Flying in the North is both the best and worst way to see the country. It is the newest thing in the North, yet it already has something of a legendary quality and in the brief years of its existence has produced a host of men surrounded with an aura of story and fable.

The great stimulus to flying came after the First World War. Canada was full of men still young, restless, and air-wise who now found no use for their wings. Increasing prosperity, the surge of mining and prospecting despite the stubborn resistance of nature, found in these young men an answer to the problem of transportation in the North. The vastness of the North and the necessity of subduing it by the time-honored, slow method of canoe and paddle had for centuries kept the white man at bay. The flier solved the riddle. Here and there, small ventures, mostly with mining and prospecting backing, began to develop. The North was vast, and gasoline depots, repair shops, even maps, were few or nonexistent, yet the North was a land of thousands and tens of thousands of lakes. It was a land largely without mountains. It was as if designed by nature for an attack by man from the air. Airplanes with pontoons in summer or skis in winter could go anywhere. Out of the preliminary reconnoitering by plane grew a new and indigenous type of aviator, the "bush flier."

By the mid–1920s, a whole series of epic flights had been made.* Most of the great network of routes over which routine commercial flying was to follow were made by bush fliers. By the late 1930's Canada led the world in actual tonnage of flown material. Long before she had established a transcontinental aerial system there were regular weekly flights to the Arctic Circle. If a deathblow was needed to extinguish the North's two hundred and fifty years of uninterrupted seclusion, the bush flier administered it.

The bush flier was and is no ordinary flier, for his flying, though now considerably more controlled, demands the qualities that the North has always demanded of the pioneer. Here, in a land that had no weather stations, he must know his weather. Here he must be his own ground crew and skilled mechanic, his own guide and mapmaker. Stories—authentic, too—are still told of those perilous and ingenious early flights in the North: landings on one ski, propellers falling off in mid-air, the plane on the lower Mackenzie on which the damaged "prop" was replaced by one carved out by hand and stuck together with glue. Extraordinary flights were made and all in the face of rigorous elements. Where the talk had once been of great hunters and pathfinders, now it was of equally great fliers; and to have flown with such and such a man was immediately a badge of distinction.

From a plane the traveler sees the North below hum as he can never see it from his canoe or from the portage trail. He sees an incredible immensity of forest and lakes that he can only visualize from the air. And yet a man can fly a thousand times over the North and see nothing of the living North, the North of a thousand and ten thousand years, the North of the people who live in it and die in it. To fly in and out of the North and say one understands it, is like driving an automobile over the broad, oiled highway over the Sierra Nevada and—while eating a perfect basket lunch—look back and claim to understand why the members of the Donner party

* A good picture of the pioneer flying feats as well as an intimate personal portrait of the northern "bush flier" is contained in: *Arctic Pilot*, by Walter Gilbert as told to Kathleen Shackleton. Thomas Nelson & Sons, Ltd., London, Toronto, and New York, 1940.

devoured each other in 1846.

The flight the next morning from Channing was a routine affair to the power dam of the Flin Flon mine on the Churchill River. A slight deviation from the route would leave me at Pelican, so the cost was not the sixty-five cents a mile and return price of a private charter but a very reasonable sum.

Two other passengers and myself crammed ourselves into the small Fairchild amidst a confusion of boxes and bags. One was a strong, large chap bound for the Churchill River to do some sturgeon fishing, and the other was a rotund icebox salesman. We ran down the long defile of Schist Lake, with a quivering and straining the plane lifted itself "up on the step," and then we were far above the dollhouse of the airport. We swung lazily over an accumulation of eccentric streets, tiny dwellings, and wriggling plumbing—Flin Flon. Forever and forever, as far as the eye could see in every direction, stretched an unbroken world of green and lakes. Sometimes the raw skeleton of the earth gleamed upward where burned trees revealed granite ridges, white and naked at this height, but again there were lakes, lakes, lakes—every conceivable size and shape. Some of them wiggling and twisting, sent off spidery glistening arms. Some were round and complacent; some had retreated to mere muskegs and bogs. Some were gigantic, some were minute. The eye became tired and the mind baffled at the endless profusion and confusion of water.

From the air the world of the North has a deceiving flatness. The spruce forest and the lakes roll on in every direction with no hill, mountain, or prominence to break the endless uniformity; only on the ground one realizes the broken and slashed character of the country. There are geological reasons for this. Most of the North is embraced by a tremendous shell of granite and other rock, which is termed the "Pre-Cambrian shield." This is an area of more than a million square miles in the rough form of a V embracing Hudson Bay and terminating in the Adirondacks and Superior Upland in the United States, and is the very core of North America. The ancient surface has withstood the convulsions of the earth since prehistoric times. Great mountain ranges were folded and twisted up, seas came and went, and always erosion ate away at every elevation. Parts of the great shield were domed upward; other parts subsided. The surface rocks were engulfed and fused with great masses of rock that forged up from the depths. The tremendous leveling process of wind and water never ceased. And the last act in the drama was the invasion of the ice sheet which in its retreat, some twenty thousand years ago, left this undrained land of lakes and islands over which we flew.

As we flew nearer the earth to pass under lowering clouds, the grim granite ridges took a more threatening form. Here and there the ancient upheavals of the earth had squeezed the granite into series of parallel bands of rock. The very structure of the granite was altered and it became a characteristic type of rock called "gneiss," which grinned up at us sullenly and evilly-fittingly, the oldest rocks on the North American continent.

In contrast to other flights I had made, we flew very low. The pilot had not been on this run for long, and practically all the flying in the North is done from ground control, recognition of the lakes and rivers. Once I saw a curious object crawling below us. It was a man portaging a canoe turned bottom-upward, which quite concealed him and appeared to be creeping along under its own power like a gray slug.

I could not help regretting a famous pilot with whom I had enjoyed flying in this region.[1] He was a veteran of the war and an older man than most flying today in the North, but he had a touch with a plane like no other flier in my limited experience. In the larger planes one is lugged along like a sack of potatoes, and the plane has as little individuality as a freight car. Careful observation of instruments keeps them on an even keel and course. But the small planes in which I had flown with Jeff were like birds. He would grin and laugh and the plane would swoop and veer. He rose from the water with the swish of a mallard and swooped down to land with the lightness of a feather. I had heard he was piloting a private plane for some millionaire mining man in the East. Anyway, I missed him here over the Pelican route—missed his exhilaration and the sight of his large red ears in front of me.

The water seemed unusually high in all the lakes, but it was easy to see the difference in the water level today from some time in the not too remote past, one of the most striking features to be observed from the air, common to much of the forested regions of the North. In many cases the old shorelines, marked by a cessation of the tree growth, are far back from the present ones. The intervening space between spruce and lake, invaded by swamp growth, affords a striking contrast in color to the dark green of the trees and the blue of the water. In some cases, entire lake basins have been drained, and cutting through their level floors are winding and meandering streams surprising in a region of rushing, tumultuous rivers.

We have come to regard the incredible feat of flying as a commonplace, but flying over a stretch of country through which you have previously passed by canoe, the magic, the profound leap into a new dimension, becomes so startling as to impress upon you the greatness of the miracle you are experiencing. Far below the plane I could see points and islands in perfect map-like form, and it was almost impossible to believe that those same points and islands had taken hours of toil to reach, and days had been spent traveling through the country, which now floated by beneath me in a few minutes.

The first time I flew out from Pelican was at the end of a summer of northern wandering which had held a particular depth in its experiences. It was the finish of a trip that happened to be particularly hard. Somehow those trips leave me with the fiercest resentment at having to leave and go back to civilization. I remember saying good-bye to my friends among the Indians. Then there was the leave-taking with the trader and his wife and children. We had become fast friends in those few days. He and his family were leaving, too, for another post. Then I flew away. It was late in the afternoon, toward sunset. As we took off, and the pitiful little cluster of Indian shacks was cut from view, we ascended; it seemed, straight into the clouds. The dying sun, filtered by ground mist, cast over everything an indescribable golden glow. The thousands of lakes partially veiled by fog burned with an unearthly burnished light. The forest was no longer visible, only the white mist, the clouds, and the golden lakes. I remember staring out the oil-spattered window and wishing with inexplicable intensity: Fly, fly, fly faster, turn and fly into the sunset so I cannot see it all.

In a little more than an hour, we were circling over Pelican Narrows. I could see the clearing along the shore of Pelican Lake, the small Roman Catholic church, the red roofs of the Hudson's Bay Company store and dwellings, the scattered clay-colored Indian shacks, the canoes on the shore. Then we were down in a low glide and taxiing into the rude wharf. A smiling brown face appeared at the window, and I climbed stiffly out to shake hands with Andrew. Andrew Cussiter, a Cree Indian, was always the first to meet the plane. Not a flicker of surprise crossed his face, though there had been no warning of my coming and it was two years since I had last seen him.

"Watchee," he said in true northern greeting. "Watchee," I replied, and walked up the dock.

I saw the short, compact figure of Bill, the post manager, coming down the hill from his house to get the mail from the plane. His blue eyes lighted in surprise as he saw me.

"Hello, P.G.," he greeted in his broad Aberdeen burr. (For a moment the sun came out and glinted on his suggestion of a mustache. Bill looked older and more drawn than when I had seen him two years before. Then he had been just a clerk, and now he was manager of the post.

We walked up to the house together. The faithful Andrew, his round face smiling, insisted on carrying up my pack-sack. Excellent Andrew! Post managers may come and go at Pelican, but Andrew always will be there. '

Everything was exactly as I had left it, even old Bozo, a decrepit and large police dog, the left-behind of a former manager, was still there. Since my last visit Bill had married, and soon I was introduced to his hospitable and kindly wife. It was easy to see that Bill had been working very hard to make this, his first post, successful—no easy task with the competition of free traders and the exorbitant freight charges. As we walked up to the house I saw a few Indians I knew. Most of my old confidants were not yet in from their spring camps. It was heart-warming to be taken in with true northern hospitality once more, particularly after the comparative coldness of the Mackenzie country, where much of this time-honored attitude has disappeared before the advance of white men and their machines.

As soon as I could disencumber myself of my city clothing, I went over to see my friend Baptiste—or, as his fellow Indians call him, "Bacheese"—Michel. I found him still the gay, rollicking Cree I had known so well. I had brought a little rubber squeaking mouse for his daughter-in-law, Eugenie's baby Marie. In my absence the little girl had died, but the household was proud in the acquisition of a new son named Pete, to whom I gave the mouse. Pete squalled mightily at the sight of me and hadn't much chance to play with his mouse as his Grandfather Bacheese found it highly amusing himself.[2]

They put on their very best victrola records for me, we chatted about past years, and I told them something about the Great Bear Lake country. It always seems strange to me, and a little comforting, to find that the Indians, except the women, change so little and are so ageless. It has made me wonder if perhaps this is not one of the reasons people go back to the North; the happiness one has found once, in the constancy of everything in the North, can more readily be found again.

Quite a few Indians came in and out. We were all a little shy. My knowledge of the Indian language is primarily utilitarian, and it is a little while before I get back into the comfortable usage of it. Soon, with the music and the laughter, this gap was closed. Bacheese occasionally jumped to his feet and executed a few fancy dance steps in the manner of the century-old "Red River Jig." Bacheese always seemed to me the happiest refutation of the notion of the stolid, impassive red man of fiction. He was small for a Cree—there are many very large men in this tribe—and possessed of an enormous vitality. It was incredible to think of him as a grandfather. He was active as a cricket and slim as a boy, an admirable and accomplished mimic, an insatiable prankster, and a fine hunter. He was the living embodiment of the mythical hero of the Crees, Wisakajak. Bacheese had purchased a small accordion. He snatched it up and began to play a few tunes, asking me slyly each time he finished what I thought the name of the tune was. When I could give the correct answer, he was delighted. He would laugh uproariously, dance a jig, and then play some more. Yes, truly here was Wisakajak.

The Crees are people from the North shores of Hudson Bay to the Rockies. They are related to the Ojibways of Ontario and to the Montagnais and Naskapis of the Labrador Peninsula. And among all these peoples are still to be heard tales of Wisakajak. His name may differ, as for instance the Ojibways call him "Nanibush," but the stories have the same familiar pattern.

Wisakajak is the Davy Crockett, the Siegfried, the Lancelot of these people of the North. No one knows when Wisakajak lived, but it was long ago before the white man, in the days when the animals could talk, when the world was young and full of giant creatures. Wisakajak was the great trickster; he went his light-hearted way in a world of terror and changed the animals to what they are today. The tales of Wisakajak are legion. As one old man told me, "You can tell a story of Wisakajak every day for a month, and still there would be many more stories."

Who made a new world by blowing on a bit of mud brought up by the muskrat when all the world was drowning? Who painted the fox red and left his ear tips and tail black? Who made the loon so squat and crushed it with his foot when it cried out to the birds and animals that their singing host was eating them up? Who sharpened with his knife the broken bill of the kingfisher? Who clothed himself in the skin of the giant frog and killed the giant lynxes? Who carried the great bag of songs on his back? The answer is always Wisakajak.

Watching Bacheese play the accordion, I thought of the last chapter in the Wisakajak saga, which he had told me one day. Bacheese had said: "You know I been thinking about that Wisakajak. Maybe he is still alive. Maybe he goes around in the 'bush' like in the old days. But you know, I was outside one time and I see Wisakajak in the move-picture. They give him different name. Maybe it Wisakajak he brother, or he father. Anyway he do all same trick as Wisakajak. I t'ink he *is* Wisakajak! He call Cholly Chaplin!"

Walking back to Bill's from my visit with the Michels, I found myself enveloped in the warmth of meeting with good friends. I reflected how fond of Pelican I had always been, what happy associations it had, and what a really attractive place it was. The trail took me down through a miserable group of mud and log huts, summer residences of the Indians. Along the curve of the shore were beached numerous canoes of all sizes and states of repair. One small birch bark canoe lay among the others, its spruce-gummed sides in curious contrast to its smooth green and gray modern companions.

The gaunt, bleached frame building of a now extinct fur-trading enterprise, Revillon Frères, "the French Company" of the North, stared with vacant windows out into Pelican Lake from the east promontory.

Ascending a small hill, the path brings to view the full panorama and delightfulness of Pelican. The small, scrupulously whitewashed trading post of the Hudson's Bay Company is set close to a sandy beach; the dwelling house, likewise white and with a red roof, lies farther back on a slight rise. From where I stood on a pleasant knoll topped with small birches, Pelican Lake, with its myriad low islands, stretched away to the west and lost itself in a great shining expanse to the south, which is known as Deschambault Bay.

Further west, a gray tin building of some size marks the Roman Catholic Mission, and around it cluster Indian shacks. The Protestant Indians live here to the east of the Post and the Roman Catholic to the west.

I have never been able to determine exactly when this particular trading post was established. It was not in existence when Richardson and Hood came through in 1820, but it was most probably established not long after that time, in 1823. The early history of many of these lesser trading posts is very confusing, for often they had brief spells of fitful existence before finally becoming permanently rooted. The Cree name for Pelican Narrows means "Narrows of Fear"—a grim reminder of the days long ago and the marauding Blackfeet from the south.

Sitting under the birch trees, the story of the Narrows of

Fear came back to me, and as it may soon be forgotten, it is perhaps worth a digression.

This spot in the sandy hospitality of the shore with its narrows so suitable for nets has always been a favorite camping spot. Once a large band of Crees camped here for a permanent summer residence. All the men of the band packed up their furs and left for the east, possibly to York Factory, which was the nearest trading post at that time. This trip, an arduous and long one all the way to Hudson Bay, meant that the women and children must be left behind. Thirty tents were pitched upon the knoll where I was now seated. Thirty tents occupied the shorefront.

While the men were off on their trip to the trading post, strange Indians came up from the south, probably Blackfeet, and massacred the entire band except for two children whom they left on the small reef a few rods out in the lake from the present Roman Catholic Mission.

When the men of the band returned shortly after the massacre, they found bodies floating along the shore. They pursued the killers down through Sandy Narrows to the south near Deschambault Lake. Catching up with them near a little creek there, they killed them all but the leader, whom they held for a special council. After some deliberation they cut off this man's hands and then, seizing him by the hair, they severed his head.

Occasionally human bones still are washed out by the rains here at Pelican.

As I wandered on up to the house, I found my thoughts entirely concerned with the world about me. It is curious how quickly, and with what little effort, one can slip from one world into another.

The fishing here in the lake was particularly poor. This was no doubt due to the excessive and wasteful commercial fishing which some white men had carried on during the winter, and to some degree accounted for the paucity of Indians here at the post this year. It was working a distinct hardship upon them and especially their dogs. It had always seemed strange to me that, with the thousands of lakes available, destructive commercial fishing should be allowed upon lakes where large bands of Indians by custom and necessity congregate.

The weather, which had been alternately threatening and clear when I arrived, had by nightfall taken a turn for the worse, and so I spent the next few days in and about the post.

An interesting attempt was being made to run a day school for the Indian children. The Roman Catholic Indians, of course, would have nothing to do with it, as their children are sent "outside" to Mission schools in the fall. The Protestant Indians were enthusiastically supporting the idea. The task was being carried on with admirable spirit and patience by a very young man named Buxton, who though he knew no Cree when he arrived, and his small charges knew no English, was getting along famously. The old Revillon Frères store on the point was being used as a schoolhouse. He was living in a little log shack doing his own cooking and was a jolly and sincere chap.[3]

Once again fortune seemed to smile, for during the evening Bill reported that a group of Indians were shortly going north to the south end of Reindeer Lake and I might go along with them. A certain Arthur Morin, a Cree from Swan River, headed the party. They were waiting for weather and an outboard motor part, which was coming from Island Falls with another group of Indians.

This seemed a particularly good arrangement. For one thing the fur season just past had been so successful that there were no new canoes available. There was one canoe, which I might have been able to get, but it was too large and cumbersome for my needs. Choosing a canoe, it is always necessary for me to bear in mind that I may do much of my traveling alone. The canoes of the northern Indians are rarely small light craft like our pleasure types. They are usually on the "freighter" model, which means greater beam and considerably more ruggedness and weight. Nearly all of them—made by an old and respected Canadian firm—are lower in the bow and stern with less sheer than the canoe to which we are accustomed in the United States.

The days passed very quickly. Excursions with Bill and his wife were mixed with calls and conversations among the

Indians. One night the old Roman Catholic priest came over to play bridge. He and the schoolteacher teamed up against Bill and his wife. It was very amusing—the Roman and Anglican churches at peace with each other and presenting a united front against the fur trade. The old priest, who had been at Pelican as long as anyone could remember, went into gales of laughter at his own description of the Indian who hanged himself from the bedpost while in the hospital.

The northern Indian does not as a rule take happily to hospitalization. It is an unfortunate and serious consideration, particularly when some epidemic such as measles or whooping cough, both deadly to them, is raging. Listening to the old priest's grisly humor, I remembered a doctor who had treated them for many years telling me: "They are strange; the minute we get them into a hospital, they seem to lose all will and effort to live. We administer to them and use everything at hand, and they will not live."

On the other hand, I recalled an old Indian telling me about a relation of his, likewise an old man, who had been sent out to a frontier town to the hospital. According to his account, the old man became weaker and weaker, and the hospital authorities completely lost hope for his recovery. The old man at last requested feebly that, as he was going to die anyway, they allow him to leave and die back in his own forests. After a great deal of entreaty and persuasion, including that of his son, whom they had summoned, he was allowed to go. He was carried to his son's canoe, and the two started back to the North. As is usual, the boy had very little food with him, but he did manage to shoot a spruce hen. The old man ate it hungrily. Later the boy succeeded in killing a young moose. By this time, the old man was eating voraciously. He began to recover miraculously, and by the time they had returned to Pelican he was once again his old self. As he naively explained, the whole trouble was that at the hospital while they were trying to cure him they had actually been starving him to death. As he expressed it, they had fed him nothing but a little meat, a very little meat with no blood in it, and all kinds of leaves. It seemed to him very odd; for everyone knows when a man is weak he needs fresh meat.

In the evenings, Bill and I talked until all hours, mostly about traveling, "tripping," and the fur trade.

Once I went over to visit a former traveling companion, Thomas. When he and I traveled together years before, he was a fine, great, strong Indian. There were few men in all the country that could challenge his load on the portages. There was no man who could approach his endurance and stealth in hunting moose. But in the intervening years the support of his innumerable children, all girls but one, had told heavily upon him, and his luck had not been good. It was sad. He was very gray now. His hunt had been practically nothing during the preceding winter. One of his smallest children had fallen ill. It was said that he would not stir, would not trap or hunt, but just sat by the little child for many days. The change in him was shocking. The bright luster of his hunter's eyes was gone, and something of the fateful resignation of the discouraged Indian was there instead. This characteristic apathy is deeper than we might suppose. Perhaps there is still, stronger than one expects, the age-old surrender of the mind to an invisible evil against which, when an Indian is convinced of its mastery, he has no defense. I will always have a very fond spot in my heart for Thomas. He was to me one of the kindest Indians I have ever known.

Bill's wife, due to her very practical training in a hospital in the south, was in constant demand. One day a very young baby was brought in to her, its face encrusted with sores. It was a very small baby and, I suspect, had never been washed. The natives will rarely carry out any medical advice, particularly if it happens to be at all on the sanitary side. For a long while Bill's wife was under great suspicion because she washed a baby that was brought in to her. Shortly afterward the child died, and everyone assumed that the bath had killed it. The fact that its parents had stuffed its digestive tract almost solid with dry breakfast foods never occurred to them as a remotely possible cause.

Arthur set the day for our start, but the day, a very fine, warm one, came and went without our even getting the canoe in the water. The missing part of the engine had not arrived, and Arthur began assembling a heterogeneous contraption from discarded parts belonging to his innumerable relatives. It occurred to me that outboard engines are more of a curse than a benefit to the North. In a brief ten years' time they have swept the country like wildfire. Today an Indian's social status may be judged by the horsepower of his engine. To begin with they cost four times what they cost "outside," and gasoline proportionately even more. There are few places where gasoline sells for less than a dollar a gallon and at some it sells for six. In this section at least no self-respecting Indian would think of going any distance without his motor; and these were at one time the finest canoe men in the North. Money is lavished on gasoline at the expense of everything else. And yet no one goes farther to trap or net than in the days before this stinking, noisy intrusion into the wilderness. The making of canoes and even paddles is a fast dwindling art. Transport by numbers of canoes and paddles—a seasonal employment in a region where employment is almost nil—has vanished for the single big freight canoe and its roaring engine towing a number of manless convoys. I remember a conversation I once had with an Indian named Charles on this matter. With a naiveté and frankness not found in white people, he said to me: "You must be very poor to travel so far up here with no engine?" I turned to him: "You know, Charles, there is a river far north of Reindeer Lake where you have never been. The Chipewyans call it, 'the place the Crees used to camp.' Your father and his father used to travel way up there every year. They never had any engine. And look at me; do I not have as many beads on my moccasins? I am even a little fatter than you."

Early the next morning, Thursday, June 29, I was wakened by a knocking at the door. It was Arthur, ready to start. Quickly gathering my few things, and calling up a good-bye to my host and hostess, I went down to the shore and soon embarked.

There were five of us: Arthur, his small son Philip, just back from the Mission School, and two young fellows, Louis and another whose name I never did know, and myself. We all piled into a seventeen-foot canoe, which had previously been filled with all manner of bundles and bags. I had contributed ten gallons of gas as my share in the expedition. It was a clear day with a gentle westerly wind and a mass of fluffy, cumulus clouds banked upon the horizon.

The route west from Pelican to the historically famous Frog Portage—the "Portage de Traite" of the voyageurs has been described so completely in the early travel works of Sir John Franklin, Doctor Richardson, and Alexander Mackenzie that it would seem presumptuous for me to describe it.*

Old landmarks of my previous trips began to appear. Nevertheless, it was remarkable to me how many stretches and spots I did not clearly recognize, though it was only two years since I had been over the same route. Curiously, the mind seems to telescope sections of a long route, pushing lakes together without the intervening river stretches. The sudden appearance of these forgotten sections is startling and gives novelty and a sense of strangeness even to an often-repeated trip.

As one moves west threading a way through the numerous islands, here and there bare rocks lift their heads above the water. These reefs are often beautifully sculptured and fluted by the abrasive action of the great ice sheet of long ago and are called by the French geologists *roches moutonnées*, "sheep-back rocks." They are more than a curiosity for they afford evidence in their striation of the direction in which the mighty ice sheet progressed.

Before long we had reached the western extremity of Pelican Lake and were at the first portage, Medicine Rapids. This is an impressive spot with high, sheer rock walls on the

* The standard works of these great northern figures all afford excellent and detailed route accounts and observations. Those referred to here are:

Narrative of a Journey to the Shores of the Polar Sea in the Years 1819-20-21, by John Franklin, Capt. R. N. London, J. Murray, 1823.

Arctic Searching Expedition: a journal of a boat voyage through Ruperts Land and the Arctic Sea in search of the discovery ships under command of Sir John Franklin, by Sir John Richardson. London, Longmans, Brown, Green, and Longmans, 1851.

Voyages from Montreal on the River St. Lawrence, through the Continent of North America to the Frozen and Pacific Oceans; in the Years 1789 and 1793..." by Alexander Mackenzie, Esq., London, 1801.

south side of a very narrow rushing stream, which plunges down a bouldery channel. At the near completion of a trip some years before, the Indian Solomon and I had run down this torrent early one evening. Seeing it now in the daylight in its higher water stage, I wondered how we had ever managed it without ripping the bottom out of the canoe.

We were joined at this spot by two other Indians in their own canoe, Tommy Clark and Johnny Merasty's son. They had a big load and an enormous eight-horsepower engine as well as a smaller one. They were inordinately proud of the former and made a great display of its superior noise and power in passing us. However, we always found them waiting for us at the portages. Philip and I walked over the portage trail and the boys lined up the canoe. Lining a canoe one or more men drag the canoe up the rapids by means of a rope, the "tracking line," while one man usually follows along and fends the canoe off the reefs and boulders. After our canoe was successfully lined up, the boys turned to the other canoe and we all pitched in to portage over the supplies. Once above the rapid, I asked the Indians to pull in close to a granite wall of rock on the north side. I wished to see if some red ocher figures, which I had previously seen, painted there could still be found. They had not changed at all. Covered with a heavy lichen growth, these painted crude drawings are of considerable antiquity. They represent dream-figures, objects seen in dreams by a man seeking his *puagan* or "spirit-power" long ago.

Shortly we disembarked once again and carried everything over the first of three very short but steep portages, granite ledges, called the three "jump-overs" or "galets" in the early travel accounts.

By noon we had reached Grassy Narrows where there is a small settlement to which various members of the Pelican Narrows band repair at certain seasons. We stopped here for lunch on the south side of the Narrows, to avoid having all our food eaten up by friends and relatives on the opposite shore. Arthur and the boys had some moose meat they had obtained from Solomon Michel before starting out, but I confined myself to a few cups of tea, as I did not feel particularly hungry. Before long I spied a small hunting canoe approaching. It turned out to be my old friend and raconteur, Adam Ballentyne. I was extremely glad to see him. Adam still maintains a recognized ability in all manner of conjuring matters and is often called in on serious cases, which defy the white man's unguents and painkillers. Behind his ancient face, a mask of wrinkles lays an enormous store of material on the past and a faith in the wisdom of his forefathers, which has kept him an honest and sincere pagan. I was very sorry that I could not stop for a fine long session with him. He was anxious to know when I was coming back as he said that he had many things to tell me. Actually, at the moment, Adam was in considerable disrepute among his neighbors. There had been a very serious case of illness and Adam had contracted to cure the man but only upon pre-payment of an outboard engine. This bargain consummated the victim unfortunately died and Adam refused to give back the engine.

As we left, I noticed that everyone rather surreptitiously left a bit of bannock, meat, or tea with Adam, an unspoken bid for good luck. I gave him a whole big bannock, and just as I got into the canoe I gave him a new pipe. His weather-scarred, wrinkled face burst into smiles, and tipping his scraggly cap, he wished me good luck. And it may have been his conjuring that kept my fortune so favorable for the rest of the summer.

It had always been a matter of regret to Adam that I had been baptized. He was quite confident that if this had not happened, under his tutelage and with the use of the proper drum, I should have been capable, in time, of communicating with him when I went away to the unknown south in the fall.

Of the many old men I have known in the North, Adam was the most vivid, most dramatic storyteller. For, as he told me one day, "These things [the ancient truths] and the old days are clearer to me than is today. I can see them inside my head. They are like writing in my head. Sometimes they are like fire. I have many things to tell you, for you do not laugh. And some of these things were told to me by my father Peter, 'The-one-who-cocked-his-head-on-one-side-like-a-chick-a-dee,' and some of these things were told to him by his father, 'He-who-watches-at-night,' and some even were told to him by his father, 'Snake-man,' who lived long, long ago before any white men and any evil came to this country."

We were soon out on a long lake some thirteen miles in length known as Wood or Burntwood Lake. The west wind had freshened, and some difficulty with the outboard engine, which Arthur informed me, was twelve years old, forced us briefly ashore. It was rather rough going for our heavily loaded craft. The Clark and Merasty boys passed us with a great roar of their eight-horse and a high sheaf of bow foam, looking very superior and disdainful.

About this time I began picking fleas off myself. They were seeking me out from their previous smaller host, Philip. Fleas seem to be indigenous to Mission schools.

By six o'clock we had made our way through several boul-dery, winding channels and slack water stretches choked with yellow pond lilies, and a last stretch of marshy country alive with "*chuk-chuk-athu*," the redwing blackbird, and arrived at Frog Portage.

Frog Portage marks the divide between the waters of the Saskatchewan drainage and the Churchill River basin. It is a portage of some three hundred yards, and the divide is so low that in times of high water the Churchill has often been known to spill over into the Saskatchewan side. Historically it is of great importance and note. At the farther end of this portage, Joseph Frobisher, in 1771, first established a trading post for the energetic Northwest Company[5] in an effort to pre-vent the Chipewyan Indians and others coming from the north and west from carrying their furs on to the Hudson's Bay Company at Churchill and York Factory on the coast of Hudson Bay. It marked the white man's first real advance into the Mackenzie Basin and the great Northwest. The post exist-ed only fitfully. The Northwest Company, pursuing its pioneer advantage, soon moved farther west up the Churchill to Ile a la Crosse.

Its name, the Frog Portage, is supposed to have come down from the time the southern Crees derisively hung a dried frog skin there to ridicule the Chipewyans' less artful dressing of beaver pelts. Today, the portage, despite centuries of traffic, is still a simple, unimproved trace, a footpath. It debouches on a lake-like expansion of the Churchill River, and here once again we "boiled the kettle." The insects were particularly attentive here; seemingly high water had done much to encourage their numbers, for I did not remember their being so bad in previous years. Blackflies were the most numerous, attending us in concentrated small clouds like plumes of smoke. Whatever divinity brought these small monsters into the world bestowed upon the man of the North a curse for which it will never be forgiven.

At this point we turned east and ran down the Churchill River, which like most of the northern rivers is a succession of lake expansions, narrows, and falls or rapids. The country is not strikingly different. The contours of the low hills are rounded, the subduing, heavy grinding of the departed ice sheet everywhere apparent. The solid bedrock is thinly disguised, if at all, by the growth of small spruce and birch. At one spot only is there much sand, and here, on a south-facing bank, the old Indians years ago were accustomed to resort to gather certain herbs and roots for their medicine bags.

There is one portage around a beautiful falls known as Kettle Falls, and this is followed by a short jump-over where the water below the falls plunges over a ledge. Here we were joined by another passenger, an extremely unsavory addition to our already overloaded craft. A very mangy and unfortunate-looking yellow dog was seen roaming about. His nose was full of porcupine quills and he was in the last stages of starvation. Apparently lost, or more likely abandoned, he was in bad shape. He was induced to enter the canoe and took up a position between Philip and me, acting as a barrier and refuge to the fleas but making up for this with a fetid and nauseous odor.

In this stretch we passed another canoe, this one was bound for Pelican Narrows. It held a number of Indians, among them one Moise Merasty with the missing engine part belonging to Arthur. Sitting amid ships among the messy remains of a recently killed young moose, was an unkempt-looking white man. I had heard a good deal about this individual, and recognized him immediately and spoke to him by name. He had no idea who I was, and I was so noncommittal that his curiosity—and possibly something more—was very much aroused. As I had been just as vague to our own group, and they were not previously acquainted with me, his questions in Cree to them, which I understood, were quite as fruitless as his questions to me. We at length broke off our conversations, and they moved on upriver with the white man looking very worried.

This is typical of the insatiable curiosity which though frequently masked is common throughout the North. Though a stranger may not be aware of it, he is the subject of widespread and continuous speculation as to his character and motives. Whenever a new face appears, the word is passed around in the district. "Who is he?... " "Where did he come from?... " and, of the greatest importance—"What does he want and what is he here for?" Once a man has committed himself to the country, though his stay may be brief, personal appearance, habits, conscious and unconscious actions, morals and general behavior become common knowledge, to be passed about and savored. This is particularly true if the person does not immediately fall into some recognized northern category, as, fur trader, trapper, prospector or policeman (Mounted Police). If many white men had any idea of what utter fools they appear in the eyes of the Indians, what distressingly embarrassing personal observations are made about them, and how completely pierced is their cloak of disdain and superiority, their life would be unbearable. The Crees— and the Chipewyans and Eskimos also—have a habit of giving white men particular names, in conversation among themselves, which are often far from complimentary if absolutely descriptive. Thus, I have heard important individuals referred to as "Shirt-tail-always-out," "Old Dirty Whiskers," "Old Cockeyed," "The-man-who-thinks-he-has lice," "Two-bung-holes," and "Big-white-belly."

I have never been able to discover my own appellation, though I have been variously known as "The Long Knife" (equivalent to "the American"), "Mimigwesso," a mythical creature with a flat face that lives in the rocks, and "The-man-who-talks-about-dreams."

By early evening we had reached the mouth of the

Reindeer River. The passage up this river is notable for the sudden change from the dark waters of the Churchill to the clear blue and much colder waters of the Reindeer. The Churchill at this point passes east, but its course is so obstructed by islands and high hills that it gives the appearance of suddenly ending. The change in the temperature of the water was very soon reflected in the chill air. The Churchill, which finally flows into Hudson Bay, down through history has been called Danish River, English River, and the Cree name, Misinippi, "Big Water."

We had now turned northward and soon arrived at the first obstruction in this river, Attik or Deer Falls. The portage passes around to the west of these and is not long. Philip and I walked across; the boys lined the canoe up part of the way. I recognized a favorite campsite of mine, a spot which I shall always think of as *Wastemancheso-mitchewap*, "Firefly camp," as the fireflies were very abundant there that night two years before and the Indians I was with made a great deal of the matter.

Arthur was treating me with as much consideration as his small son. It was unusual treatment for me, and I could not make it out. I did not entirely like it. It stamped me either with the ineptitude of a child or a false and paradoxical superiority, which I neither felt, not relished.

A short distance above this spot the combination of darkness and a stiff headwind, which kicked up a nasty sea, made it inadvisable to go on. We stopped at a small island and made camp for the night. This consisted of the usual boiling of the tea pail and each finding, as best he could, a place to lie down on a minimum of boulders. It was not a very good camping spot, which is unusual traveling with Indians.

Despite our load and the archaic engine, we had made excellent time and were about halfway to the south end of Reindeer Lake. The cold was sufficient to keep the mosquitoes in check. Arthur was worried because Philip had a stomachache, and I was distressed that I had nothing to give him for it.

Our progress on up to the south end of Reindeer Lake the next day was uneventful. Reindeer River, like the Churchill, is a series of lake expansions, and only in the narrows is there much of a current. There are a number of portages, though none of them is particularly long. Steep Hill is a rather difficult one in wet weather because it is an abrupt climb over a clay ridge. I had a moment of retrospect and gratification passing over this portage as I remembered how arduous and difficult it was the first time I tackled it. It was much easier this time though my load was much greater. Since that, my first trip, my neck had increased in girth and my balance painfully improved.

Portaging and the North are inextricably identified. When an obstruction is met in canoe travel, a falls or a land barrier to be crossed, the canoe is beached, everything taken out and the canoe, turned over, is transported across first. This is usually done by one man, the middle thwart resting on the back of the neck and on the shoulders. The hands and arms are used merely to balance the load. Usually the paddles are tied in loosely and the flats of the blades interposed between the thwart and the body. The loads come next. The tump-line is fastened around as large an accumulation of boxes and bags as the person can manage. He then kneels, back to this, and slips the leather strap over his forehead until it pulls directly down on the front part of his head. At this juncture it is advisable to take the heaviest unpacked object near at hand, a fifty-pound bag of flour is admirable, and wedge it in against the back of the neck. The victim then struggles to his feet and staggers forward, gradually accelerating his pace until he achieves a shuffling scramble always on the verge of plunging to his knees. The hands, grasping loose miscellaneous objects which do not easily pack, such as guns, axes, and tea pails, are useless to comb off the hordes of black flies and mosquitoes which seem by long patience and intelligence to have congregated from all parts of the North at these portages to attack their unarmed and defenseless victims. While the mosquitoes favor forming a massed cover upon the forehead and backs of the hands, the black flies indulge in more insidious attacks on the neck and exploratory invasions of rents, tears, or openings in one's clothes.

The packing and portaging abilities of the Indians, and in

particular these Crees, is unbelievable until actually seen. Every portage calls forth a contest of speed and load carried. The year that Thomas and I traveled together, his son-in-law Solomon Michel, a small man, scarcely a hundred and forty pounds, carried over three hundred pounds of Hudson's Bay Company freight on each of his trips over the portages. At a contest at Pelican Narrows between some Chipewyan "packers" and the Crees, a big Cree Indian named Joe Morin packed for one hundred yards the incredible load of six hundred and twenty pounds of flour. For a long while there was a photograph in the Company store as proof of this great feat.

Later on we came to Devil's Rapids, or as the Crees call it *Manitou-powstik*. The Cree word *manitou* is used interchangeably for god, devil, and spirit. This portage, which can be made on either side of the river, goes around a spot of remarkable beauty and not a little danger. The river is closely contracted and after flowing over a ledge rushes down into a caldron-like space bounded on one side by high vertical cliffs against which the water foams and rebounds in nasty, twisting eddies and a larger, slow-swinging whirlpool. It is the custom to run up to a small island and with engine and poles and later rope work the canoe up to the quiet water above.

Unfortunately, Arthur insisted that Philip and I walk around on the portage, so I was unable to watch this exciting and interesting operation. As we hurried through the open forest of young birch, we could hear the cries and exhortations of Arthur as he directed the two young men. From the volume of the directions and commands it sounded as if the whole outfit was being carried down into the maw of the whirlpool. My apprehension was relieved when, bursting out at the head of the portage, we saw the complete crew placidly rolling cigarettes at the brink of the rapid.

The Manitou is a particularly vivid memory to me, as it was the first large rapid Solomon and I ran together. We were nervous both of each other and the rapid, which is very formidable looking approached from downstream. It is one of those deceptive stretches that look infinitely more savage than it is. You rush straight down at the towering cliff and just as you seem about to be dashed to bits or swamped by a tremendous white curling wave, the rebounding current throws you off into more quiet waters.

After the Manitou we had but two more portages, White Sand, which derives its name from a glacier-deposited ridge of brilliant sand on its east side, and Rocky Falls.

White Sand is a dangerous place though it has a deceivingly mild appearance. The portage trail rounds a long chute and falls of tremendous wildness and violence and comes out at the very lip of the rapid. Here and for some space upstream the water moves quietly and with scarcely a ripple through a rock-encased channel of great depth, twenty-eight feet in one spot. Because of its depth, the water is so little agitated as to give the appearance of having far less power and current than it has. Within memory, the rapids have claimed six human beings and one ox. The most recent victims were two young Geological Survey men two summers ago. They were going upstream and, deceived by the mild appearance, allowed their canoe to get out into the vicious grip of the current proper and tried frantically and unsuccessfully to reach the other shore. They were carried down through the falls and madness of the rapid. Miraculously, one of them escaped unharmed, but it was a long time before the body of the other was recovered.

Several years before, a Pelican Narrows man and his son had set out from the portage path here full of confidence with their new outboard engine. They had gotten only a few yards when the engine went dead. The man clasped his son and, putting his faith in the white man's god instead of his forefather's paddle, began praying. The two were swept over the edge of the falls to their death.

A miraculous and quick-witted escape was once made here when an Indian attempting to cross found his paddle breaking in his hands. Flinging it aside he grasped a broom that happened to be in the canoe and made his way safely to shore.

The last portage on the Reindeer, Rocky Falls, had changed a great deal since my last trip. Here the river splits into a number of small channels. These had been dammed with logs and concrete in order to control the Reindeer Lake level. This was no mean feat with only Indian labor to call upon and all tools and exterior aids being flown in by plane. This work had been carried on as subsidiary to the Island Falls hydroelectric plant many miles to the south and east, which in turn supplies the power for the mine at Flin Flon.

The portage, now off to the left or west of the old one, is a strenuous lift-up over a granite ledge. When we had reached the other side, we saw a boat near the east shore which we soon identified as the *Lac du Brochet*, a gasoline-powered craft of some twelve-ton capacity which the Hudson's Bay Post at Brochet at the north end of Reindeer Lake used in summer to take up its supplies from its warehouses at Rabbit River. This was a very fortunate event for it meant that I could obtain passage all the way to Brochet, and I would not be subject to the delays of canoe travel over a hundred and seventy miles of lake with which I was already acquainted.

The boat had stopped off at the house of Alf Olsen, a well-known old-timer in the country who had been appointed guardian of the dam. It was nice to see him again and to have him recognize me. The last time I had seen him was at Brochet. He was living with his Cree wife and seven children on a small island and feeding and caring for eighty dogs. The children, I soon discovered, had increased to eight.

I abandoned Arthur and his canoe and joined the company of the Lac du Brochet. Soon we chugged north to the small trading post at the bottom of Reindeer Lake known as South End.

It being well after sundown, we tied up for the night with the intention of leaving in the morning for Rabbit River, loading on freight there, and then going on up to Brochet.

But it is impossible to leave the Reindeer River without some reference to the supernatural inhabitants and travelers on it. For all the rivers in this section, the Reindeer is most famous for its *weetigos*. The Reindeer is known as a particularly favored route for *weetigos*, and in fact there is a great possibility that *weetigos* are still there.

The *weetigo* is the Cree embodiment of all the fear, all the horror, all the starvation and misery and terrible cold of the North. The *weetigo* is a man, yes, but a man who is a cannibal. He is a man who has eaten human flesh and thus has taken unto himself not only the flesh of another being but also his spirit-power, and thus has become supernatural. Though the Christian missionary has succeeded very thoroughly in establishing new and Christian fears for the old pagan ones in the North, he has not succeeded entirely in eradicating this most persistent horror. In the summer time (when *weetigos* become perfectly indistinguishable from normal humans) the younger men may laugh at the tales, but in the winter, during the long dark nights when the wind is howling down from the Barrens, when the trees cry out with the agony of the cold, when the Reindeer is muttering beneath the ice, when the little death-bird begins to perch, then the matter of the *weetigo* is another thing.

Descriptions by those who have seen *weetigos* differ only in minor detail. Certain features are always more or less evident. The *weetigo* is a man. He is usually naked. His face is more often than not almost black with frostbite. His eyes are glaring and staring, protuberant, and of a ghoulish ferocity. He has long fang-like teeth, and occasionally his lips are entirely eaten away. With the changing of summer to winter the *weetigo* gradually begins to assert his true character. By middle winter, *weetigos* are haunting the forests looking for human victims to devour.

Tradition has it that a *weetigo* lived on Reindeer River. In the summer he would appear with several children. He came from the east and usually late in the season. In the winter he ate the children.

Though a number of people affirm either that they have seen a *weetigo*, or preferably that some friend of theirs has seen one, it is impossible to find anyone who has had much actual contact with these creatures. Obviously the only thing to do is to hide or run away when anything like a *weetigo* appears.

Some years ago, a Cree at Reindeer Lake found that some other Indians were camping a little too close to his own trapping grounds. During the night, he went out barefoot in the snow and made a series of flying leaps. The next morning the Indians discovering huge barefoot footprints around their camp hastily moved off to a less *weetigo*-infested area.

According to the most competent authorities, a *weetigo*,

being possessed of supernatural powers, cannot be destroyed by any ordinary methods. When a *weetigo* invaded a village in the old days, it was necessary that he be combated by the man in the village acknowledged to have the strongest occult powers. The two men then wrestled. The combination of their physical combat and the accompanying spirit-power wrestling of their two psychic powers resulted in a veritable whirlwind into which the two contestants sometimes disappeared. If the *weetigo* was unsuccessful, he would at length succumb and in a state of exhaustion would be plunged into the fire and burned to ashes.

My old companion, Solomon, had a harrowing experience when he went out to civilization for an appendectomy. For the first time in his life he traveled on a train, and he mistook the Negro chef for a *weetigo*. Fortunately his attempts to leap from the train were unsuccessful, but the shock of the experience was frightful.

Solomon's terrible encounter was circulated about with great dispatch upon his return. A short time later a cousin of his was flown out for hospitalization. He never got as far as the train, for he leaped out to his death from the plane somewhere between Pelican and Channing. How much Solomon's experience had to do with his leap will never be known.

Just before rounding the bend and heading ups for South End, a peculiar, very rounded island came in view. I was reminded that the Reindeer is known for other beings beside its *weetigos*. For on that island lived at one time three mimigwessos. Possibly, too, they still live there, though current opinion is that with so many baptized people around there is little chance of it.

The *mimigwessos* are a strange and elf-like people with flat faces and just two holes for a nose. If one comes upon them unexpectedly, they are inclined to bend over and hide their faces with their hands. Though they are small and prefer to live in rocks and particularly near rapids and falls, they are possessed of more than ordinary abilities. Rarely have they been known to exercise these powers, usually confining themselves to merely capricious pranks. But this was not the case with those three who lived on the island I have just mentioned.

Many years ago, three young and rather irreverent youths from the south, Lac La Ronge, were journeying north up the Reindeer to trap north of Reindeer Lake. As they approached the rounded island, they saw some movement on the shore. Stealthily drawing nearer, they saw, to their amusement, a very small canoe and in it three very small people. The little canoe began to draw away. The young men, either from curiosity or deviltry, overtook the all canoe by dint of great effort and the bowman grasped its gunwale. By this time the dwarf-like people had ceased paddling and sat crouched over with their faces in their hands. Obviously, they were *mimigwessos*.

The first young man who had so rudely seized the small canoe hailed the bowman in it with the usual greeting and then followed this with the usual question on the trail: "Tell me some news?"

The small figure in the bow, without lifting his head, spoke between his hands and said: "You will never see the snow fly!"

The second young man in the middle of the canoe turned to his *mimigwesso* and repeated: "Tell me some news?"

The second *mimigwesso* said: "You will never see the New Year!"

The young man in the stern turned to the *mimigwesso* in the stern and said: "Tell me some news?"

The *mimigwesso* replied: "You will never see the spring!" Then before the young men could say more the strange little craft and it's stranger little crew disappeared. The young men lingered for a moment, and they could hear a soft laughter from the rocks. But they, too, in their youth and exuberance, laughed and paddled away to the north up beyond Reindeer Lake and set their traps.

Oddly, the one who had been in the bow died just before the first snowfall. The two others, terrified, abandoned their traps and started back for Lac La Ronge. On the way the second one died on the day before New Year's. The last one's grave is to be found at Lac La Ronge.

There are many tales of the *mimigwesso*, but this account is the one actually identified with the peculiar humped island at the Reindeer Lake outlet. It is an excellent lesson for any-one's comportment, and a check on rash impertinence to the odd or strange when one travels the Reindeer.[6]

Typical Section
of
Reindeer Lake
near Rabbit River

0   2   4
miles

from
aerial map

★ Wapos River H. B. Co.

CHAPTER 3

Reindeer Lake

The gathering that night in the lamplight of the tiny Hudson's Bay post was an entertaining one of old friends and scenes. There were a number of Brochet people who had come down with the boat; the outpost manager from Swan River, a tremendously broad, muscular, and soft-spoken man; the Provincial Game Guardian, a giant of an old-timer; my old friend Father Egernolf, a missionary of thirty-four years' service in the North; and the boat crew, Mistigosso and the pilot, old Henry Thomas, a Cree who had been piloting the Company boat on the lake since he first started as a young man in the old York boats.

We gathered in the log store for a while, and later moved into the house. The small trading store was a miniature of a hundred trading posts. In one corner were stacked bags of flour and burlap sacks of salt pork. The high counter, running the length of the store, barred the inquisitive from the ceiling-high shelves packed with cotton print, plaid, and other dry goods, including face powder and an assortment of ten-cent-store baubles. From pegs in the walls hung traps and tea pails, rifles and tump-lines, axes and hardware. Suspended from the rafters were two pairs of gigantic women's pink silk bloomers.

We were royally entertained in the house by a man new to this part of the country. He was very young, very obliging, and very sincere. He was married. The first time I passed through South End the former post manager had asked eagerly whether I could deliver a baby.

As is often the case when northern men gather for even a little while, the evening passed very swiftly with countless stories of the country and discussions of illegal buying of fur.

This is a matter for serious consideration in the North wherever marten and beaver are still to be found in commercial quantity. Of recent years, the record of the big, long-established companies has been very clean on the whole, but it is common knowledge that many of the fly-by-night "free" traders' very existence has often been staked on this illegal traffic. The morale and respect of the Indians for the law of the white man is not encouraged by this dishonesty. They know it is illegal, and they also know that the fur-buyers to whom they sell illegal fur are committing a breach of the law. Further they are all quite aware that other white men know who these are; and they see the same white men go uncaught, unpunished, unapprehended year after year. It would not seem to be an impossible thing to check. After all, the burden of guilt lies directly upon the buyers, who are well known. No Indian is going to trap what he cannot sell.

I sat enthralled in the lamplight. The big and small men crowded into the little low-roofed room caused a grotesquerie of light and shadow, and through it all rose and fell the conversation and comment. There was no intrusion of the "outside" in this world. And though the conversation was all of the North, it was not the North of any circumscribed small spot. Names mentioned brought other names, and reminiscences wandered with the fluidity of the shadows from the Arctic Ocean to Winnipeg and from the Yukon to Hudson Bay. Time, too, in these conversations seems to lose all importance; twenty years or yesterday live alike in this timeless land. The geographical immensity of the country is staggering, yet so few are its white people, that among those who have spent any real time in the country there is an invisible bond and connecting web of acquaintance all over the North. This is strengthened and increased by the custom of both the Hudson's Bay Company and the Royal Canadian Mounted

Police to shift their men repeatedly about. Tomorrow the man who is in Alberta may be uprooted and find himself in Ungava. When you yourself arrive in Ungava, ten years later, everyone in the community has heard about you for ten years.

As the web of conversation was spun from one to the other with the speed of these men about to leave for different and far destinations, I found that without effort I was drawn into it. For I too had traveled and lived a little bit in this world of our thoughts. And as my contributions, observations on parts of the North some of these had known thirty and forty years before, or timid suggestion of anecdotes in parts of the North they had never seen, insinuated themselves into the fabric, I had a warm feeling of an inward growth in stature, not of arrogance, but of an approach to equality; I became an individual and here at last a person.

The next morning we set out for Rabbit River, a small inlet some thirty miles up the lake. Before leaving, I had some words with Arthur, who was very disconsolate. The outpost manager from Swan River for whom Arthur had worked the preceding winter as a tripper that is a roving fur buyer, was due for a transfer to Souris River, and Arthur, who was very fond of him, was quite downcast. Furthermore, he did not know whether he could secure the same job again with the new outpost man.

He asked me whether I would consider his going along with me north of Brochet. He admitted he did not know a foot of the country in that section. It was hard to refuse the mute questioning of Arthur's round pleasant face. He had been as congenial and as considerate a traveler as one might find, but I refused, for I did not wish to waste any more time than was absolutely necessary in trying to find the way. My desire was to get to Nueltin Lake as quickly as possible so that I might have the maximum time to devote to that country.

As the *Lac du Brochet* pulled away from the little log wharf, I saw Arthur gazing after us with an utterly forlorn expression. At the moment I wondered if we might ever travel together again; the probability seemed zero, but I should have remembered that lack of probability is the chief jest and delight of the strange fates in the North.

As we plowed up great Reindeer Lake, I could see the little clearing where I had always camped. The small opening brought a flood of thoughts. There was the morning when Solomon and I had started forth to paddle to Brochet in September. The time we returned there, defeated and hungry, and some Indians coming up from the south handed me a soiled scrap of paper. Solomon asked me to read it, for it was for him. The note, in a childish schoolgirl hand, read: "Dear Husband, I am lonely. Please come back. Our little girl has died while you have been away. Your wife."

Solomon was little surprised, and later thumbing through my diary I found an entry on the day the little girl had died: "Today Solomon says he has been feeling his devil again. He says that he does not know what it is but it's about the size of a match box and trembles when something bad is either going to happen or has happened at home. He says that it is inside him just above his heart."

Yet in the sadness of the moment there was the quiet gladness that the lake was now behind us, the great lake with its perpetual roaring winds and waves, the little island where we almost starved and ate seagulls. On that small island, prisoners of a relentless wind of eight days' fury, I said I hoped it might stop and Solomon said, "You do not 'hope' in this country; you do not hope, you just do the best you can."[2]

That small clearing now almost lost from sight was where the boy Sageese had thrown rocks at my tent and old George had given me a most beautiful pair of moccasins in recompense. There I had talked with the old trapper Bill about the world of long ago. There I had camped after I flew down the lake and the Indians thought I was the Bishop, flew in with Archie Turnbull, whose body and plane were found a charred wreckage the very next year—Old Reindeer leveling once more the impertinence and lack of respect of the white man.

Thoughts such as these crowded my mind as I watched South End fade from sight. Then the high hills to the south were cut off by the first of the thousands of islands that choke this mighty lake.

Reindeer Lake is one of the really great lakes of the North, a distinction in a world, which often seems more lakes than land. It was first partially explored and mapped by the indefatigable David Thompson, who passed through it in 1798 in an endeavor to open a new route for the Hudson's Bay Company to the rich Athabaska and Mackenzie country. The Northwest Company with its competing posts on the Saskatchewan and upper Churchill River was so successfully and strenuously thwarting the Hudson's Bay Company over that established route that a new one was necessary. Thompson, by more than heroic efforts, managed to get through to Athabaska, but the route via Swan River-Wollaston Lake-Fond-du-Lac River was deemed by him quite impractical. He very nearly lost his life on the return trip. He established a post and wintered on the west side of Reindeer Lake, probably not far from the present-day Swan River outpost. He called it Bedford House. The site has never been found.*

Some fifty years later a post was established at the northern end of the lake. This post, Brochet, was for years known primarily as a "meat" post rather than a source of great fur catches. It is difficult to turn the wandering Chipewyans from caribou hunting to fur trapping. Even in the days of Thompson the area was very sparsely inhabited by the Chipewyan Indians.

Cochrane in 1881 and the Tyrrell party in 1892** [3] completed the first adequate survey of the lake, and since that time considerable topographic work has been done.

The Chipewyan population seems always to have been indigenous to the area and at one time extended down to the boundary of the Churchill River, which marked their country off from that of the Crees to the south, and has over the years gradually withdrawn to the north and west, still going

* An account in Thompson's own words and interesting observations upon this country are afforded in: *David Thompson's Narrative of His Explorations in Western America, 1784-1812.* Ed. by J. B. Tyrrell. Toronto, The Champlain Society, 1916.

** A very detailed and accurate account of this entire region with emphasis on the geological aspect can be found in: Report on the *Doobaunt, Kazan and Ferguson Rivers and the North-West Coast of Hudson Bay*, by J. Burr Tyrrell. Ottawa, The Geological Survey of Canada, 1897.

to Brochet to trade.

A few members of the Inland or Caribou Eskimos used to come down from the north to trade at Brochet, but of recent years, the establishment of posts inland from the sea coast, like Padley, has stopped these long and arduous treks down from the Barrens.[4]

The remote position of Reindeer Lake, off the great travel routes, has kept it more or less inviolate from the hordes of civilized mongrels, which have invaded other less fortunate parts of the North. And unless on its granite and gneissic shores some considerable mineral discovery is made a possibility which from known formations looks unlikely—this happy state may last a little longer.

Reindeer Lake is a body of water some hundred and forty miles long—one hundred and seventy by the canoe route—and at one spot thirty-five miles wide. Its axis is a bit east of north. Innumerable long bays trend northeast and southwest following the linear distortions of the rock structure, and except for one portion the lake is filled with literally thousands of islands. Despite the myriad islands, there are some large traverses and openings, which make it a difficult and dangerous lake for canoe travel, particularly during periods of high winds, which come often and without warning.

The southern end of the lake is hemmed in by comparatively high and rugged hills gradually lessening to the north. Here sand-girt islands begin to appear and the whole effect is of a more subdued topography. In the southeast corner is a large and perfectly symmetrical round bay quite devoid of island and tremendously deep. This huge bay, utterly out of character with the rest of the lake, is a spot usually to be avoided. It is too deep for nets, affords no shelter from the wind, and is supposed to be inhabited by a gigantic fish of miraculous abilities and voracious appetite, inclined occasionally to come up through the ice and select itself a young caribou.

The lake has long been famous for its winter concentration of the Barren Ground caribou, and also for fine lake trout and whitefish, which thrive in the extraordinarily clear, cold water. In fact the waters of Reindeer Lake compare favorably, in their lack of suspended sediment, with the clearest lakes in the world—Baikal in Siberia and some of the Scotch lochs.

The clarity of Reindeer Lake water was demonstrated in a very interesting way just before we left. Down very deep I could see a large jackfish (northern pike) swimming slowly about with a herring in his mouth. He had the herring by the middle, crosswise in his lean jaws, and by a series of leisurely bites he gradually worked the smaller fish along, slowly approaching the head. Then with a last rapid twist he turned the fish about and popped it head first out of sight. Just the end of the tail protruded for a brief instant, and then that too followed.

The course followed by the *Lac du Brochet* differed some-what from the established canoe route. The latter naturally follows the course most protected by islands and swings over to the eastern shore after passing through a long channel known as Birch Narrows. In these narrows, some years before, I had seen a group of the same type of red ocher figures as at Medicine Rapids. These drawings—a wolf, a buffalo, some canoes, and a number of less distinguishable geometric fig-ures—were created in the distant past in the same way as the Medicine Rapids figures. They are notable not only for their artistry and antiquity, but also for the fact that they occur so far north—at a northern extremity for this sort of thing, if one excludes the Pacific Coast. As we passed through Birch Narrows it occurred to me that with the heightened water level due to the dam these figures now must be entirely sub-merged.[5]

The practice which gave rise to these pictographs de-serves more than a passing reference, for it represents the very crux of the ancient Cree spiritual life and has received scant treatment from professional recorders of these people.

Few writers seem to realize the tremendous importance of dreams and the dream-life in the world of these northern hunters. The latter was so intimately bound up with the wak-ing life that the entire religious concept of the Cree centered around it. To the pre-Christian Cree a well-defined theism was quite lacking. The "Great Spirit" motif of popular fancy did not exist with either great effect or conviction. Vague conceptions of a "Great Spirit" were held to some degree, but as the Great Spirit was no doubt good, i.e., not harmful, little attention was paid to it.

However, to the Cree mind, all the world was spirit bearing and animistic every tree, every animal, every insect, and even the rocks and sand and water. His life was spent in placating and observing a host of spirits. He and the world about him were a completely dual world of the physical and its spirit counterpart.

To help him in his struggle in this world of spirits, each individual possessed a very secret, personal guiding and helping spirit which he could call upon in time of stress, which often visited him in dreams, which was his and his alone. It might be the spirit-half of anything—a certain animal, a sunbeam, the rainbow, a grain of sand, an unknown human, in fact anything in the world. This was a man's "pagan." On the strength of a man's *puagan* rested his success in the physical world about him and his survival against the evil, which the spirits of enemies might direct against him.

I knew of one man whose *puagan* was a skeleton, another a sunbeam, another an old man with glass moccasins and a plug hat. Of great significance was that fact that as a man became older and approached actual senility, his *puagan* likewise lost its power.

To obtain and recognize his *puagan*, the individual, just following his adolescence, secreted himself from his fellows for an indefinite period of fasting and intensive dreaming. It was often the custom to go off and construct a sort of nest high up in some secluded spruce tree.

Gradually from the dreams, hallucinations possibly brought on by the self-imposed starvation, one figure or one dream object would disentangle itself and become increasingly clear and dominant. When this dream object became so fixed that the neophyte could establish a rapport with it, it was recognized as the lifelong, personal "manitou," power, god, spirit-in short, the *puagan*.

Rather marvelous tales are still told of some of these searches through the dream world. Marvelous too are the tales of the extraordinary achievements of people whose *puagans* were of a particularly powerful and effective nature. For to these people there was no natural world, as we with rather sterile imagination see it. There was no "luck," bad or good. Bad luck, because it breaks the normal chain of circumstance, indicated that someone or something was directing a more powerful *puagan* against one. A man died because his *puagan* was beaten by another antagonistic *puagan*.

To the Cree the full menace of completely amoral, crushing, destructive nature was revealed. As one old man said to me: "This religion of yours is very well, but why should one pray to God, who you say is good? It seems only sensible to me to pray to the Devil, who is bad and who will harm you."

But let a Cree be wind-bound on an island. Let him see the mad force of a mighty lake churned into a maelstrom of foam. Let him see that in an inexorable mighty world he is a grain of sand, and all his past virtues or sins, his wishes and desires are nothing. In the foaming rapids, whether he is good, bad, ambitious or slothful, brave or cowardly, intelligent or a moron, death waits a mistake. In the crying of the wind and the rumbling of the falls he hears that he has no one to help him, no one to change the way of destruction. Then, and then only, perhaps does he cry out in his heart for a personal, a visible, *puagan*. He may even curse a way of living and an environment which has stripped him of an ancient succor.[6]

In a few hours' time we arrived at Rabbit River, "Wapussipi." From the two ancient and dilapidated warehouses we all began to load boxes, bales, and bags with speed and determination. A great deal of the load was "Treaty," rations of flour and clothing to be distributed at the Treaty ceremonies in July. At these annual functions, the Indians are given five dollars each in payment for their forfeiture of individuality, their dependence upon the Government, and their abdication of all land ownership. Various goods are rationed out to the indigent and old. The money immediately travels back over the counter of the trading post, and the day is proclaimed an enormous success.

Most of the bags of rice had been attacked by mice, but the flour had not suffered so badly. We carried aboard four tons of flour in hundred-pound sacks, of which I tallied one ton, myself. I stumbled walking up the narrow, high-pitched gangplank with a hundred and fifteen pound box of tea, but managed to hold on to it in a very undignified and ludicrous pose, much to the amusement of the Indians. But Mistigosso dropped a large bale of pants into the water, and it was my turn to laugh. Everyone pitched in with a will, particularly the venerable and jolly Father Egernolf, who hitching up his cassock rolled gasoline drums out of the warehouse.

There were a good many cases of ammunition; .3o-.3o's to be put on board. This caliber is still the standard in the North. The total cargo amounted to about ten tons. By afternoon we had finished, and after much prying with poles got the heavily loaded *Lac du Brochet* off and headed north for Brochet.

I was very thankful for the work; I knew that real portaging lay ahead of me, and this, with the Reindeer River preface, was a good introduction and warm-up.

It was a somber gray day. The fire-blackened forest and high, steep, grim rocks of the shore gave one a feeling of the sullen savagery of this lake. It is curious the human characteristics various rivers and lakes in the North take on. Many of them are commonly known as "good" or "bad," and this has little to do with their size or appearance. Reindeer is always spoken of as bad.

At dark we tied up at an island. The eight aboard, passengers and crew, had been increased to seventeen with the addition of Mrs. Olsen and her eight children, bound for Brochet on a "holiday."

When night came, we turned in en masse below the deck, each seeking for himself the most comfortable couch he could find on the rock-like sacks of flour and boxes of ammunition. Every cranny was chinked and the hatch closed to keep out mosquitoes, and the already thick atmosphere was heavily sprayed with Fly-Tox. At least one of the Olsen brood set up a howl. It wasn't long before I left my uneasy berth suspended among the flour sacks, stepping on two people and gashing my toe rather badly on the way out.

The morning of July 2 dawned, still overcast and gloomy, and as I uncoiled from a very wet and soggy tarpaulin I was greeted by the sight of old Father Egernolf conducting Mass for the two Indians of the boat crew. They were kneeling together among the rocks and moss. It gave me an odd turn to see them, their straight backs silhouetted against the early morning light upon the lake.

Later I went off in the bush for a homely function, and when I returned the boat was already some distance from the island. In the confusion of departing they had quite overlooked me. After much shouting—how embarrassing to hear one's own voice in the stillness of a great lake—they at length turned back and hauled me aboard with much laughter and badinage.

As we plowed up the lake we alternately watched the procession of low islands and lying on the flour bags below the deck, followed in hypnotic coma the spinning flywheel of the laboring engine. Observing Father Egernolf quietly reading, it occurred to me that he was one of the most extraordinary men I had ever known—a person of whom, when someday he was covered with the winter snows, one could say, "He was a man!" He does all and more than all that the world asks of him with no reward and through it all has kept himself a man, with the humor of age and the vitality and heart of youth.

Sixty-two years old, he was still as energetic and full of enthusiasm and jollity as a man half his years. His electric energy is a legend. For thirty-four years he has administered to the Chipewyans at Brochet. He is a marvelous linguist, one of the very few white men in the world who can really speak the Chipewyan language. He is a jolly raconteur and a man of infinite kindness and generosity. It is rare that one meets a man in the North who has what you might clumsily call the "feeling" of the country. Father Egernolf is almost the only one I can remember. I studied his face. Long, frightfully hard winter trips, blizzards, searing cold, and the exhausting self-denying labors he had conducted so long had lined his face very deeply. No one who has ever passed through Brochet can fail to remember some kindness of "Eggy's." I suppose that there is no one who knows the strange oblique mind of the Chipewyan better.

Our course was now directed up the lake to Halfway

Island, where a camp had been established by a group of men who were attempting to fish the lake commercially. It was an ambitious program. The men went off in canoes and boats, set the nets, and later returned to the base camp with white-fish and lake trout. Thence, after being iced, the fish were flown out to Flin Flon. The venture had been tried before but not with marked success. The only thing that made it at all feasible was the excellence and largeness of the fish in the lake.

Our stop at Halfway Island happily coincided with the lunch hour. We were hospitably received and had a tremendous feast. An elderly Finnish couple who had partially underwritten the project also ran the camp. We had pie cooked on the premises. It was almost unbelievable. In my wildest imagination years before when I had been windbound for eight days and our food supply had dwindled to those two execrable seagulls, I had never dreamed of pie in the middle of Reindeer Lake!

Father Egemolf was very amusing. He kept showing me off like a curiosity, saying, "And he is going to Nueltin Lake!" Through all his travels he had never seen Nueltin in summer, and indeed few white men have. He seemed very proprietary and proud of me.

The men had returned and were busy gutting the large trout. I could not help resenting them somewhat. There are so many lakes, even this small intrusion of the "outside" seemed in a way a blasphemy—the ever greedy, shouldering, aggressive white man. Someday there would be no place left to wander.

After this kind treatment we were once again on our way. On the islands diminished and we crossed a very large, open traverse. It is here that the full majesty of Reindeer begins to be apparent. The shoreline disappears to the west, a great inland sea. A few islands huddle against a high point to the east and mark Pasquachi (Stump) Bay, and its dangerous northern shore Porcupine Point. By canoe, this is the most feared crossing in the lake. In Stump Bay I had previously had the experience of being lost in the company of a Mounted Policeman!

The day was clear now, with a low, dark bank of clouds clinging to the western horizon. I watched the lake. For once there was no roll, not a ripple upon it. How tremendous that great expanse was! And over these waters had passed how many canoes and boats, York boats loaded with meat and pemmican for the brigades to the south, their great oars dipping endlessly to the tune of the voyageurs' song, soon swallowed up in the great emptiness! How many canoes had made the darting fearsome crossing, pointed Chipewyan canoes, rounded longer bark canoes of Crees!

But of all this, as ever in the North, there was no sign, just the silence and the faint line of the eastern shore and the lake waiting.

When I went below amidst the flour sacks to meditate, the Olsen children constantly popped in and out like mice from behind bales or bags. Despite their fair, obviously Swedish faces, their conversation was entirely in Cree.

We stopped at length and boiled up the teakettle on a low sandy island. And not long after a solitary lobstick came into view and then the red roof of the Hudson's Bay Company post, the scattered Indian shacks, the withered crosses of the graveyard, the Mission-Brochet.

CHAPTER 4

Brochet

The approach to Brochet by the "schooner" route is up a narrow bay of some length. A solitary sentinel spruce with its limbs trimmed off in a striking and eccentric pattern—a "lobstick"—signals the entrance. The settlement is almost entirely on the west shore on a level gravel ridge. First one sees a large log cabin, used by transient white trappers, then a forlorn and populous graveyard, barren and dominated by a forest of pitiful, small, bleached crosses. This is followed by a huddling cluster of Indian shacks built of logs and chinked with mud; in some cases grass grows from the roofs, giving them a curiously hairy appearance. Beyond them and dominating the scene is the gray Mission church, and at some distance are the three buildings of the Hudson's Bay post, white and gleaming and with the usual startling red roofs.

As we neared the shore, I noticed immediately that something was different. There was the usual audience of Indians silently squatting on the bank to watch us come in. I could even see the familiar faces of Frank Henderson and Jack Hogarth, old-timers long associated with Brochet. The Mission church, the square Hudson's Bay store, and the 75 dwelling house still dominated the skyline. Then I realized it was the old Revillon house that had been torn down in my absence. As we pulled in to the old scow now made into a dock, a few of the squatting Indians came down to the boat, and the wailing of the dogs, which had long since signaled our approach, rose to a great crescendo.

Brochet was established in 1856. Since that time, literally thousands of pounds of caribou meat and pemmican have left this post for the voyageurs of the fur brigades to the south. This traffic ceased a great many years ago and the emphasis is now strictly on fur. It has had very prosperous years; in one year alone it had a harvest of eighty-seven thousand dollars' worth of fur. The trading competition was very keen here in the past. At one time the Hudson's Bay Company withdrew, leaving the field to Revillon Frères.[1] This was temporary, however, and with the absorption of the latter competitor in 1936, they once again actively took over Brochet. At the present time their only competition was from a small Jewish trading outfit[2] which maintained a miserable little shack at the other end of the "village."

About 1926, with fur prices high and an inrush of money to the south around The Pas affording capital, there was a great deal of excitement and a very active enlargement of the whole fur trading field in this area. Outposts and more formal trading posts were established in a rash fever of competitive eagerness and optimism far to the north of Brochet and indeed right up to the edge of the Barrens. Revillon had posts to the north on Kasmere River and well into the Nueltin Lake territory. The Hudson's Bay Company followed suit and penetrated to the habitat of the Caribou Eskimo on Ennadai Lake. An independent trader, Del Simons, long associated with Revillon and a man to be counted in when anything big was in order, established posts at Rabbit River and also northwest from Nueltin Lake near Windy Lake not far from the only present relic of these ventures, the Nueltin Lake Post of the Hudson's Bay Company.

Costly rivalry, falling fur prices, mismanagement, incompetent personnel, and a total disregard for expense combined with the great and arduous distances shortly to level off these advances. Almost as quickly as they sprang up, they disappeared. Only the Nueltin Lake Post remains an active remnant of these endeavors.

The result of this flare-up is not at once apparent, but to the inhabitants of the country the effect is more far-reaching than might be supposed. The coming of traders and money brought an invasion of Cree trappers from the south and in their wake a number of white trappers. Both of these peoples, and particularly the latter, are in general far more thorough and ruthless exterminators of fur than the natural inhabitants of the region, the Chipewyans. The age-old primary interest of the Chipewyans is caribou. Their local name, the "Idthen-eldeli" ("caribou-eaters") is significant. When there are caribou or, as they are called in the North, "deer," to the Chipewyan there is nothing else.

A rather full account of Brochet,[3] something of its people and much of its birds, has been written by Captain Angus Buchanan, an English amateur-naturalist who wintered here in 1914.* A lake some distance from the post is still referred to as "Buchanan's Lake." On its west shore a small depression in the ground and a few fragments of photographic film mark the spot where his cabin stood.[4]

The people who resort to Brochet—Chipewyans, Crees, half-breeds, and whites—total about four hundred and fifty souls of which possibly three hundred are Chipewyans, or more properly "Idthen-eldeli." These, the original inhabitants, are divided into two bands, one the Hatchet Lake Band, which hunts and traps in the neighborhood of Little Hatchet Lake west of Wollaston Lake on the Black River, and the other the northern or Barren Land Band, which roams over a large tract north of Brochet and in the main concentrates on the Nueltin Lake drainage. Unlike the Crees to the south, neither of these bands are inclined to spend much time at the trading post. They arrive in summer, a week or two before "Treaty," and leave very shortly after it. Most of the year, Brochet remains a tiny village of six white men, the two fur-trading establishments, the Mission, and a few half-breed and Cree families who have some connection with their activities.

In the last twenty-five years the number of the Chipewyans has dropped to almost a third of what it was.

* *Wild Life in Canada*, by Capt. Angus Buchanan, Toronto, McClelland, 1920.

The chief of the Hatchet Lake Band at this time was a pleasant, rather fine-looking man named Pascal Benouni, and of the Barren Land Band a disreputable-looking old man called Denarl. The term "chief" is an artificial creation fostered originally by the fur trade for these northern Indians. Originally they never had any such distinction. Each family's whims were sufficient unto itself, and they made no attempt to follow any particular person at his command, though they might on occasion more or less and of their own will be temporarily advised and influenced by some outstanding individual. Thus for many years the Barren Land Band has been to a degree dominated by a very old man named Casmir or Kasmere, who had considerable weight among them.

The country around Brochet is very subdued and quite sandy in marked contrast to the south end of the lake. The post and Mission stand on a sandy ridge, which represents an ancient level of the lake, some forty feet above its present level. What an incredible world this must have been at the last melting of the great ice sheet! The whole north must have been a succession of gigantic lakes, an almost continuous floating immensity of water and islands. Here at the north end of the lake the sand represented a dying and weary last phase of the ice sheet. The withdrawing wall of ice, its scouring and abrading activity over, deposited floods of ground-up rock and gravel. This, filling the depressions, resulted in the flat landscape, which is characteristic of the section.

As it was already late, it was decided to do the unloading the next day. Frank, planted solidly on his single leg on the top of the bank, waved a greeting to me. I gathered together my small sack of belongings and went up to greet him. We all went up to the house and soon were seated over a fine meal. No business is contracted, no wayfarer questioned until after a good meal, if one has come any distance, in the North.

There had been a change in the personnel since my last visit. The former manager, an excellent Arctic raconteur, had been transferred to a post "on the line, near the railroad, and his place had been taken by a man with many years' experience in the country east of Lake Winnipeg.[5] He proved to be an extremely well-informed person with a diversity of interests unusual in a fur trader. The "family" was further augmented by two white trappers who had come in, one from the country to the west, Wollaston Lake, and the other from the north.

When the dishes were cleared away, the time for reminiscence, news from the "outside," and general conversation began. The opening gambit is frequently the same. The visitor searches about for someone he has met or knows who knows or has met someone in the gathering. The intricate and far-flung web of northern acquaintance rarely fails, and it did not this time. The hours passed swiftly with the aid of a mellow quart of Scotch until the gathering eventually broke up at five o'clock in the morning.

The talk, as if in deference to the visitor, touched at first lightly on the"outside." But this was soon forgotten and brushed away, once the convention of its mention had been observed; then, with mounting enthusiasm, the conversation became solely and entirely the North. As I sat listening and occasionally contributing, it struck me what a huge area our discourse covered. Alec, the post manager, covered a tremendous country east of Lake Winnipeg and out to Hudson Bay; Frank could draw from all the Pelican Narrows–Brochet area and also the Ile á la Crosse and upper Churchill region. Old Jack represented the country north of Brochet up into the Barrens and the Kazan River, not to mention British Columbia. Curry had the Swan River and the east side of Reindeer. John, the trapper, was conversant with Wollaston Lake and the country to the west of that, and I had a brief smattering from the Mackenzie River, the Eastern Arctic, and Labrador. Through our mutual recollections from the previous post manager, both Frank and I could speak of the west side of Hudson Bay and the interior to Baker Lake. To round it off were the interwoven and interlocking innumerable hearsays and common acquaintances.

The depth of years lent the conversation its greatest savor. For almost all but me were men of twenty or more years' northern background. A good story in the North remains intact and untarnished regardless of its time. For the North is timeless; the vintage of its heroic, its pathetic, and its comic is undated.

On the practical and immediate side was the general opinion that I should have no difficulty in finding some Indian to go along with me. Fur prices had not been high, fur had not been plentiful, and many of the people were in rather bad straits. There was comment on the activity of a mining outfit which had been doing some reconnaissance work far to the north of Brochet. It was reported that they had fifteen men in the field. Of particular interest to me was the pilot's report that the lakes were still frozen.

There were innumerable small items of local interest. The winter just past had been a difficult one for the Indians and particularly the northern band, which had lost five members from some sort of influenza which was believed to have been transmitted from Lake Athabaska, the Goldfields mining area, by some Chipewyans who had come from Fond-du-Lac and met the northern band at Kasba Lake. The price of gasoline was dropping and at the moment was only $2.75 a gallon.

The following day, the boat was unloaded, and once again it turned south to make another trip to Rabbit River. The time went by very quickly and pleasantly. There were old acquaintances to see and much to talk about. But there were very few Indians in at the post. What few had arrived were off on the islands fishing. As I rambled about, the rather disquieting fact began to be apparent that it would be next to impossible to get anyone to go with me. As the Barren Land Band had not yet come down from the north, there was no possibility of returning with them until after "Treaty," a date too late for my trip. What Indians were around either did not like the prospect of such a long absence or else were engaged in their own pursuits and unable to go. There remained but one possible person, but when he learned of my destination he became obdurate, which was perhaps fortunate as I later discovered that he was subject to fits usually brought on by the excitement of any critical event.

I was daily in more of a quandary. I had never been beyond the post here. Although there existed a large-scale[6] map of the Cochrane River, from the river to Nueltin Lake there was no known map worthy of the name. No one at the post had ever made the trip by water, so it was impossible to get much information. One hundred and twenty-five miles of the route was upstream work in a river reputed nasty, full of rapids, and difficult for one man to ascend. However, I daily become more determined to go. With everyone else busy at some task or another, I felt more and more the imposition in my staying and doing nothing. I had about made up my mind to start out alone, when John, the white trapper from Wollaston Lake, offered to go along with me. This presented a new problem.

John did not know a foot of the way, and indeed had never been north of Brochet in that direction; it would be a case of us both finding the route. I had never traveled inland with a white man, and I was not sure, on such short acquaintance, just how things might turn out. Knowing the usual white man methods of travel, I had always preferred the company of Indians; and, in particular, much of my wandering had taken its real value and substance in my association with them. He could not speak Chipewyan or Cree. It would thus be difficult to secure information, topographical or otherwise, even if we succeeded in keeping to the route and met Indians coming south. Furthermore, and particularly vexatious, was the matter of an intangible mutual responsibility which I did not relish.

For the next few days we talked the matter over from every angle. There were a number of factors in John's favor. His reputation as a canoe man, particularly with the pole, was very well established—not an insignificant thing in a country where criticism is great and judgment stern and reserved. He was known as a good and a tough traveler. He was a seasoned and experienced man in the North. He seemed to be enthusiastic about the trip.

An interim of perplexity and inaction was now forced upon me, anyway, for since my arrival the wind had become very violent. Mostly from the south, these winds whirled over Brochet with a tremendous force. Sometimes there fled with them shreds of black clouds, but there was no rain. They had a peculiar character. They were like walls of air that pressed forward with a terrible eagerness, shrieking and menacing. Sunset would bring a brief interlude of calm, and then once again they would start to roar through the pale night while the moon, nearly full, rode blood red in the sky.

There is nothing quite like the northern night at this time of the year. There is no real darkness. After the sun has gone down, the western sky stays a pale greenish hue. There are no stars, but the zenith is darkened to a deep blue. Small birds keep up their noise throughout the prolonged and endless twilight. There is over everything a hush that seems unnatural, as if the world is waiting for a darkness, which for some strange reason will not come.

In my perplexity I went over to see Father Egernolf. My call was ostensibly just a social visit, but it became immeasurably more than that to me. Sitting in his small room with its Spartan simplicity, it was impossible not to catch his infectious gaiety and something of his enthusiasm, which, by some subtle alchemy within myself, was transformed to a new enthusiasm for whatever might lie ahead. We chatted of the Indians, the fur, and the travelers of many years ago. We talked very little of my plans, but the effect was beyond the words.

Father Egernolf's command of the Chipewyan tongue was a wonderful thing. The Chipewyans, although they are neighbors of the Crees, differ from them completely in language. There are not two syllables in the two tongues with the remotest similarity. The Cree is a soft, liquid tongue; the Chipewyan is harsh and guttural, and extraordinarily tonal, the same syllable-consonant combinations meaning entirely different things if spoken either from the more remote parts of the stomach or the passages of the nose. Particularly baffling to me was the fact that it has innumerable sounds that do not exist in our language at all. Somehow, it had never occurred to me that there could be sounds in a language for which we have no letters. An old North story illustrates this very well.

Some years ago, a young man appeared at Great Slave Lake. Fresh from the outside, he caused mild speculation at the small trading post at which he stopped, for he did not have the appearance of the usual trader or trapper. He was not long in identifying himself to the manager of the post. It seemed he was a scientist and furthermore a man of action and enterprise who expected and demanded quick results. He was armed with small pile of notebooks and a pair of spectacles. He explained to the post manager that he was in this district to study the Chipewyan tongue, or rather the Athapaskan, of which the Chipewyan is a dialect. He was horrified to find that no white man there, particularly the trader, was capable of conversing in Chipewyan. It seemed incredible to him that men who had been twenty years or more in the country could not talk fluently a tongue that, as he pointed out, was basic and simple. At last, with a good deal of rummaging about through the country—for he paid his bills and had come armed with official letters—an old trapper, a white man who had been married for years to a Chipewyan woman, was summoned. The weary old man was brought to the company store where the young man sat with a pile of fresh notebooks at his elbow, his pen poised and a frightening interrogative stare behind his glasses. He explained to the old man, who had taken advantage of the occasion to get the advance of a plug of tobacco, what he intended doing. The old man was to repeat in Chipewyan a number of words that the young man would dictate. But, before this, explained the scientist, he wished some fundamental and root syllables.

"What, for instance, is the most common syllable; what sound do you find most typical?"

The old man looked wearily about him. He scratched his head without removing his battered travesty of a cap. He looked around the store, at the young man, and then at the pot-bellied stove which was roaring with spruce knots. He chewed reflectively for a moment and then spat a long stream of tobacco juice on the hot stove lid. A sharp *zsst* broke the silence.

"There!" he said. "Write that down, that's the first syllable!"

For a long time Father Egernolf and I talked about the Indians, their vagaries, their peculiar ways of thinking, their indirection, and their strange subjective rationalizations. The Chipewyans, and particularly this branch, the Idthen-eldeli, seem more than the others to have some of that odd indirection of thought which they brought with them thousands of years ago from the unknown steppes of Asia.

To him they were like a man in a darkened room. Like a man whose eyesight is so failing that when you ask him what some object is he might say a chair and then asked again might say a bureau. But as we talked I began to wonder, particularly when he told one story which seemed to me to reveal a great deal without his intending it.

"You know," he said, "these people sometimes seem to me as if they never can understand, they never can learn. Perhaps our Lord intended it to be thus; perhaps it was not given to them to learn as we do. Like the birds and the animals, their God-given sphere is limited to what they know. Let me give you an example. During the summer here I have a catechism class of the children every day. Every day through the summer I go over the same thing, the identical questions and answers. Do you think they learn?

"There was a little girl in my class. She looked very bright—most Indian children do. Every day I took special care of this little one. I went over the questions and answers with her alone. You know, there is a part in our catechism where the question is asked, 'What is the most beautiful thing that God created?' The answer is: Man and all the angels.' But do you think I could teach this simple thing, that this little mind could learn? Every time I asked: 'What is the most beautiful thing God created?' She would look up at me and say: '*Idthen!*' the caribou!"

The old priest rocked in his chair for a while. He buried his lined face in his hands. He was thinking.

"You know," he burst out in his abrupt manner, "years ago when I was a young man I left Prince Albert. I was ordered north. I remember saying to my friends—I had many there—as I left, 'good-bye, good-bye, see you in two years' time.' " He smiled at me and then said simply: "It has been thirty-four 'Thirty-four years here and I have perhaps done nothing.'" [8]

But the greatest gift that Father Egernolf gave me was in the few words we spoke about the Nueltin Lake trip. How his old eyes lighted with enthusiasm! He laughed and joked. "Sure, start out with John. He's a good boy. Think of the deer you will see and that big lake. Ah, you are lucky to be still young! You have traveled in the North! You have traveled alone! The good Lord is always with us! You will see what no one else has seen! Good luck! I wish I were going with you!"

All my enervating doubts dissolved in such tonic as this. We laughed and joked for a while, and as I was leaving he pressed some pemmican and a few caribou delicacies upon me.

I went over to the Company store and got together my outfit and grubstake: a new tracking line forty feet long of quarter-inch light Manila rope, an extra pair of moosehide moccasins, fifty pounds of flour, some lard, tea, and plenty of tobacco. Salt and sugar I already had, and I purchased a tin of baking powder. With a little luck this should last the two of us for six weeks.

I did not sleep for a long while that night. I went over in my mind the events which had preceded my arrival: the plane from Channing, the fortune of Arthur's coming up to South End, the lucky chance of the *Lac du Brochet*, John's being in from Wollaston. All of these were consistently good fortune. The signs appeared to be right. There was no more perplexity and perturbation; with the wind dropping tomorrow, it would be time to go.

As I lay listening to the small sounds, the *cheep* of the white-crowned sparrows, the rustle of mice, I watched the blood red, full moon. The buildings stood out in a stark and unearthly whiteness. I saw one star, but the green of the western sky flooded the world with a subdued, unnatural, eerie light. Somewhere some children were playing football. I could hear their thin, piping cries. They seemed to come from nowhere, disembodied, shrill sounds like the noises of shorebirds migrating across the moon in the fall. Then high in the semi-darkness I heard three loons calling. From one to the other they flung their challenging notes, that strangely haunting cry they use when flying high. On they swept in the night. The children's voices stopped and then they too in chorus took up the quavering call. A shot rang out; once more there was silence, and then, in defiance and exaltation, I heard the loons crying out again far down the lake.

I remembered that when *magua*, the loon, calls in flight he is saying, "Wind! Wind! There will be wind!"

The next morning, July 6, John and I gathered our outfit

together. John contributed an extra cooking kettle, purchased his own tobacco, and we were ready to start. Before leaving, we agreed upon various details, the most important, perhaps, that if anything happened either of us, in the way of getting lost, the other would make no attempt to look for or save him which could mean a disruption of the year to come.

This may seem a curious and rather brutal agreement. The fact was that each of us was entirely dependent upon his particular job, which in both cases commenced in the fall. To get back to them meant leaving the country of our projected trip well before "freeze-up." If either of us was detained for any reason until freeze-up, it meant the ruination not of a month's but of a whole year's work. We both knew that when something really serious happens in a country like this, so vast, so unknown and confusing, the time it takes to get out and get back even with aid is so great, and the possibility of this aid being any use is so small, that it is nothing but a gesture to convention.[9]

Odd as this may seem, between us we had an understanding and a freedom that in reality meant a stronger bond. The biggest worry was thus cleared away.

While we were making our preparations, the *Lac du Brochet* returned from Rabbit River. We secured from the Hudson's Bay Company a stout, freighter model, seventeen-foot canoe. Before long, the heavy southeast wind died down. We went down to the shore. A few curious Indians as usual were squatting along the bank. The white men gave us a little send-off. John paddled stern and I bow. We pushed off from the small Brochet wharf in the late afternoon. We headed the canoe northeast toward the mouth of the Cochrane River. I could feel John digging in with the big, deep strokes you use when you start. Neither of us looked back.'[10]

CHAPTER 5

The Cochrane

The Cochrane River is the main contributor to the waters of Reindeer Lake. It has its source in Wollaston Lake some distance to the west, flows from the northeast quadrant of that unusual lake, and pursuing a northeast course suddenly turns very abruptly upon itself and flows south through a series of lakes into Reindeer, which it enters from the northeast corner some three miles from the post of Brochet. It is named for A. S. Cochrane, who mapped and explored its length in the year 1881.

In 1894 it was ascended and geological and physiographic comment were made upon part of it by Tyrrell. He, as we proposed to do, left the river just before its great bend and struck off to the north and east.

A small-scale map of the river was made in 1914, but this map traces only the actual canoe course followed by the survey party, and the shores of the larger lakes in the course of the river remained uncharted.

Wollaston Lake, from which the Cochrane rises, deserves at least a passing mention. It is a very large, clear lake with islands and bays similar to those of Reindeer in shape and alignment. It was discovered by Thompson in 1798, and he gave it the Cree name for spirit or god, Manitou Lake. Tyrrell changed the name to Wollaston Lake, as it is known, at least to the whites, today. It has the unusual formation of a height of land passing through the lake itself so that it has two discharges into entirely different watersheds. Another peculiarity is the fact that the Black—later Fond du Lac—River and the Cochrane, starting close together at the north end of Wollaston Lake, drain, respectively, northwest into the waters of the Mackenzie Basin and thence to the Arctic Ocean, and southeast through Reindeer Lake and the Churchill to Hudson Bay.

After Brochet had disappeared behind us, we followed a small channel between islands to northeast, each secretly hoping, I suspect, that we would discover the mouth of the Cochrane River without any trouble. It would be embarrassing to have difficulty finding the way at the very outset. But despite the short distance, the mouth of the river is not obvious either from the lake proper or from our approach.

As we glided along, we were each, I am sure, making judgment upon the paddling abilities of the other. We had started with auspicious speed and soon settled down into the routine strokes customary in the North—which appear utterly amateur to those on the "outside," who do not live by the paddle. It is the northern practice to paddle two or three strokes on one side and then shift and paddle the same number on the other. When two men are paddling they usually shift to opposite sides conversely and in unison. A rhythm is set up, and in the long hours of constant paddling this procedure is less fatiguing than the eastern method of steering and paddling confined for long periods to one side of the canoe.[1] The paddles themselves are quite different. A factory-made paddle is something of a rarity in the North; most of them are made by native craftsmen, chopped out with an ax and shaved down with a crooked knife into long narrow blades with very stout handles, usually without a grip or expansion at the top. The blade itself does not flare out into the conventional oval pattern but is straight, more like an oar. The reasons for this shape, and their size and weight—they are heavier and never less than five feet long—is at once apparent when one travels over any northern river. The paddle must have a weight of its own in the fast currents or rapids. It must be stout enough to be used alternately as paddle, pole, and pry. The blade must be narrow so that the swirling force of erratic currents is mastered by the paddle rather than the paddle mastered by them. When Indians paddle a canoe alone, they often sit in the middle of the canoe. Their maneuvering, as they solemnly swing the paddle from side to side, often raising it vertically upward into the air, appears deceptively deliberate and slow. Actually their strokes, very short, but very powerful, drive the canoe at a rate the slow arc of the paddle does not suggest.

A silent acknowledgment passed between us that neither would prove a burden in the canoe, and we began watching anxiously for some indication that we were near the mouth of the river.

Pursuing our course and crossing a large bay, we could just see in the fading light a dark, disturbed band of water moving out toward the lake from behind a wooded point or island. Rounding this, we felt the current and, much easier at heart, paddled northward. So complex and extended and clogged by islands was the bay opening that only the slight pull of the current gave us any assurance that we were on a river.

In this first brief three-quarters of an hour I had already noted one thing, which was very comforting. John did not display any of the small mannerisms, which can make long association with a fellow paddler torture. These eccentricities or petty habits take on an unimaginable importance. I remember particularly an Indian who once traveled with me paddling stern. He had the most aggravating habit, after an hour or two, of breaking into a timed series of small body noises. The evident complacency and satisfaction with which these regular sounds issued by the end of ten hours' paddling would drive me to a state of suppressed and sullen rage. They seemed to mock every effort I extended myself. Another time, I traveled down a long river in a canoe so small that three of us were all but touching each other. I was in the middle, and the Indian paddling bow had a peculiar crackling noise in his left shoulder. Hour after hour, my ear scarcely three inches from his imperturbable but noisy back, I could hear the grinding of his shoulder socket. Whenever I asked him about it, in a tone of curiosity rather than reproach, he stopped and grinned and then, holding the paddle upright, ran his tongue along the blade for a drink of water. Turning without a word, he would recommence his inexorable paddling, and it always seemed to me the lubrication stimulated the horrible noise.

The problem of finding or keeping on the route while ascending a river would seem to be the simplest in the world. But in these large northern rivers infinitely broken up by islands and frequently expanding into lakes, it is not as easy as it might appear.

Long bays extended off to the northeast and west, and the river was so cluttered with islands, with frequent stretches in which the current disappeared, that the pursuit of the correct track became at times entirely a matter of hunch.

Before long, we passed a number of small shacks, and shortly after this the river contracted and rushed down upon us through a narrow channel split in the middle by an island. As we had not expected rapids so early in our ascent, we had not provided ourselves with poles. We attempted to paddle up the channel to the west of the island, attacking the rapid on the inside curve, but we found it much too strong for us. We then tried to cross over to the other side and in the process, despite frantic efforts, found ourselves swept some distance downstream. Keeping close to the west bank we crawled upward again. The water was very heavy, though fortunately deep. By dint of paddling, pushing, grasping the willows on the bank, and clawing the shore with our paddles, we managed to defeat the rapid and reach a more quiet stretch. After resting a moment and rolling a cigarette, we discovered that another long rapid lay ahead of us. Since it was already late, we decided to camp.

Our camp, the first of the trip, was made on a fine, open, sandy ridge. It was a very pleasant spot, with banksian pine, called "jackpine" in the North, and stands of small spruce, in the open, glade-like forest carpeted with white sphagnum moss. The only possible drawback was the continual roar of the rapids above and below us. Some Indians with whom I have traveled will never if they can avoid it camp within sound of rapids, not only because of the noise, but as one told me: "The sound make me have a feeling inside I do not like."

John as by agreement set about preparing our supper while I wrote up the day's events. Neither operation took very long. Some of our flour we had previously baked up into bannocks, circular, indigestible cakes baked in the frying pan consisting of flour, water, lard, and baking powder. There was the inevitable tea pail boiling, and we had some lumps of pemmican.

John worked deftly and quickly. He was a small man, about my own height, five-feet-seven, with disproportionately long arms, a small head, and a very broad chest and back. I never saw him with his cap off, but I believe his hair was dark. His eyes were small and extraordinarily deep-set and divided by a beak-like nose. Even at this initial stage neither of us presented a very aesthetic picture. John wore a black sweater with a thick roll collar, dark patched pants, and moccasins. I had made a tremendous improvement over former years in the acquisition of a ski cap, dark blue and with yellow-lined earmuffs. This cap was admirably functional; the padding in the top was a buffer in packing, and I wore the earflaps down to protect me against mosquitoes. I also had a fringed deerskin jacket, my new pants, which were already parting at the seams, and the usual moose skin moccasins and rubbers. The thought of wearing rubbers over moccasins may seem odd, but it is everywhere in practice in the North. In fact, special moccasin rubbers are now made. Moose skin or caribou skin, locally cut, tanned, and sewed, makes the most comfortable and at the same time most porous and moisture-absorbent footwear possible. Besides, unprotected moccasins wear only a very short time in the summer. In the canoe, of course, one can flip the rubbers off by simply stubbing toe against the heel. My own moccasins were very elegantly and heavily beaded, one of my vanities, but John's were of a plainer style.

We did not bother to erect the balloon-silk tarpaulin as the night looked clear. We did, however, each set up an enclosing mosquito netting arrangement over our sleeping bags. Without these, Indians and whites alike would find sleep impossible. It is the most essential traveling article one can carry next to fishhooks.

I have never favored a tent. Bulky, inconvenient, and good for only one use, they can be more of a nuisance than help.

Once I purchased from a very elegant store a miraculous and ingenious tent guaranteed to have been used in all manner of conditions and climates by everyone from Livingstone to Peary. This tent—a very expensive one —I never used until on one occasion the rain was so bad it seemed imperative. After a great deal of trouble disentangling its simplicity, I managed to erect it and, thoroughly soaked, crawled inside. The next morning I discovered that the only waterproof part of the tent was the ground cloth which, refusing to allow the dripping through the roof to run out, kept me surrounded by almost two inches of water.

The next day was very eventful. Having cut two good dry tamarack poles about sixteen feet long, we commenced to pole up the long rapid in front of our camp. The maneuver of poling up a rapid is the most delicate and difficult of all that canoe travel demands. Standing up in the canoe, each man sets his pole and thrusts the canoe forward. It is imperative that the thrust with the pole is made not with the arms but the whole body and particularly that the impetus is directed so that the canoe is not forced away from the pole. The entire procedure is a combination of balance and timing, which in the face of the swirling, plucking current, the bouldery bottom, the ledges and reefs, the submerged rocks, and the instability of a canoe is a great art. Immediately John proved himself a past master.[2]

The roar of falls was soon heard, and crossing the river below them we disembarked and made a portage of nearly a quarter of a mile on the east side of the river. The portage, though long, was a good one. We scrambled up a steep sand and clay bank and the trail led through a fine, open banksian pine forest and over comparatively level ground. The footing was firm, sand and river-rounded boulders. These boulders were so aligned and smoothed they suggested that at one time this had been the river's bed. We made two trips over this four hundred and thirty yard portage, on the first trip carrying the canoe together. In the smooth water above where the falls plunged over a gneissic ledge, I saw some sort of fish just breaking the surface. From their position and action I assumed them to be grayling, a fish not unknown to these waters.

John was in considerable pain with something, which had gotten into his eye during the night. Our combined efforts to remove whatever it was were unsuccessful and he was finally driven to tying a large red bandanna handkerchief around his head. He made a pocket in it and filled it with steeped tealeaves, which thus plastered against the eye seemed to bring some relief.

Along the stretch of river we were now traveling, the formation of the banks was unusual and interesting. From their sculptured form it could be seen that the river had once flowed at a higher level. In the remote past, the pressure of ice in the spring had forced large boulders into a flanking wall of continuous rocks. They were almost like man-made stone facings or walls bordering the river. Very shortly we were forced to portage again, this time around a falls with a drop of about eight feet. The river, squeezed through a narrow opening and plunging over a ledge, spouted up in a high, curving, solid green wave. As we approached this spot, I saw a bald eagle and four tremendous ravens, which at our approach glided away croaking dismally. This portage was not long but it was more difficult to find as it led off from a small, partially concealed bay to the west.

We boiled up the kettle here, and while we were eating, a canoe with four extremely ragged Chipewyans appeared. They were bound for Brochet, and one of them could speak a little English. I do not know when I have seen a dirtier, more ragged and tattered group. We shared a bit of tea with them and then we were on our way.

A long rapid, which the map indicated involved a thirty three chain portage, lunged down upon us, but we decided that we could manage it with poles and did. Following this, we encountered two more short rapids, and then we were relieved to paddle a long stretch unimpeded. We had one moment, which might have been disastrous when, poling up the last of these rather sharp, steep "chutes," my pole became lodged between two boulders and was snatched from my hands. It was a matter of grasping the paddle quickly, and with John still poling we managed to get up without serious accident. My admiration for John's prowess was steadily increasing.

Clawing up the steep pitches, where the full force of the current sweeps down, there always seems to be one critical point, which determines the success or failure of the attempt. The bowman must keep the canoe headed slightly toward the bank, for if the current strikes the shore side of the bow, the whole canoe is seized and swung around. However, the poling by the bowman must be from the shore side, usually, for on the other he is likely to find no bottom. Any large rock is taken advantage of for the slack water in back of it. Then, by imperceptible degrees, the canoe is inched out and around it.

Sometimes it seemed as if we were literally stuck in the midst of the current boiling by on each side of us. The canoe would be suspended in motion while both of us frantically strained on the poles. Afraid to relax for even a fraction of a second to gain a new grip, I cast a wild glance at my companion to see what he was doing and found him repeating my own agonized position and expression. For an interminable time, with the full throaty snarl of the river drumming in our ears, we hung poised between advance and retreat, and then the river rather than the canoe seemed to give way, and we crawled on.

John's eye became the worry of the moment. His piratical-looking bandage did not seem to do any good and he began to have trouble with the other eye. In my mind it became a question whether or not he should go back with any Indians who might appear on the way to Brochet, where he might have a chance to be taken outside to medical attention. If he went back with the Indians, I would retain the canoe and go on alone.

To his great credit, John would not agree to give up yet. He had unshakable confidence in the tealeaves, and he was sure that he would be all right in a day or two. In the meantime we rested, as John found the glare of the water on his good eye coupled with the pain of the bad one almost unbearable.

When we had started out once more we saw a canoe bearing down upon us under sail. It proved to contain an Indian and a white man. At first I did not recognize the latter for a white man, he was so darkly tanned and his clothing was so faded. He was an old-timer in the country and the only one I have known who had been married to both an Eskimo and an Indian. As he was known to have some acquaintance with the Nueltin Lake country, I asked him a few questions about the route, in particular the Kasmere River, which we expected to follow. His report was not in the least encouraging. He remarked that the Kasmere was a very bad river, full of rapids and with at least five long and arduous portages. His information on the whole seemed very vague and lugubrious with a note of disapproval as if it were presumptuous for us even to think of making Nueltin. He was obviously skeptical that we could.[1]

In the haphazard but surprisingly effective way of the North, I had been given a letter for him with the idea that I might happen to meet him somewhere. This I turned over to him and we parted company.

Toward sundown, we came on two most unusual sights. Rounding a bend in the river we saw the whole western shore apparently veiled by a cloud of smoke. It seemed to hover in a layer about thirty feet high. As we could smell no smoke, we went over to investigate and discovered a solid mass of small, gray flies. They had all just hatched simultaneously from their watery home.

Later, while it was still very light, I saw off in the northwest quadrant of the sky a brilliant blue meteor. It plunged downward; leaving a great trail of sparks, and looked to be traveling rather slowly. The light was equivalent to late afternoon in lower latitudes, and not a star was visible. I heard no noise.

We poled and tracked up two more rapids before making camp on a nice sand ridge. I found evidence that we were not the only ones to have selected this spot. Here and there in the sand were small flakes and chips of white quartz, mute evidence of a camp long ago when they had been splintered off by Indian hands making arrowheads. Such evidence of a prehistoric past is often encountered and never fails to bring back to me the timeless continuity of the North.

The following morning, after poling up a short, swift rapid, we came into a large lake with a long bay running off to the south and west. This bay connects with an alternative route, which is frequently traveled when going upstream. It passes through a series of lakes parallel to the river, rejoining it farther downstream. It was by this route that Tyrrell had come, avoiding the series of rapids up, which we had toiled. It is probable that the river itself may have followed this course some time in the remote past, for a low wind-gap type of saddle could be seen in that direction.

On the west side of the lake rose a truncated, elliptical hill of brilliant yellow sand, and connecting with it a long, high sand ridge which looked for all the world like a perfectly constructed, level railroad embankment. These sand ridges are so typical of certain parts of the North that they deserve some explanation. They are sometimes as much as eighty feet high with very steep slopes, and some are sinuous, winding and stretching over the flat country for miles like great snakes. They are composed of coarse sand and gravel. Seen from the air they are particularly striking for they are the favorite highways of game and are often worn bare. They must have originated in the last, dying phase of the ice-sheet. For if the ice front was still moving forward at the time of their making, they would have been destroyed. Some geologists hold that they are the deposits carried by rivers and streams within the ice. With the disappearance of the ice the deposits, a sort of riverbed in reverse, a negative print, a cast rather than an impression, was left. This is not the place for a detailed discussion on the matter, but it is not certain that this explanation is entirely correct. Their technical name is an "esker." They have been found in the United States—Maine and Wisconsin particularly—and classic examples also exist in Finland and Sweden.

From this point on, the river widens and changes from a rushing, boulder-impeded stream to a bewildering network of channels intersected by low islands of mud and alluvium. From the air I believe it would look like a "braided" river like the North Platte or the lower Yukon—rivers, which are split into innumerable small channels, interwoven and intricate, finally coalescing into one main stream.

Signs of old caribou kills began to be frequent. Bleached horns and occasional hides became numerous along the banks. Ducks too were more frequent. It is characteristic of the pre-Cambrian country that ducks are scarce, and only the mergansers, locally called "saw-bills," occur in any numbers. This has a reasonable explanation. Because the pre-Cambrian region is underlain by granite and its stretched and malformed derivative gneiss, the shores of its lakes are usually steep and deep and do not afford the various shallow-water plant growths necessary for food. The shallower limestone lakes to the south and west are more hospitable.

This unusually lush span of country did not last very long. The river resumed its old character and flowed narrow and swift between high walls of sand. There were more boulder pavement terraces as well as rounded hills of fragmental boulders and rocks which Tyrrell has named "ispatinows." These hills all run in a trend or direction coincident with the ancient glacial flowage and are supposedly laid down upon an irregular bedrock floor.

Around suppertime we passed through a small lake and then suddenly came out into a much larger one. To the north of this we saw a very high sand hill which the Indians call "Thy-cho-nili," the Big Sand Hill. We crossed the lake and reached a very small islet of solid rock sup porting a solitary, tall spruce trimmed to give it a striking tufted appearance. This was a lobstick like the one at Brochet, created to act as a signpost or, as is sometimes the case in the northwest, to commemorate some event or person. They seem to say, "It's all right, you're on the right track."

We made camp a short distance below a small log house then occupied by the white man whom we had passed the day before. It is known as "Le Pensie's" for a white man of that name who maintained a trading post there for a number of years. I had met him in 1937, when after many years in the country he was preparing to leave with his Indian wife and many children in two canoes for the "outside" to get the children some education. None of them, I believe, could speak English. He was a rather faded little man but I thought, very courageous. He asked me with quavering doubt, "Do you think people will laugh at the children 'outside'?"

The next morning we entered a small narrows and saw four tents pitched up on a sandy knoll. We stopped to investigate. They were tents of some of the Northern Band who were on their way south. All the men but one were off hunting, but there was a small group of women and a few children. I dickered in Chipewyan-Cree-English for some whitefish and took a few pictures. One of the women seemed ill. She sat in front of a tipi-type tent-a rarity in the North today—alternately suckling a child and dipping an old rag in a basin of water and applying it to her bleeding nose. Bleeding at the nose seems to be very common among these northern people, and I have heard that it is particularly so among the Eskimos.

They had a blown-up bear bladder tied to a pole. What its exact use was I could not determine, but I believe they sometimes melt down fat and fill the bladders with it.

The whitefish were very welcome. Of all the fish of the North the whitefish is the most sustaining and the least tiresome to eat over a long period. Most important of all, it has a thick abundance of fat, which one always craves as the work and labor of the trail increases. The mouth of the whitefish is so small and tender that it is customarily caught in nets. Having none, we were dependent upon chance meetings such as this to secure any. The usual method of cooking it is to spread the fish on a stick and broil it. It is delicious.

We pushed on and now found ourselves on a large lake, which rapidly became very rough, as the wind had risen. We were forced ashore on a low, sandy island, and this too, by its litter of ancient bones and quartz flakes, indicated a very old and much used campsite. As we rested here, the wind increased in violence; jagged, ragged, storm clouds raced across the sky. We were forced to lie by for the rest of the day.

Nothing is more exasperating than to be wind-bound. Instead of welcoming the respite, we were seized with an overwhelming urge to get on. I wandered about our small island prison. On a ridge I found a single child's grave. It had been fenced in with a hand-hewn, tiny picket fence. It looked very lonely. I began musing about the bear bladder we had seen, and I wondered if the Chipewyans had the same extravagant regard for bears as the Crees. Among the older Crees, the bear always occupied a unique position. To them the bear was the most powerful of all the animals from a spiritual point of view. He was an object of sincere regard and great respect, so powerful that a curious circumlocution was used in talking about him. He was spoken of as the "black one" or the "old man" but never directly as "bear." The parts of his body were referred to as human parts—as his toes and his hands. After a bear was killed his skull was always suspended in a tree out of reach of lesser animals as a mark of respect and so that his spirit might not be offended. Women were not allowed to eat certain portions of the bear, the head, the paws, the heart, or the fat above the heart.

A story told by a very old Cree who lived on the reservation across the river from The Pas illustrates this reverence.

"You know, the black one is a very powerful being. He is like a man, though he looks different. He is the only animal that stands and walks like a man, and he can understand what a man says. You have been talking to me about telling of the future. Well, this is one of the best ways, which we used to use long ago. Because the black animal is so powerful, when one was killed, a man would cut out the long gut and clean it. Then he would think very hard about what he wished to know concerning the future, and he could ask the bear's spirit that which he wished to know. He would then hold the end of the gut to his ear and listen. After a while he would hear a rumbling. The noise would sound as if it were coming from far away. Before long, the gut would speak to him and tell him what he wished to know.

"You white people are strange. One time a white man came over here, and I told him about this. He laughed and said that I was a foolish old man to believe such a thing.

"I turned to him and said, `Why do you laugh at me and say that I am a liar because I can hear things from this long tube? I have gone over to the town. I have seen you white men go into a little box. You take down a small black thing with a string on it nowhere as big as a bear intestine. *You* say *you* hear things! How can you say I do not hear things?' "

Even today in the North, one occasionally runs across an old bleached bear skull in a tree, a nearly forgotten courtesy to "old grandfather."

It is not so much the temporary halt that is so annoying when one is wind-bound as the fact that it is impossible to tell when one will be able to resume the journey. For winds in the North are often quite different from summer storms elsewhere. They cease at their own whim, and this may be in an hour or a week.

Next morning the lake was once more at peace, and we were soon on our way. Again the landscape began to change. To the north were high, bold hills, while on the west side of the lake was a vertical cliff of red granite. Off to the northeast, bordering a long wide bay, we could see some very high sand hills. From this bay there is a route, called the "Maria Lake trail," which leads to Nueltin through innumerable small lakes. But we understood this to be a winter rather than a summer route. Now the shores were hemmed in by severely glaciated rock, and at the water's edge was a continuous barricade of great jagged fragments. The gray lowering sky threw a pall of gloom over the whole country, and the teeth of the fractured rocks grinned upward. The trees had been burned off—everything spelled desolation and destruction.

We poled up a short rapid and came upon a thunderous cascade called Chipewyan Falls. Running the canoe up to the foot of the falls, we hoisted it over a rocky ledge and then poled up close to the shore, where we encountered another swift rapid. In this treacherous stretch I felt the bow of the canoe slowly turning despite all the pressure I could put on the pole. I jumped out into the water and held the bow in toward the shore until we managed to get up above the falls. The water was very cold. John, who had been championing the difficulties of his own part of the North, began to admit that the Cochrane had its ugly stretches. We found the poling of this section particularly difficult. The river was so narrow and flowed down such a steep grade that the force of the water was tremendous. It had carved a channel of such depth that we were unable to find bottom with the poles when we ventured more than a foot or two from shore. Ledges and boulders forced us out from the bank again and again, and several times when I set my pole it slid off and plunged unexpectedly down carrying me over the side of the canoe until my arms were half under water. But John, standing firm and immovable in the stern, kept the canoe headed into the current with a silent and intense ferocity. Throughout, the black flies feasted on us unmolested.

Resting after this short but bitter struggle, I began to feel the inevitable aches of the first few days out. The small of my back was the first to rebel, and my hands had begun to assume a claw-like crook from their constant grasp on the pole. I did not ask John how he felt, but I noticed that his hands too were a little awkward as he rolled a cigarette and that he too had small streams of blood running down from behind his ears where the black flies had been feeding.

After the peaceful crossing of a small lake, we came upon another rapid. This one did not appear long, but it was violent, and as we approached it seemed to be a veritable slide of water running downhill. At the foot of the rapid we could not see the level of the lake above, which we had seen when approaching it from the distance. There was a drop of six feet in less than thirty yards. A placid bit of river followed, but it did not last long. A portage on the east bank, indicated by cuttings and a well-defined trail, caused us to disembark. After climbing a steep clay bank, we found the portage to be a moderately level one, but it was over a mile long. There were toboggan tracks in the sand of the trail. It is not unusual in this country, where the portages are long and frequently sandy, to drive dogs and toboggans over them even in summer. In fact, some white trappers take along an old toboggan for just this purpose. Long and heavy and unlike our own, they are usually shod with "irons," two long strips of steel.

The portage, which had cut off some six miles of the river, brought us out on the low shores of a lake known as Jackfish Lake or Lac Brochet. It is twenty-two miles long, the largest lake in the course of the Cochrane, with very low shores and off to the southwest some high hills. There was much smoke everywhere, and we could count a number of forest or bush fires to the north and west. These fires are annual events throughout the North. They burn on until they die of their own destruction on the shore of some large lake. Their slaughter of animals and the livelihood of the people—fur—is tremendous.

The lake, though large, was very shallow, and boulders disconcertingly appeared just below the surface even at some distance from shore. As we went along, we speculated on just what we could do if we were caught on the lake in a high wind. The waves would let the canoe down upon these immense submerged rocks and smash it to pieces.

Well after sundown we camped on one of the five small Spider Islands in the middle of the lake. For the first time we discovered no vestige or sign of anyone ever having camped in the same spot. Apparently the Indians follow the shore.

Discussing the day's work before a cheery campfire with a revitalizing cup of tea, we reflected that the day had really been one of achievement. Despite the endless rapids and falls and the portages, all in the face of headwinds and constant up-river work, we had accomplished nearly thirty-five miles. Best of all John's eye was much better; and he was in a good humor. As we were going along, he had said: "Those god dam sand flies, they don't suck blood, I can see one eatin' and chewin' a piece of your meat."

The following day, at the northwestern extremity of the lake, we had our first serious disagreement as to route. By my calculation, at this point we should turn north up a narrow contraction to another long lake. Jackfish Lake itself ran pretty much westerly. The route, which our map indicated—it was now reduced to a twenty-miles-to-the-inch scale—however, gave no indication of a river at all. There was not the slightest suggestion of a current, though we were passing through a very narrow opening. John was openly skeptical and had decided very definitely and pointedly that we were wrong and that it was utter folly to continue in the direction I suggested. After a good deal of cajolery and allowance for the excellent basis of his argument, we used up sufficient time (following my route) to find ourselves out on the lake we wished to reach. This lake, a long unnamed one, ran north and a little east. It then became apparent that, despite our map, it was not really a separate lake at all but a twelve-mile extension of Jackfish which made the total length of the latter some thirty-four miles.

A heavy wind made rough going and fanned the flames of four separate fires to the north of us, which with the fires behind us to the southwest completely encircled the horizon.

As we approached the end of the lake, we saw a little gathering of Indian shacks and one large one, which we knew, must be the Hudson's Bay Company outpost operated from Brochet in the winter. There was no sign of life in the place at present; a solitary, abandoned dog howled mournfully as we paddled by. This is known as the Misty Lake outpost, and is supposed to be on Misty Lake, although as we have seen this was not Misty Lake at all but a continuation of Jackfish or Lac Brochet. This is typical of the hazy geographical notions of white men in the North. Though it is so vitally important to have correct geographical information, observations as to locations, distances, and route details, even by men who have lived and traveled in the country for years, are always conflicting and questionable. To one white man a river may be impossible, while to another it is just the opposite. Some will judge that there are ten portages on the left side of a certain river; while others are just as sure that there are only three, and all on the right side. Distances may range from one to five miles on the same stretch.

I was traveling alone one year down the great and majestic Slave River.[4] My canoe was very small, with room enough for just one man and his tea pail. I knew that very shortly I was to reach a certain rapid and was anxious about it. Seeing a cabin on the bank, I pulled into the beach, and an old man with an enormous mat of hair came down to see what I wanted. A white man, he was apparently one of the old trappers to be found along this river. I asked him about the rapid and which side people were accustomed to run it on. He meditated for a long time looking over my canoe carefully, then went into a long detailed description of the violence and general appearance of the rapid, ending with the judgment that it was impossible for me to get through it in my small canoe. I had better portage around it. Further detailed advice followed, including reassurance that the roar of the rapid was so great that I should have warning of it before I was too near. This information was topped off with a long account of a previous traveler who had lost his canoe and entire outfit in the rapid. Needless to say, the rapid was uppermost in my mind for the rest of the day. However, as I went on there seemed to be no indication of it, only a few swift stretches of water no different from any previous ones and never remotely resembling the maelstrom of the old man's description. In the evening I came upon some Indians and asked them how much farther I had to go to get to the rapid. They stared at me as if I were a lunatic, and told me that, unless I had flown, I must have passed through the rapid about eight miles back.

Indians are not so vague. Either an Indian does not know a route or he knows it in extraordinary detail. They seem to have an almost eidetic imagery. But one must take into account their peculiar attitude toward distance. Few of them are acquainted with our rigid system of miles. To them, distance is infinitely more relative than to a white man.

For instance, at Ile á la Crosse, where there is still a strain of the old voyageur, the custom persists among a few very old men, of referring to a distance as so-and-so many "pipes." This dates back to the days of the fur brigades when the crew was allowed to rest at definite intervals of time and smoke.

To the Indian, distance and time have a very close relationship, as becomes obvious if one has anything to do with their maps. A map of a difficult river route may be stretched out spatially much longer than an easy river route of the same length because it takes longer to travel over it. The same distance, in an Indian's mind, is shorter to a good and experienced traveler than to a poor one.

Passing by the deserted shacks, we turned north again and ascended a very rough rapid called White Spruce Rapid, up which I dragged the canoe with the tracking line while John fended it off the sharp rocks. Above this was a stretch of fast, deep water, which we both thought might harbor a fish or two.

John threw over the trolling hook with its big spinner and tied the line to his leg. Paddling slowly upstream, he was soon rewarded with a swirl and a lunge followed by a quick jerk on his leg. I stopped the canoe and watched him pull in a fine long jackfish. The jackfish, though not a pleasant-looking creature, is tolerable eating and a boon to the North, for the traveler can catch him almost anywhere by trolling. Its teeth are so savage that John, in the customary manner, pulled it to the canoe and sinking his strong fingers into its eyes held it wriggling and squirming while he removed the multi-hooked spinner with his other hand and his teeth. We were assured of supper at least.

We now paddled out into the real Misty Lake. This lake is much larger than it is shown to be on any map and its east and west shores are quite undetermined. Despite its size it is extremely shoal. Going straight up through the middle of it, we had to be constantly on the alert for sharp rocks and loose boulders. Without warning we would find ourselves almost aground on shoals which seemed to have no reason for existing—not current-controlled sand but large, angular rocks. The whole lake seemed so obstructed with islands, large and small, that it was difficult to establish any reasonably consistent direction.

Toward dusk, we approached one of these islands, which was high and rocky, and saw near the shore a cluster of tents. We had intercepted the main body of the Barren Land Band. Coming closer, we could see people running about, and soon a knot of dark figures came down to the shore to see who we might be. As we drew near the camp, another canoe appeared from the north loaded with men. We touched the shore in front of the camp almost simultaneously. After a moment of strained and expectant silence, a tremendous clicking of tongues and explosion of gutturals burst forth on all sides, to which the dogs as if awaiting a signal immediately responded, making the most discordant uproar I have ever heard.

We did not immediately land, allowing the occupants of the other canoe to go up to the eight tents first. Though members of the band, they seemed the objects of almost as much comment and attention as we were. I surmised that this was a rendezvous and that these late arrivals were members of the band who had come down from some other part of the North to join the main body. Women, children, and dogs crowded around the new arrivals, and by this time a number of men, young and old, had assembled to add to the general din.

There was something strange, dark, and splendidly barbaric about the whole thing. Children rushed about for sticks, and the campfires were stoked up. The sky in back of the camp was a dull, sulphurous yellow with black clouds. The women, in their red silk bandannas, shrieked and clubbed at the dogs. The men were wild and shaggy, their long coarse black hair matted about their heads.

For a few moments we fiddled around our canoe at the water's edge. Both of us felt a peculiar reluctance, an old wariness at boldly going up to this group of strange people. For by this time the women had gone back to the tents and the men had settled about the fire and everyone was looking at us. As we left the canoe and went up to meet them, the talk died down. We were met by a ring of dark faces, black, staring eyes, and complete silence.

In the center of the group was one very old man, still broad, squat, and powerful looking. He was wearing a ten-pound flour sack sewed together into a hood with a high peak. It gave him an odd gnomish look. I recognized him immediately. It was old Kasmere. Next to him was another old man who looked for all the world like an apparition out of a child's fairy tale. He had a big beaked nose and craggy eyebrows, an upturned chin, and black beady eyes. Him I recognized also. It was Edzanni ("Gull-droppings"), reputed to be a great rascal. These two older men seemed to dominate the group, and I went straight to them, shook hands, and called them each by name. They immediately broke out into voluble, guttural Chipewyan, simultaneously streaming through the worn brown teeth of both so that it was impossible to make out a single word. The others of the group but one were much younger men.

This outburst stopped abruptly, and everyone looked at us with an intent and expectant stare as if waiting to see what we were going to do. I felt very nervous. My own Chipewyan was fragmentary, and the Cree Edzanni could speak, when he tried to, was so guttural that it was quite impossible to understand. Apparently not a soul in the camp could speak any English, or, if they could, they did not reveal it.

I ended the embarrassing pause by passing my tobacco

pouch to Kasmere and Edzanni. The latter dexterously shifted a good portion of its contents into his hand beyond what he put in his pipe.

I drew out the crude sketch map I had of the way to Nueltin, and we had a very amusing time trying to find out something about the route. I did gather that the best track to Windy Lake and the Hudson's Bay post was not along the shore of Nueltin, where one was very likely to be wind-bound, but to portage over and pass through a series of small lakes to the west of Nueltin just before the main narrows of the lake.

Looking about us we saw that the camp was entirely without meat, which would indicate that the caribou were not yet down from the Barrens. They had a little dried whitefish, and for some of this we traded some tobacco with Edzanni. I remembered Edzanni very well from my previous trip to Brochet. He had quite a history and reputation. One year he went about in the winter exacting tribute from everyone with the threat that he would put a spell on whoever did not give. One look of his evil eye convinced most of the band. At last, through community effort, he was tied to a tree and left to freeze to death while everyone fled. But his daughter returned and saved him. I remember a conversation he had with the free trader at Brochet, which went something like this:

"Ah, Jim, I see you have a big woodpile."

"Yes."

"With such a big woodpile you must be very rich! Give me a little tobacco."

"No!"

"What! You cannot give me even a little tobacco, which is so small, when you have such a big woodpile and are so rich?"

"No."

"Tell me, then, will you give me your woodpile when you go away, for you cannot use it then?"

"I'm not going away."

"Oh, yes, you are, for you are going to fail. Everyone knows that. Look, the Company [Hudson's Bay Company] has had a boat come in with many fine things today and you have nothing. No one is going to trade at your little store; you are going to fail!"

"Get out, you old fool!"

"Ah, Jim, what a nice smooth skin you have. But what is this? I think it is changing. Let me feel it." Edzanni stretched out a black and inquisitive long-nailed finger. "Yes, I feel it changing. Yes, I believe you are having horns grow from your head like the devil. Possibly you are the devil! For certainly you are a wicked man and the devil is wicked, for that is what the Father tells us. Give me a little tobacco?"

"Get out of here, you old——!"

"Oh, well, life is hard, very hard..." And with that, Edzanni wandered off, chuckling evilly to himself.

It was unfortunate that I could not converse at any length or in any detail with old Kasmere. He was an unusual man. No one knows how old he really was; he was by far the oldest of all the Indians in that region. In years past, he had traveled over the country far into the Barrens, and he probably knew more about routes and the Barrens than any Indian alive. He was the only Chipewyan I had ever heard of who could speak Eskimo and speak it well. In the days when the Eskimos used to come down to Brochet, Kasmere had a camp on Theitaga Lake and exacted tribute from them for passing through "his country." He looked quite different from the other Idthen-eldeli around him. Old as he was, everything about him spoke power. He was short, with a very broad back and deep chest. His face was wide and the lower jaw square and unusually heavy. There was a massiveness about him that none of the rest possessed. His teeth, worn almost to the gums, were large and like an Eskimo's. He had a deep, bass, and guttural voice. Even his fingers were short and thick, unlike the characteristic long delicate Indian ones. Many tales are still told of his prowess. He was the first "chief" of the Brochet band. To him was first given the blue coat with the brass buttons, the hat with the gold braid. And along with these, the Indian agent had presented him with a new canoe. For two years Kasmere held this honor. On the third year he demanded another canoe. The agent refused to give him one. "What," cried the fiery Kasmere, "this great King you have told us about, he is too stingy to give me a new canoe?" He stripped off the coat and flung it down. That was the end of his chieftainship. But the Idthen-eldeli never forgot, and it was Kasmere in the years to come who dictated whatever complaints and slight policy they had. For Kasmere was the greatest hunter and the most expert gambler of them all. No one but Kasmere went to the distant Barrens and there gambled at "*udzi*" for dogs with their hereditary enemies, the Eskimos.

Talking with the old man in painful pantomime and jargon, I felt some of his power. Listening to his rumbling gutturals, I would not have believed that the winter to come would bring the death of Kasmere on the trail.

Little did I think that another summer would find me passing a sandy hilltop where, beneath a cross, stood the buried body of Kasmere. "When I die," he had said, "bury me standing up. Bury me on the high hill at the narrows. For there I shall stand and watch you, my people, as you go north to hunt the deer. I will see you all as you pass and I will wish you luck in the killing of the deer."[5]

By this time the tension had entirely dissolved, and we were all sitting around the fire and laughing. Edzanni had fixed me with his evil eye and was pouring out a stream of Chipewyan and Cree, which I caught at the tail end whenever he paused to spit on the ground, which was very frequently.

The sun had now gone down, and the clouds were dark and threatening in the west. The whole scene—the tents, smoke-blackened and torn, the scaffolds of drying fish, the suspended strips of bloody bear membrane, the fires and black kettles, the lean wolfish dogs, the confusion of dark faces, all set in the gloomy wildness of the desolate lake shore—was strange and barbaric.

It occurred to me that few white men in recent years had seen quite such a thing—the last little fragment of these truly wild and nomadic northern hunters in their own country in their thousand-year-old migration to the south. It was a picture I knew I should never forget. Here was none of the timid, white-shirt, silk-handkerchief show of the trading post gathering, the servile lounging around the Company store, the wheedling, ingratiating begging of the impoverished and misfit. Here they were free, here they were the hunters, here they were men and we were the timid strangers; we were the askers and they the givers. Remnants, proud remnants of a departed great host, like the caribou, they were moving south from the Barrens to the unknowing death that waits all free animals at the hands of the white man.

As it was getting dark, we decided to move on. If we had not been pressed for time, and for food if we lingered, I would have liked to stay here for a number of reasons, not the least that the light was so dim I doubted whether my photographs would reproduce at all.

We set out, after cheerful farewells, in a northeasterly direction toward a small peninsula, which nearly bisects the lake. Here there was a rapid marked on the map, but we found it to be only a trickling stream that would not allow canoe passage even for our lightly loaded craft! We decided to camp for the night. Thinking about our visit with the Chipewyans, it occurred to me that I had never seen such Mongoloid-looking children and that an unusual number of them were cross-eyed.

While we were boiling the tea pail and roasting our jackfish on a stick, two men suddenly appeared in the firelight. We had not heard the slightest sound of their approach, but happening to glance up we saw them standing a couple of feet away silently looking at us. They had come over the portage and had apparently been hunting. They both squatted down at our invitation and helped us finish the meal.

Relieved of the pressure of the crowd, I managed to get along a little better with the older of the two, whose name was Pierre Edzanni, a son of old Edzanni. His English was limited to about three words, but, by piecing these together with a scrambling of Cree, a little Chipewyan, and our mutual grotesque pantomime, I managed to extract a considerable amount of information. Our conversation opened something like this:

"*De-juli-son…*" (There are lots of mosquitoes.)

"*En.*" (Yes.)

"*D' inth owsa?*" indicating John. (Does he understand Chipewyan?)

"*Muatz.*" (Cree: No.) "*Hilya…*" (No.)

"*Edlini tu-lu?*" (Is this the correct route?)

"*En.*"

"*Lots portwuth?*" (English and Chipewyan: How many portages, many?)

Pierre put up eight fingers.

"*Denne ota?*" (Chipewyan and Cree mixed: Chipewyans here?)

"*En,*" indicating a spot on my sketch map.

And so, in the dying firelight, we continued. I gathered that by the time I got to the Barrens I would be so fly-bitten I would not be able to see, for my eyes would be swollen tight like the Eskimos! He said there were more Chipewyans farther along and that we should meet them en route. He explained that the camp where we had recently stopped was waiting for these more northern Chipewyans to join them, whereupon they would all move down to Brochet in a body. There was still another group camped at the mouth of the Putahow River, which empties into Nueltin Lake. He understood when I said that I was an American, a *Bescho*, "Big Knife," but it had no meaning to him and he could not understand where I came from. He exhausted, in inquiry, the only two places he knew from which white men came, Fond-du-Lac, a trading post at the east end of Lake Athabaska, and Churchill on Hudson Bay. When I denied living in or coming from either of these two places, he was completely mystified, and it was beyond my ability to enlarge his geography. He said further that in two Sundays we would begin to meet the caribou at Nueltin Lake.

When they had gone, John paid me the dubious compliment of remarking: "By gosh, if you hang around this country much longer, you *will* turn into a Chip."

After these "conversations" I had renewed admiration for Father Egernolf's linguistic talents. The amazing range of gutturals, nasals, and unsounded prefixes certainly had no counterpart in any language I knew. A dialect of the basic Athapaskan tongue, as I have mentioned, it has an enormous number of related dialects; variants are spoken by the Dog-Ribs, Slavis, Hares, Yellow Knives, Sastuden-eh, and even our own Apaches in the Southwest.

Though these people are Chipewyans, and more accurately

a small branch, the Idthen-eldeli, they refer to themselves simply as *Denee*, "*the* People."

During the night, the hard northwest wind brought a downpour of rain. I could hear John rustling about, but the scourge of mosquitoes was so terrible that I refused to risk bleeding to death and did not stir, just let it rain.

The driving wind continued through the next day and with it an increased deluge. We constructed a shelter from the balloon silk tarpaulin, which we fastened to the half-overturned canoe. It made a very satisfactory refuge.

At this time, we were both beginning to be "meat-hungry." The strenuous work of continual poling and portaging demands heavy food. Bannock is at best a filler and an obstruction in the digestive tract rather than a sustainer. Though whitefish is adequate, we had not had much of it, and the leaner jackfish leaves one very hungry after a short spell of labor.

Though it was several hundred miles from civilization, the country through which we had passed had proved absolutely destitute of game or recent signs of it. In fact, all we had seen in a hundred miles or more was one porcupine. We were north of the moose range—though moose have been moving steadily farther north throughout great sections of the country—and the caribou had not yet been reached. More surprising, there had been no sign of bear or the smaller animals, as foxes, yet the sand ridge type of country would seem excellently adapted to the latter. The popular notion that the North is teeming with wild life is completely erroneous. A region may in certain seasons or for a very brief time seem to be overrun with game, then just as suddenly there is no trace of any, and often the farther one goes north the more inexplicably empty it becomes.

Around our forced camp was considerable evidence that the spot had been a semi-permanent winter camp for the Indians. Old tipi poles were still standing, most of the trees had been cut for firewood, the ground was littered with caribou bones, many of them split lengthwise for the marrow, and the whole area was deep with white caribou hair and many torn fragments of hides. From the numerous stakes to which dogs had been chained, an overpowering stench arose, and this, with the effluvia from the rotting hides seemed to attract flies and insects. Though the wind kept them somewhat at bay in the open, they congregated in concentrated masses in our shelter. In defense, I tied strings around the bottom of my pants, but those miserable products of a salesman's iniquity had now sprung gaps at pants' most vital area and caused me much mending and discomfort.

The following morning, we saw a canoe sailing toward us, and were soon joined by two Indians. Over the teacups, we learned that they were both named Louis, though the older one, who had but one eye, was named Louis Naygli (Nah-i-glee. "Born-twice"). He proved a most genial and informative person, though he spoke no English. He confirmed the information Pierre had given us. Becoming autobiographical, he told us that he had first gone to Nueltin Lake when he was a boy of five, when a twig had snapped back and put out his eye. He concurred with Pierre that we would not see any caribou until we reached Nueltin, and said that there were no trees on the whole north shore of that lake. He explained that one time the white man had taken him up in an airplane and he had directed them over the route to Nueltin Lake to look for the trading post, though with what success I was unable to find out. Finally, and most important, he drew a map for me which was to prove surprisingly accurate and helped from time to time not to *show* the way but to satisfy us that we were on it.

The younger Louis did not add a word to the conversation, but he did give it a genial background with a fixed and continual grin.

On the trip across the upper part of Misty Lake our first miscalculation brought us into a blind bay. When something like this occurs, it is very disheartening because one can only find out where the mistake was made by going back over what may be a very long distance, a distance previously gained by sweat and effort. The lake crossing had been a battle against a fresh head wind that called forth all the strength we had. It was tiring work; if we once relaxed, the canoe would come to a stand still and begin to inch backward.

Happily we discovered our error before very long and found ourselves moving off to the northwest and out upon another all lake. Then we were once more in the river, which was very narrow and swift. Every change in direction was signaled by a rapid. Here the shores were lower, and there were long stretches of muskeg and tamarack swamps. Occasional sharp bends would reveal high cutbacks of sand, undercut eskers. Caribou trails began to appear in great abundance, looking like well-worn footpaths. They crossed and recrossed the river from one bank to the other, and the entire country seemed interlaced with them. Most of the advance was made by poling with tracking in the heaviest rapids. In many ways, it was some of the best, country we had seen. As we passed particularly inviting sand ridges and knolls, we would speculate to each other on the adaptability of each location for a mythical cabin we might some day build.

As we went along, we did not talk very much, not that either of us was excessively uncommunicative, but each was too busy paddling or poling or searching the shore for any sign of life or any indication of human passage to show that we were on the route. Every two hours or so, we stopped paddling and rolled a cigarette or took a drink of tea. We always left some tea in the kettle from our "boil-ups."

Sometimes before the campfire at night, John would tell me a bit about his experiences in the war. He had enlisted as a volunteer in the old Imperial German Army and was captured at the Somme. He was glad that those days were over. Here he had come to peace and his own life.

As we progressed up the river, both of us paid increasingly sharp attention to the east bank. From my calculations, I felt sure that we were approaching the big bend in the Cochrane at its northern apex. It became absolutely necessary to know just where we were, for somewhere in this stretch we were supposed to leave the waters of the Cochrane and portage over into a small chain of lakes that led to the Kasmere River drainage and thence to Nueltin. It was a very critical point in the trip; unless we could find this initial portage we would be unable to go on. But a very close watch showed us nothing, which indisputably suggested a portage,

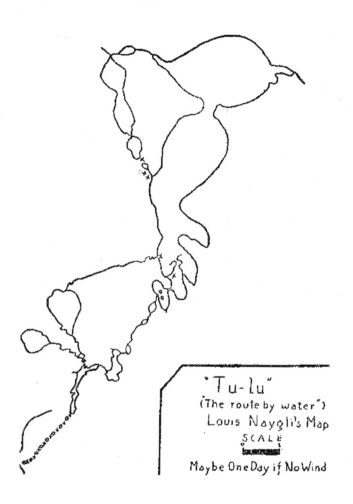

"Tu-lu"
(The route by water")
Louis Naygli's Map
SCALE
0 1

Maybe One Day if No Wind

although the caribou trails were very confusing and tempting. In the trail itself there is nothing to distinguish the two. For men use caribou trails as portages and caribou use portages as trails. But at a portage there is apt to be some small shred of evidence that men have passed that way. It may be very slight—a stick thrust in the ground from an old fire and tea-pail-boiling, small branches broken where they have rubbed against a portaged canoe, a few old ax marks, small trees cut down for firewood, a green branch half-floating on the shore where canoes have been pulled up.

One night when we camped I felt that we must be within a mile or so of the spot. It was the thirteenth of July, which, with two wind-bound days, constant headwinds, and the impediment of rapids and falls, we felt was not unsatisfactory traveling over a route previously quite unknown to us. We were in the neighborhood of one hundred and twenty-five miles from Brochet, and by my route a little over five hundred miles from the end of "steel," the railroad.

We made a fine camp, feeling that this should be our last on the Cochrane. It was on a high sandy terrace above the river. Above us ran a long straight esker, the moss-covered embankment stretching far below and above us. The river had paralleled it for some distance and a few miles below us had cut through it, but the esker kept up its straight-backed march through the country; terminating we knew not where.

While we were sitting and smoking we saw a muskrat, the first sign of animal life since our porcupine of several days before. '

We talked by the firelight for an unusual length of time. Each of us felt that the next day was in a sense momentous, for we would be striking on into unmapped country, and success, at least preliminary, demanded our finding the correct departure from the river. At least, we had conquered the Cochrane, and if the rest of the going was no worse, we should get through. We made a resume of all the rapids and bad stretches up which we had come. Finally we put out the fire.[7]

Inside my sleeping bag, I killed the last mosquito that had entered the bar as I was erecting it. I lay for a long time listening to the small noises of the night and in the drowsy exhaustion of a hard day's work allowed the happiness of a silent and forgotten land to come over me.

CHAPTER 6

The Little Lakes

The next day our search for the portage began in earnest. We had obtained specific information as to its appearance, the most distinguishing feature, according to our white informants, was a high sand bank over which the trail climbed. The river itself supposedly cut this bank so that the trail could not be missed even cruising past in a canoe.

With this in mind, we moved north and poled up through two rapids to the foot of a large and violent one that had a portage around it on the east bank. From our map and other information, I was sure that this spot marked a limit beyond which we should not go and that the portage must be below us.

However, there had been not the slightest sign of a portage in the stretch below us, particularly none, which fitted the description we had received. We had given the bank such a close inspection; it did not seem possible that we could have missed it. In a quandary, we dropped downstream again, keeping very close to the shore.

It was now debatable whether we were as far up the river as we believed. Everything seemed to tally except a long bay, which ran off to the southwest and was not indicated on our map.

To go back through the rapids we had just laboriously poled was aggravating, but there seemed no alternative. As we

Little White Partridge River

Unknown

Kasmere Lake

Kiyuk I.

Kasmere Por.
Revillon Frères
(abandoned)

Center I.

Kasmere Falls

Fort Hall
(abandoned)

Fort Hall Lake

Kasmere's grove

Trout Lake R.

Cabin

Smith House Lake

Blue Lake

The Esker

Wolf Island Lake

Cochrane R.

Sketch
Cochrane R.
to
Kasmere R.
Scale
1:450,000
Approx.

went downstream, I followed along on the top of the sand ridge to see if I could discover the trail on the land itself. To the north and east I could see hundreds of small lakes, but there was nothing to indicate that they were the right ones to follow. I perched in the top of a dead spruce tree and searched the country with my binoculars for some sort of sign. There was none. We continued downstream searching the country both from the land and water until we reached our previous night's camp. John came ashore here and began a long reconnaissance to the east.

While John was gone, a feeling of helpless futility crept over me. I began to debate in my mind what we should turn to if we were unable to find the trail. The type of country we were in is particularly well adapted to concealing any sort of trail. It is sandy and overgrown with stands of jackpine, very open, there being no underbrush, and carpeted with white caribou or sphagnum moss. Wandering through this mockingly delightful country were literally hundreds of caribou trails, crossing and crisscrossing in every direction. When I started to analyze the problem and set various bits of description and advice one against the other, I became confused and as baffled as if I had tried to follow one of the beguiling game trails. My scientific approach completely broke down, and there seemed nothing left to do but call on my *puagan*. Unfortunately I was deprived by birth and circumstance even of this.

John's report when he returned was not at all encouraging. He had gone in as far as one of the lakes, but there was no indication there of human passage except some old cuttings which seemed from their height to point to a winter camp but no through travel. We discussed what to do as we boiled up the tea pail for the noon meal. I was very much against a blind attempt in a generally northeast direction. If we did this, we would have to cut out our own portage trails and we might get into a maze of lakes without end leading us anywhere. There was so little evidence of a connected, well-defined drainage pattern that it would be quite possible to go on almost indefinitely and arrive nowhere. If we could not find the first portage, I thought we might best stick to the Cochrane and go on to Wollaston Lake, changing our entire course, direction, and itinerary and going through to Lake Athabaska—a route of historical and geological interest, which was very sketchily known. John agreed to this plan as a last resort, but we both were determined to make at least one more attempt.

As we had so thoroughly explored the east bank from the land, we once more poled up the two rapids and crept along the shore in the canoe. Just above the second rapid—a very bouldery affair—I saw a small opening in the willows that looked very innocent and natural. An almost concealed little strip of sand suggested that it might be a convenient place to land. We had twice passed the spot before. Going ashore here, more from weariness and discouragement than expectation, we found to our surprise and delight a trail. The location was entirely out of keeping with the descriptions we had been given, but it was a trail and human beings had passed over it. As we followed it, we became increasingly sure that it was a portage; whether it was *the* portage was a different matter. We must both have crossed it previously, but as it passed through a burned area soon after leaving the river, we had seen no indication of it.

The trail led straight up the very steep slope of the big main esker, which followed the river. But here the esker was some distance back and concealed from the shore. The ascent was very abrupt, a sixty degree slope, seventy feet long. It then made off in a northeasterly direction across the top of the esker, which was unusually broad and pitted with small depressions and holes, and after about half a mile it dropped down almost vertically into a small pothole-like lake. The plunge down the sandy side of the esker into the small lake was such a vertical pitch that we had to use our hands to claw up it again. It did not seem possible to me that canoes or loads could ever be portaged either up or down it.

This portage, so difficult to find and then to maneuver, is a good example of a typical phenomenon in the North. I suppose that through the centuries literally thousands of people, Indians and a few white men, have gone over that stretch, yet nothing has ever been done to change or improve it. It remains as it was after the first prehistoric caribou trotted over it—a mere trace.

We carried everything over in three trips. I recorded my impressions in my diary at the time:

"It seems like suddenly coming into some strange new world. I have never in all my northern travels seen country just like this.

"Now our real task begins, straight exploring or rather route finding. We must follow a chain of eight all lakes until we hit Tha-nai-tua and the Nueltin watershed. (Tha-nai-tua, "Sand-ridges-around-the-shore" Lake is the Thanout Lake of Tyrrell and the Fort Hall Lake of the traders.) The country is all sand, almost dunes only higher and more rounded, typical moraine-esker topography of the most extreme and recent sort. Further, we seem to be in some sort of an abandoned river course; we are deep within precipitous sand walls. The country is quite open—and the caribou trails! There are thousands of them! They are stamped out and so plain in the sand that you would swear they were human trails. They all come down to the water's edge. You can see them everywhere you look. They lace every hillside like a web.

"There is no apparent outlet to this lake yet the water is beautifully clear and fine..."

As we started out we had the comforting sight through the clear water of a number of long green jackfish lazily getting out of our way as we passed over them. The humble and cannibalistic jackfish—how scorned by sportsmen "outside," how blessed in the North!

Dragging the canoe over a low barrier beach that seemed to divide this lake into two, we went on and at length arrived at the end of the lake. Here it split up into three bays. We selected the east one, which turned out after a long paddle into a marsh to be the wrong one. A large bog terminated the bay, and to the east a high black cliff of shattered and frost-fractured rock gloomily stared down at our intrusion.

We found the portage at the end of the middle bay. Like the other, it rose very steeply over a sand ridge and some two hundred yards further along plunged just as abruptly into another small lake. These lakes were almost perfect "finger" lakes in form; their southern extremities had odd rectangular shapes as if cut off with some giant ax.

The second lake—the first two were actually one—resembled in setting the one over which we had just come, but it was more complicated and had a number of eskerine points dividing it up, particularly at the northern end, into numerous complex bays. Again we selected the northeast bay, and as night was coming on we stopped. We camped in the middle of a short portage, but something about it gave me the feeling that it was not the correct one. The "something" at first was too indefinite to place. Anyway, my feeling was strengthened by John's contrary conviction that it was the right one.

The next day, instead of following the portage where we were camped, we made a reconnaissance of the other bays. My vague uneasiness about the portage had increased, and I prevailed upon John against his judgment at least to take a look at the other bays. It was raining hard and the going was unpleasant. The first bay we investigated led off to the west and developed into a baffling labyrinth of small enclosures and twisting points, islands and channels, hills, knolls, promontories, and even lakelets within lakes. It was incredible country. Returning from this maze bewildered and a little frightened by the confusion of sand and water, we discovered in the bay next to the one where we had camped a much more evident and used portage trail. The experience we had just been through brought home to us with renewed emphasis the absolute necessity of staying on the correct track, for any divergence could lead us into a complexity of near interlocking bays and lakes that would prove fatal.[1]

Ever since we had left the Cochrane I had been faithfully mapping the course. This was a rather crude performance, but the result was not as erratic as I felt it might be at the time. I constructed the map in one of my small notebooks on a scale of one mile to the inch. To ascertain distance I used a time ratio that we had previously established when we were traveling by the map. That is, our usual pace was about four miles an hour when we were paddling under normal conditions. Every half-hour I would stop and take bearings with a Brunton compass and fill in the various details we had passed. Further refinement of the map had to wait until the trip was over and I home again. These stops for sights and bearings were done from the canoe, and many times it was unnecessary to stop entirely; John kept paddling slowly and our progress was not materially affected.[2]

The portage we had found was short and similar to the previous two—a clawing scramble over the top of an esker and a sliding descent to a small canyon-like bay steeply walled in by eskers on either side. And as in the preceding lakes, this long narrow funnel opened out into a larger expanse.

In the northeast corner we found a small stream entering from the north. The previous lakes had exhibited neither inlet nor outlet and the drainage was apparently entirely through the sand. From this point there was an alternative, highwater route to Cochrane.

The lake on which we embarked after a half-mile portage was much larger than the others, and about two miles down it we saw tents on a large island. As we approached I could see through the binoculars small figures scurrying about and coming down to the water's edge to watch us. It was another encampment of the southward-moving Chipewyans and must have been the group Pierre and One-eyed Louis told us about.

This camp seemed entirely made up of women and children, with no elderly men at all and an unusually large gathering of youngsters. As we paused to take photographs and trade for whitefish, of which they had a fine supply, a thunderstorm rolled up from the south and so we moved on. We gained no information about the route, and the three young men there were either utterly uncomprehending or very stubborn.

We found the trail out of this lake after a hunt that carried us into two small bays and behind several islands. It turned out to be the longest and most difficult we had encountered. The ascent up to the top of the sand ridge was a fifty-foot climb almost straight up from the lake. The approach was across a patch of quicksand followed by a treacherously boggy stretch. The trail stretched and wandered a mile or so over a flat sandy plateau and dropped precipitously into another lake. There were trails in the sand where the Indians had driven their dogs over with loads.

Exploring about for a possible shorter route, we ascended some of the higher sand hills. I noted at the time...Lakes, lakes, lakes innumerable. Some seem interlocking, some do not. This is all a crazy jigsaw puzzle of sand and water, dry potholes, coulees, kettle holes. God help the man who gets off the route in this country! Nothing—nothing to go by, just up and down, around sand hills and dry washes, and thousands and thousands of caribou trails."

Packing over the portages has a peculiar limiting and brutalizing effect on the mind. Personally, I found myself becoming less averse to it. For one thing, when you are traveling in company there is a silent but inescapable rivalry. And here I was competing with a white man, not an Indian, so the competition was within my range. There is an odd, savage, masochistic joy in finding yourself able to pile on more and more until you can just stagger to your feet. As you trudge on, unable to turn your head to right or left, unable to lift your eyes more than a few feet from the ground, the whole world begins to shrink into a focus of pain and short gasps of breath; the deadening pressure of the strap on the top of your head seems to be forcing it down through your shoulder blades. After a few hundred yards, your neck muscles begin to shriek in remonstrance, and it is an aid to grasp the two straps on each side of the head and pull them and the load forward. If the load is properly balanced, not the back but the legs tire first and begin to give way at the knees. As you go along, sweat and blood spattering to the ground, you concentrate in a fanatical, blind struggle with the load and the length of the portage. Instead of a desire to rest, a furious impatience begins to fire you with dull sullen rage. The crushing weight, after a while, sets up a rhythm with the pounding of the blood in your ears, and to break this oppressive thundering you alter your pace to a faster shuffle. The struggle between you and the load becomes a murderous and vengeful obsession and you hear your mind saying: "I'll show you, you bastard. I won't stop and let you down on the ground. I'll lug you over if it's twenty miles..." At the end of the trail, you slowly crouch down until the bottom of the load touches the ground.

Bent over backward, you stare up into the sky and carefully remove the top of the load from the back of your neck. You twist your head and are free from the strap, and flopping down in the cool sand and mud like an animal you suck up great draughts of water. Then rising to your feet you untangle the tump-line from the load. You feel curiously light. With a savage exultation you dogtrot back over the trail with feverish impatience for the next load and the secret anticipation that if you hurry you can, maybe, catch up with and pass your companion.

There are few sweeter words to the man of the North than: "By God, there is a man that can pack!" The North is so crushing, it gives away before the ineptitude of man so slightly, its rewards are so withheld, that these small conceits are magnified out of all proportion and are warming wine to the spirit.[3]

This was our sixth portage since we had left the Cochrane the day before. Once again we plunged down into a trough seemingly gouged out of the sand and into a narrow cut-off lake with endless ramifications of islands and channels as it opened out.

At last we came to a tiny narrows scarcely fifteen feet wide. There was a strip of recently peeled spruce bark hanging from a bush on the bank. This sign, left by the Chipewyans we had just visited, indicated by its freshness to those on how long ago they had passed. Numerous trail signs like this are used in the North, but their use is rapidly dying out. The Crees used to put up a diagonal stick and an upright intersecting shorter one to indicate direction, length of journey, and time of possible return.

Paddling silently through the narrows, we nearly collided with two large canoes full of men. Neither of us had heard or seen the other. By instinct we both stopped abruptly, drew off a short distance from each other, and just stared. There were two big twenty-foot canoes jammed with men and one woman. In one canoe was a man I recognized, Bedzi-azzi, "the Caribou Calf." In the other was the chief of the Barren Land Band, old Denarl.

After a moment of questioning silence, we drew near and

passed around some of our fast dwindling tobacco.

Soon we were trying to communicate with one another, but the effort was not too successful. We did manage to make them point out the route. I told them as best I could of the people below and explained where we were going. They obligingly posed for some pictures. The woman, who maintained a stony and reserved silence, had a baby done up in a moss-bag.

Our efforts seemed so fruitless that we had begun to pull away when to our astonishment the woman called after us: "Say, boys, have you any tea with you?" in perfectly good English! We immediately turned back, gave her some tea, and began to ply her with questions, where-upon she became very reticent and gave only monosyllabic replies. She said that we would not meet any caribou until August and made a few comments about the portages.

From the appearance of the men and the loads of food-bags of dried caribou meat and pemmican—it was obvious that they had come straight down from the north. Happily we were able to secure a little pemmican from them. They were a fine, strong body of men. Apparently the women and children had been sent on ahead to fish and feed the dogs while these stayed behind to hunt until the last moment.

This was a lesson to us to be careful with Indians who apparently speak not a word of English. I was embarrassed now about some side remarks I had made to John concerning them. However, with the exchange of tea and meat and the discovery of the excellent interpreter, they all became very smiling and affable. Since there was little more to be gained, we all shook hands and parted. A few minutes later we arrived at the portage.

This portage passed over three-quarters of a mile of extraordinarily forbidding and sterile country. The sand ridges gave way to barren, stony, morainic hills, some of these solid masses of gray, lichen-covered boulders and shattered fragments of rocks. The trees had been burned off some time previously and had not grown up again. It was all very grim. The rolling, gray waves of rock, the fire-blackened, dead spikes of spruce, the gleaming white ghosts of birches all

Top: Hudson's Bay Company building, Brochet. This trading post and Oblate mission, founded in 1859, was one of the most isolated of northern settlements. Here, its heyday long past, it drowses through the summer of 1939.

Bottom: Fr. Joseph Egenolf, OMI. He served at Brochet from 1905 until his death in 1957. "A person of whom," Downes reflected, "when someday he was covered with the winter snows, one could say, 'He was a man!'"

Top: Chipewyans at Brochet, 1937. Identifiable (left to right) are Jazzi, Denarl, Bedzi-azzi, and Edzanni. Jazzi reminded Downes of "an Italian fruit vendor." Edzanni means "gull-droppings."

Bottom: Chipewyan camp on the Cochrane. These Indians were bound for Brochet, where Treaty Day payments and pageantry awaited them.

Top: Drying meat, Misty Lake. Here, at the main temporary campsite of the south-bound *Idthen-eldeli*, Downes felt "something strange, dark, and splendidly barbaric ..."

Bottom: Boiling the tea-pail while windbound on Misty. One-eyed Louis Naygli, mapmaker, is in the foreground; "He proved a most genial and informative person, though he spoke no English."

Top: Padding silently through the narrows, we nearly collided with two large canoes full of men." Barren land Chipewyans, the Little Lakes.

Bottom: John posing with antlers, Fort Hall Lake, July 19. "During the morning we came upon the most enormous pair of caribou horns I have ever seen. I stopped and photographed these." (Downes's journal)

Top: "The next morning the sun was shining and a fine southwest wind blowing. Taking advantage of it, we cut poles and set up the silk tarpaulin as a sail." Kasmere lake, July 20.

Bottom: Early evening, July 28, 1940, Kasmere Lake. Downes grips the hindquarter of a caribou he'd shot. "I suppose I shall never be so happy again."

Top: Alfred Peterson (l) and "Eskimo Charlie" Planinshek at the latter's demesne on Putahow Lake, 1940. The skulls on stakes are nearby.

Bottom left: Lop-i-zun. "Crooked Finger was a tall, well-built man…. On the 'outside' he would be considered a handsome man." **Bottom right:** Zah-bah-deese. "Within him seemed to burn a constant feverish flame of impatience, restlessness, and search."

Top: The HBC's Nueltin Lake post, Windy River, Northwest Territories. It was abandoned in 1941. The main building still stands.

Bottom: Charles Schweder and his lead dog. "He obeyed no one but Charles."

Top: Caribou Eskimos at Nueltin Lake post. "They would sit motionless for hours watching the hill for *tuktu*, 'caribou.' "

Bottom: Mary Fortin and her children, South Knife Lake. "The whole family was a fine example of the traditional family struggle against a common adversary, the North."

backed by a lowering dull sky streaked with rifts of lighter gray added a Goyaesque touch to the scene of abandonment and desolation.

The lake now before us was just a few yards wide and hemmed in on the west by the almost overhanging mass of the hills over which we had portaged. Here the wall rose seventy or eighty feet straight up from the water's edge. The lake is called Blue Lake by the Indians and Tyrrell reported that it is noted for its fish at certain seasons of the year. He further commented that it marked the height of land, the divide, between the south-flowing waters of the Cochrane–Reindeer Lake drainage and the northeast-flowing Nueltin Lake country watershed. We had some grounds to question this. The lake, according to him, was fifty feet lower than the one over which we had just passed. However, with the exception of one, none of these lakes exhibited any drainage, and these and later indications were to make the matter doubtful.

We camped at the foot of Blue Lake that night, and proceeded up the narrow gorge-like lake the next day. We noted some very large spruces on the west side, which was bounded by a steep and high esker. The report of 1894 recorded that one was found with a seventy-six inch circumference three feet up the butt. We also saw considerable poplar that had long been absent. Not only were the trees the largest we had seen over the entire route, but also their presence was in striking contrast to the barrenness of the stony hills we had just crossed. The lake itself was only about one mile and a half long; indeed none of the lakes in this chain had been over four miles in length.

This portage went up over the esker to the west and doubled back southwest to a small lake, an arm of which ran parallel to the one we had just left. This did not seem a natural or consistent course to follow and seemed as though it might very well be a trail coming into Blue Lake from the south from some alternative route. The indistinct print in the sand of a canoe keel and a few bruised twigs finally convinced us that this was the right way.

This next lake sometimes called by the Indians Smith-House Lake,[4] was the most complicated and erratic one we had seen. On the east side we found a small, almost dried-up creek exhibiting some flowage to the south. This too made us question Tyrrell's height of land demarcation. A narrows at the end of the lake brought us to a pleasingly brief jump-over of scarcely twenty yards at the foot of which was the opening to Tha-nai-tua. This lake was a full seven feet below the level of the last of the little lakes. The portage was distinguished not only by its welcome brevity and the fact that it marked the end of the little lakes, but also for several fine white spruces, an uncommon species here. From now on we would be following running water downstream, water draining northeast to Nueltin Lake and Hudson Bay.

The little lakes through which we had successfully found our way seemed all to be in a chain embraced by one great continuous esker. Some of them were apparently bounded by it only on one side, and others were within the esker itself. A fitting name for them as a group would be the "Esker Lakes." Three of them had individual and distinguishing names. The one where we had seen the camp of women and boys was called Wolf Island Lake, and there was Blue Lake, and this last one, Smith-House Lake. The latter name derived from the permanent camp of a white trapper named I. H. Smith many years before. His custom of trading for wolf pelts at Wolf Island Lake was the source of that lake's name.

The whole problem of lake and river names in the North could stand clarification and some regulation. For it has more importance than anyone who does not travel the country can realize. In the old days, it was the custom of explorers to name lakes and rivers for their various backers and friends. This is all very well, but it clutters the map with a confusion of names totally unknown to and usually never adopted by the people of the country and which bear no relation to distinguishing characteristics and features. The next step was naming in the native tongue, a custom legitimate and excellent if the native dialect or language is compatible with English spelling, as is Cree. The traveler can use these names and the people of the country will know what he is talking about. However, in the North dominated by any of the Athapaskan or Eskimo dialects the practice breaks down. The cartographer and explorer ends up with a series of names which he alone knows, and to the traveler to follow he bequeaths a jumble of words unknown to the white man and entirely unintelligible and meaningless to the native. The only solution of the dilemma in this region would be, first, to find the native name for the various geographical features, and next, to render these in English. Then the traveler has descriptive names, and further he can almost always find some native who can understand a little English and translate it back into the native tongue.

All along we found the error and fatuity of attempting to reproduce names in the Chipewyan tongue itself. This was the practice of our predecessor of forty-four years before; and these names that have since been officially fixed on some maps are totally without meaning or use to either the white men or Indians in the region.

CHAPTER 7

Fort Hall Lake and the Kasmere

Fort Hall Lake, the headwaters of the Kasmere River, Nueltin Lake's chief tributary, has been known by a variety of names. In the Tyrrell report it was called Thanout Lake or Gravel-ridge Lake. To the Chipewyans it was known as Tha-nai-tua or "Sand-ridges-around-the-shore" Lake. To the few white men, trappers, and traders, it is known as "Fort Hall Lake." This latter name, now used by both Cree and Chipewyan, seems by far the most appropriate and apt. It derives from an abandoned trading post originally called Husky Post but of later years Fort Hall, from its founder.[1]

We approached the lake through a winding, weed-choked bay. It stretched away to the north before us more like a river than a lake, for both its east and west shores seemed nearly straight and tended just a little east of north. The total length of the lake was thirteen and one half miles, and it was divided nearly in half by a transverse esker, which was pierced through to form a narrows. The first part of the lake was singularly free of islands, showing only one small and conspicuous one near the southeast corner.

In the southwest corner of our approach there was obvious evidence of a winter camp of some size. Cracked caribou bones and tufts of white caribou hair were everywhere. We even found a spear for killing caribou. It was crude but effective-looking with a long steel point affixed to a peeled wooden handle by a thong, about five feet long.

The custom of spearing caribou is still prevalent among both the Idthen-eldeli and the Inland Eskimos. When the caribou are on migration they are intercepted at certain advantageous river crossings and lake narrows, and the Indians or Eskimos set upon them while swimming. They are speared from the darting canoes, the thrust made from the side and behind. An upward stroke then severs the spinal column. The victims then either float or are pulled ashore where they are cut up. When a large number of caribou are attacked in the water the slaughter is at times tremendous. It is an effective practice, saves precious and expensive ammunition, and does not make enough noise to drive away oncoming herds.

As there was a fresh northeast wind blowing, we crossed over to the lee side. Here the land was everywhere low and covered with immense boulders, erratic, massive rocks perched and jumbled indiscriminately over the land, transported and left by the ice sheet. What exposed rock we found was a very beautiful and interesting type of gneiss, squeezed and contorted granite, which gave the rock the appearance of wavy bands of alternately gray and whitish streaks bending and flowing in wonderful convolutions and whirls. These were cut across by yellow streaks of an ancient volcanic material called "pegmatite." The huge erratic boulders were usually of a quite different composition, dense gray and pink rocks called quartzite. This of course is proof of their transportation from some other source.

A short distance up the east shore, we noticed a small cabin. Going ashore to investigate, I found it without flooring and vacant except for a starving dog, a rifle, and a huge church bell!

A short distance beyond the cabin, a good-sized stream came in from the east, and I understand that an equally large stream comes in from the west on the opposite side of the lake called Trout Lake River. On the west, long low hills paralleled the lake. As we went along, we could see boulders of immense size lying thickly jumbled together on the bottom of the lake.

This whole country is a vast glacial dump.

Traveling easily along the east shore, we arrived at a beach so inviting and sandy that we went ashore to boil the kettle. It lay at the foot of the esker we had previously noticed, which rose at the narrows to a high prominence with a fine commanding view of the whole southern portion of the lake. This was to be old Kasmere's last resting place.

We passed through the bisected esker, the cut-bank face of which, being of brilliant yellow sand, can be seen far down the lake, and noticed, high on the top of a sand hill on the east side, two graves. The lake now narrowed but maintained its almost straight sides and northerly axis. It contracted more until we passed through a short passage broken up by two tiny islands composed, oddly enough, of marble deeply pitted and eroded. The surrounding hills became higher, and to the east of us one hill reared itself up to a dominating height and fell away to the north in steep cliffs and a wide apron of shattered rock fragments. It was very beautiful; the gray rock was streaked and splattered with brilliantly orange, yellow, and white lichens.

More and more the lake took on the character of a river, but there was no appreciable current. Then the long narrow passage suddenly opened up into a large lake, and we were forced by the increasing northeast wind to seek shore and camp.

The hills everywhere had now become bold and massive. But they were so glaciated and smoothed that the country had an almost undulous look. Our camp was in a fine sandy spot.

After making our camp—starting a fire, thrusting a sharpened stick diagonally into the ground, and hanging the tea pail on it—we discussed the problem of where we might be. If this was Fort Hall Lake, as we had assumed, where was Fort Hall? The old buildings were known to be still standing, and certainly we could not have missed anything so obvious. If this was not Fort Hall Lake, what could it be, and where had we gotten off the route? Could our error have been back at Smith-House Lake at the peculiar south-trending portage?[2] With the wind now increasing to gale force we could not come to any conclusion or solution of the matter. John busied himself making some "dumplings," and I wandered off to see what I might find of interest.

I ranged far up and down the lake, but not a track or trace of a living creature was to be found. Tramping along the high sand ridge near the shore, I came upon ancient campsites and quartz flakes indicative of arrowhead making centuries before. These spots always excite my imagination. In my mind's eye I could picture the caribou skin tipis, the small fires, the old hunters in their brown, fringed, pointed deerskin shirts sitting here before their lodges working away and, just as I was, searching the shores and the lakes for signs of game. How many years, centuries, ages have passed since these mute fragments were chipped off from the small white pebbles under the pressure of lean brown hands? Were they Idthen-eldeli, or Crees, or possibly some now forgotten and unknown race of who there is legend but not record? Now they had vanished; they had followed the bird trail of the Milky Way; they were the *Cheepai*, the ghosts who danced at night, the aurora.

I discovered, concealed with great skill, a merganser's nest and in it twenty-four greenish eggs. I did not disturb the nest when the mother straggled off in her feigned crippled and distressed manner through the water. If I had been a Chipewyan, the eggs would have made a fine dish, for they were nearly ready to hatch and to them nothing is more delicious than duck eggs when the young birds are about to break forth.

Back once more at our wind-bound camp, I found that John had brought the dumplings to a happy conclusion. Cooked with some pieces of dried meat, they floated about like soggy cauliflower in the yellow and iridescent broth. They were excellent and descended into the stomach with a leaden finality, which promised their residence there for days to come.

The insect life was teeming. We found the ground alive with ants and during the next day were mysteriously set upon by clouds of the common housefly. They came from nowhere and covered everything. I had on my buckskin jacket, and every time I moved and swished the fringes a great swarm would rise from me with an angry roar. Neither John nor I had ever seen them before in any abundance in the North. In fact, the insect world seemed to attack us on an organized and well-timed schedule. Early morning would find the mosquitoes dominating the offensive. Awakening, we would hear their drumming roar and find hundreds of them eagerly assaulting the mosquito netting, thrusting their blood-hungry long noses through the netting while, others seemed to push and squeeze the nearest ones into the small openings. These lasted throughout the day but the more persistent frontal rush would be taken up by deerflies with the rising of the sun. By noon, the great "bull dog" and moose flies had begun to zoom about. These could bite through clothing. Black flies would then have come on, more stealthy and insidious and preferring the tender parts of the body, the eyelids and behind the ears; no portion of the body was inviolate to them as they entered the clothing through buttonholes and up the pant legs. As sunset approached, they gave way to the microscopic sandflies with a bite like the burn of a spark. As the sun descended, the mosquitoes, rested from their labors and madly hungry, took up the pursuit and constantly increased in numbers and voraciousness. Unlike our own mosquitoes, these did not rise or attempt to escape when one made a move of self-defense; they simply descended in blankets and had to be scraped off. They seemed to permit this from courtesy to their fellows whom it gave opportunity immediately to take their place in a new black mass. Sometimes, if you were sitting silently watching for game, you could hear the whole forest vibrating and roaring with an indistinct, trembling hum.

I saw several pairs of beautiful pine grosbeaks at this spot. Other birds beside the common gulls, terns, and ravens had been a tree swallow, a purple martin, a duck hawk, robins, yellow warblers, and nighthawks. The Crees call the nighthawk *"pee-squa,"* with the accent on the last syllable. Among these people the habit of naming birds from their characteristic sound is quite common. In the case of the nighthawk, the correct Cree inflection to the name reproduces admirably the cry of the bird as it darts through the dusk seeking insects. The same is true of a number of other birds as the redwing blackbird, "chuk-chuk-a-thu"; the herring gull, *"kee-ask"*; the owl, *"oohoo"* or *"kuku-ooho"*; the robin, *"pee-pe-chew"*; the loon, *"mah-gwa"*; the rough-legged hawk, *"kah-kak."*

Another realistic and admirable use of language by the Cree is the way they name articles which are new to them and for which their tongue has no preconceived words. This is particularly the case with new foods with which they have become acquainted since the advent of the white man and the trading post. Thus, the words for rice, *"ochay-sa"* literally means maggots, dried apples are white man's ears, dates are moose droppings, prunes are black man's testicles, barley is little girl's genitals, and beer is known as baby's urine. To one who is acquainted with the language, the use of these terms may seem a little startling, particularly within the proper confines of the trading post store. But when the required articles are handed unhesitatingly over the counter the propriety and aptness of the names become obvious.

For two days the winds refused to rest and we, impotent, uneasy, and impatient, roamed about our camp watching rifts in the clouds and lulls in the winds with short-lived hopes and despair. The rocks of the immediate region engaged much of my attention. Their origin was different from others we had passed. Here they represented the most ancient and primitive of formations; originally formed below water, they had been engulfed and completely changed or metamorphosed by later masses of rock which had come up from the most profound depths. Molten and enormously heated, they had created out of these infinitely ancient remnants an entirely different rock than the original type.

The weather still held threatening on the morning of the third day, but we decided we should push on though we might be forced ashore a few hundred yards on. To the north, the horizon was crowded with huge billowing pillows of gray and white cumulus clouds. These seemed to unpeel from their bed and be shredded and swept across the sky before us. With the relentless wind driving into our faces and the sharp crash of the steep waves against the bow our progress was slow, but we eventually pulled by two high islands, and then, as the lake narrowed, we saw to our joy and relief the gaunt, abandoned log and mud buildings of old Fort Hall.

Investigating it, we found that one of the two buildings had been used the winter before as there were several caribou skins lying about and the walls had been partially covered with them. On the roof was a decaying head and horns.[3]

The abandoned buildings occupied a very pleasant site, well cleared of trees, on the west bank near the end of the lake. They were set back about twenty yards from the shore. Crumbling to ruin, they stood surrounded with a wonderful high growth of purple, flaming fireweed in full bloom. There is something tragic and forlorn about old abandoned trading posts. And the two bent and staggering buildings here seemed particularly woeful, left behind to an unkind fate. All the life and bustle, all the cheery warmth, which they had harbored, had disappeared. Their old bones creaked in the wind. They had done their part, and now deserted and forgotten they were left to face the bitterness of the north wind and the killing frost alone. Much better that the sturdy, faithful old beams had received a pyrrhic funeral in some warm camp-fires than neglect and a crumbling, ignominious death before the all-conquering winds they had fought so long. But the old post was not going to its fated end alone; behind it was a small graveyard with eleven humble mounds, the crosses already leveled and the sand mercifully covering the tattered strings of rosaries.

As if purposeful to the end, the old post with its sightless eyes had done one more favor to man for it gave us a "fix." At last, and for the first time in many miles, we knew where we were. Our restored confidence gave us new vigor and impetus. We paddled on. The lake narrowed and became really a river for in places current began to appear. As if annoyed at our turn of good humor, the billowing clouds opened and it rained wildly and furiously. Before long we heard far off the sullen thunder of some falls. We were approaching the famed and feared Kasmere Portage.

At this spot the river makes an abrupt turn to the east and plunges down through a gorge for about a mile and a half. In this stretch, which is hemmed in by towering cliffs on the east, the river drops approximately sixty-five feet. It makes a deep, thunderous roar that can be heard for a long distance.

We paddled away from the river into a small pond where the portage takes its beginning. Here on the bank was another abandoned old trading post, called Kasmere Post, which had been operated some twenty years before by the now defunct Revillon Frères. Around this spot was much evidence of camping both comparatively recent and ancient; three quartz arrowheads were proof of the latter.

A short distance from the small log building stood a round, pink granite boulder with a cross-chiseled into its top. This marked the spot where certain observations for magnetic declination had been made in 1922, and was great help in the later plotting of my map for it gave an absolute control as to latitude and longitude.[4]

As it had begun to rain really violently, we delayed going over the long portage. We had heard so much about the grueling length of this trail that we felt we should fortify ourselves with a meal before tackling it.

The portage starts out very innocently, rising up from the small lake over the sand ridge, and then winds along it to the northeast. It continued to gain altitude and distance and the river valley was lost to view. After three-quarters of a mile it began to descend into a valley and the going became more difficult. The sandy footing, which had been good, now disappeared, and we stumbled and staggered over stretches of sharp knife-like rocks and shorter spaces—of oozing mud and swamp. Fallen logs added to the difficulty. After what seemed an interminable distance it suddenly twisted out onto a sand ridge again and then dropped sharply down to the river. The mosquitoes and the weight of our loads probably exaggerated our estimate of its length, which we judged to be two miles.

I hurried back, after dumping my load, and found that John had deposited his own burden about halfway over. He had then gone back. I ran back and met him with the canoe. Loading up with a mélange of incidentals I followed him as he lurched along with the canoe. After a while he stopped and we exchanged our loads. I took the canoe. It was very heavy now; not being a new one it had had years to accumulate sand and was equipped with a very stout oak keel which added to its weight. Slipping and sliding on the fractured rocks, crashing through the dripping and overhanging bushes, soaked through by the rain and the wet brush, we slithered and struggled on. Once more we exchanged loads and at last put the canoe in the water. John suggested that we stop and rest. He said we ought to have a smoke and talk this trip over. The fear flashed through my mind that if we stopped to talk it over we might not go on, there was something so weary and so discouraged in his comment.[5] Besides, I seemed to have been possessed with some of the Indian's mad impatience to get everything over a portage no matter what the cost. I said nothing but scrambled up the embankment and once more rushed back for the load that John had left. From the top of the bank I looked back at him. He was sitting in the canoe, his head bowed in his hands, a thin little wisp of smoke trailing about his head. Even from that distance I could see the blood trickling down his face from the black flies.

Cursing the portage, the weather, and the flies, I brought the last load over. It had been heavy packing but had finally been done in a little over three hours. To crown our labors, a dense swarm of mosquitoes, reluctant to have us go, swarmed down over us, and we were almost immediately faced with a long swift rapid.

As we approached this rapid we saw at its brink a veritable forest of poles, left there, no doubt, by the Indians who would have no use for them above this point, at least in ascending the river. We looked the rapid over carefully to see if we could run it. We were so heartily tired of portaging that we might have run it anyway, but we felt we should make a preliminary survey. It was a wicked-looking, confused stretch of boiling, mad water that shot down a narrow channel and then foamed up into a curling, white wave parted by several glistening black boulders. After this, its force shattered, it became more diffused and then disappeared around a bend.

Of all the hazards of traveling in the North, the running of rapids with the paddle demands the quickest decision, the most desperate of straining maneuvers, the surest of immediate judgments and actions. You cannot make a mistake or turn back once you have committed yourself to the raging water. It is totally different from running rapids for sport or pleasure, where an error in judgment means only a wetting and a swim. You are always conscious that if the canoe strikes a ledge or is swamped and overturned, everything is lost, if not immediately, then in a longer and more hideous fashion, for with the outfit gone, there is no escape but the end of the starvation trail. When one first runs rapids the impulse is always to stay near the shore. Unfortunately this is rarely possible, the current, the channel must be followed; usually the fastest water means the deepest channel, and this, more often than not, is to be found in the middle of the maelstrom rather than near the shore. Always and constantly you try to follow the slick, oil-like thread of the deep water. The beauties of artistic and rhythmic paddling are forgotten. You claw and paddle with all your strength, in any fashion, manner, or method you can command at the moment. If possible, the canoe is kept moving faster than the current and so you paddle madly down the rapid to keep steerageway.

As we watched the rapid swirling and roaring down below us, we decided that we could make it. The channel was very narrow but not impossible if we could keep the canoe out of the big wave and run very close to but not on the boulders. Silently we went back to the canoe. Each of us was sunk in the vivid picture of the rushing flood and working out in his mind what course was to be followed. We got into the canoe and exchanged a few, matter of fact words: "Down the slick water and we'll take the big boulder on the left, cross over to the eddy, swing in close to that big rock, pick the way from there. Well, let's go."

Down we shot on the first black, oily slick of the deep water. As we watched the water so intently, the canoe did not seem to be moving at all. A glance flung to the shore brought the shocking realization that we were flying along. The big boulder—we clawed away from it with crablike motions, frenzied and brief. Part of the big wave shot up for a moment and hung just to the left of the bow. But we were by. Now it was left and then right, in and out. The boulders reared up like magic from beneath the water, and on and on we rushed. It seemed endless. Then abruptly we were out in still water; we stopped paddling and the canoe drifted. The rapid behind us rumbled and snarled, cheated. It was odd, it looked just the same; for some obscure reason I felt it ought to be different. I looked back at John. He was grinning to himself and had already begun to roll a cigarette.

I grinned back at him; "Well, John, not so tough!" He poked the end of his cigarette with a match, "Naw, not so tough—for us!"

It was not long before the river discharged into a very large lake. Looking to the northeast we could see neither shore nor end to it. We pulled the canoe up on a fine sandy beach and made camp on a bare knoll. We were confident that we were looking out on Tyrrell's Theitaga Lake, the Thy-n'-ara-tu-eh of the Idthen-eldeli, and the Kasmere Lake of the traders, trappers, and Indians. From this point we knew that our course should lie in a northeast to easterly direction following the east arm of the lake out to its discharge, the Kasmere River again. It had been a long twelve-hour day and we were glad to boil up our humble meal and get beneath the mosquito netting. We felt fine, for the long portage was behind.

The next morning the sun was shining and a fine southwest wind blowing. Taking advantage of it, we cut poles and set up the silk tarpaulin as a sail.

Few experiences are more exhilarating than canoe sailing, particularly when traveling in the North. The same craft which had been so stubborn, so heavy and lifeless, which has wearied arms and backs, which has been pushed, poled, and paddled, which has been dragged and hoisted and carried, becomes almost alive, quivering, straining and rushing forward with a will and eagerness of its own. Ascending the waves slowly, it hesitates for a moment and then rushes down while a great wave seems to rise up in the stern and overhang for a moment and then slips quietly under the keel. The canoe shudders, the hands on the gunwales, the feet against the ribs can feel them working and a movement seems to have transfixed the entire craft as if it were pulsing with a life and vitality.

As we sailed east, the lake became larger than we had at first imagined. A long bay choked with islands extended away to the north. It was up this arm that Tyrrell had traveled in 1894 on his way to the Kazan and down through the Barrens. He had not traveled the shore we were now following, and we found the lake much different than it had been represented. The shore was low and subdued and thickly barricaded with boulders, a nasty coast if we were forced to land.

After some time the wind began to swing more to the west and north, and we were forced to take down the sail and resort once more to the paddles. A long bay, whose end we could not determine, now opened to the south. We pressed on across it, and our course became more northerly. Near the mouth of this bay was a large conical island called "Kiyuk Island" from an Eskimo of that name. Here he had killed a boy by striking him on the head with a block plane or, as he said, "I did not kill him; I just tapped him gently on the head and he died." At right angles to us was an almost continuous chain of islands, which fused and merged into the points and bays of the north shore of the lake; both were so complex and low that it was impossible to distinguish which were islands and which might be mainland.

Our own extension of the lake began to narrow, though there was another enormous bay stretching far to the north. High on a hill we could see a solitary cabin. It was in an unusual position, much too far from the water and very unprotected and isolated. Upon investigation, it proved all the more puzzling. It was much too well built for the usual Indian shack and had far too many windows. However, there were no old rusted tin cans to indicate that it was the house of a white man, trader, or trapper. It was a complete mystery, and not until a year later did I discover that this was one of old Kasmere's redoubts in the days when he was lord and master of the domain and exacted tribute from passers-by which he spotted from this perch. On the shore below the house I found in the sand a very curious knife. The blade was short, broad, and highly tempered, and the handle, made of caribou horn, was engraved with a studied geometrical pattern.

We paddled on to the eastern extremity of the lake, but there was no sign of a river discharging from it. We searched the shores very carefully with the binoculars but still there appeared no break or opening to suggest a river. We had almost abandoned hope of finding it and were preparing to shift our inspection to the north, when I noticed a pile of boulders almost completely obscured by the low willows. As a matter of routine, we paddled over to the spot. It was the outlet!

The Kasmere River, as it is known today to both Indians and white men, was called, sight unseen, the Thlewiaze, "Little of Poor fish" River, by the Tyrrell party. This has led to much confusion in the country, for the Thlewiaze in reality refers to another river two hundred miles away. The first Chipewyan name for the river was the Nare-lin-dessa, "Water-flowing-down-hill" River, but of late years the river, particularly since the days of the Cree packers and canoe men, has been identified with the various other features of the country which have taken their name from old Kasmere, and is known as the Kasmere—or as one report had it, "Cashmir"—River.

Here the river discharged from the lake in a long bouldery rapid. It was not wide, less than fifty yards, and the whole stretch was so impeded with rocks of every size and shape as to seem almost impossible to navigate. We ran down this rapid with the aid of poles and paddles, dodging and twisting in and out among the boulders. At their feet the river expanded into a long narrow lake whose shores on both sides were fairly studded with caribou antlers. Here it runs easterly to turn very abruptly north at the foot of a high north- and south-running esker.

We disembarked at this elbow in the river to investigate the evidence of a winter camp we could see lining the shore. It exhibited the usual litter of bones and tufts of caribou hair, and from its size and the accumulation of offal and refuse it had evidently been a long and populous camp, probably a gathering point of the Northern Band the previous spring. Back of this spot on the top of a sand hill was a graveyard enclosed by a crudely constructed picket fence. In it were twenty-five graves. In the soft sand we found the recent tracks of a wolverine, which had entered the enclosure and excavated the small grave of a child. There was something frightfully depressing and pitiful about this little graveyard on the hill. Each grave had a handmade rickety cross, weather-beaten, unpainted, and gray, and from each hung the deceased occupant's rosary. The Christian God had not guarded it very well if the wolverine tracks were any evidence.

From this depressing scene of death and abandonment we moved north and then made a very abrupt turn where the river sliced through the esker and turned south. This is an important spot in the country, for it is a famous caribou crossing at certain times of the year. The caribou coming from the north follow the top of the long esker and ford the river here resuming their course along the top of the south-trending ridge. At this point too is an alternative route to Nueltin Lake which goes north, avoiding the Kasmere River and passes through a series of lakes to one known as Putahow, "I Missed,"[6] Lake, and thence to Nueltin by the Putahow River. We turned south, though the Putahow route was tempting as there was a chance of running across a famous and already legendary recluse who was known to be living somewhere around Putahow Lake. He was called Eskimo Charlie. A white man of disputed age and nationality, he had made, many years ago, a canoe trip from Reindeer to the Gulf of Mexico, and had returned, still by canoe, to Montreal, the whole voyage taking three years and one day. This remarkable and almost mythical person is heartily feared and detested by the Chipewyans and is reputed to guard his camp with Chipewyan skulls erected on poles.[7]

The river course now bent to the south, and we were soon on another narrow lake that turned back to the northeast. Running parallel to the lake, but some distance back from it, we could see a long, absolutely straight, very high escarpment or ridge. It seemed far too high for an esker and its amazing straightness and uniformity, its unbroken height, so strikingly unorthodox in this land of irregular knobby topography, made me wonder just what it could be. John too was impressed by it and we discussed it at great length.

At the end of the lake the river turned abruptly to the east and plunged down a very long rapid with great force and violence. The shores of the rapid, which was narrow and appeared to be in the low-water stage, were a mass of foliated splintered rocks, black in color and resembling slate. These had split along the cleavage planes making them knife-like and very ugly either to walk upon or run the canoe against. This peculiar type of rock is called "schist," and its origin is comparable to that of the rocks I had found at Fort Hall Lake.

With some difficulty we found the portage following the left or north shore. It ran far back from the river on a high river terrace or bench and was very long, so long that we never did follow it to its conclusion but came back to the river again to see if we might possibly run it. It looked absolutely impossible. The irregular bottom and the endless boulders threw the rushing water, which was traveling at a tremendous velocity, up into great green curling waves. Added to this, the water seemed in places to be dropping over step-like ledges, which dropped it into a swirling series of caldrons. John felt that one man might be able to pole down the rapid alone in a lightened canoe. The venture seemed to me very dubious, but his experience was greater than mine. From the appearance of the rapid, and from previous descriptions, I felt sure that this was the one in which an expedition from the University of Iowa some years before had lost part of its outfit and turned back. Also here, a canoe-load of four of the most experienced and expert travelers in the North had swamped and had a very difficult time.

Keeping the gun and a few other articles, I stayed at the side of the river, and John walked back prepared to pole the canoe down alone. Before long I could see his small blue-skirted figure in the canoe as he began to pass by the island, which slits the rapid at its head. He came down very carefully, the canoe swinging this way and that, as the current seized it. Sometimes, when he checked it with the pole, it would rise and fall in one spot as the big waves rushed beneath it. Most of our outfit was in the frail canoe, and more than just that was at stake and held by a thin tamarack pole in John's steady hands. Slowly he came nearer. His small erect figure swayed and balanced with the leaping, bucking craft. I watched him tensely. Once he lost bottom with the pole and the canoe leaped ahead as if shot from a gun. But he checked it again and with agonizing slowness brought it under control. It was the most masterful performance I had ever been privileged to see. When he at last drew opposite me I embarked and we poled down the rest of the visible stretch together. As we drew near to the bend it became obvious that nothing but a fish, and a strong one at that, could travel alive down the rest of the rapid, which dropped in a series of thunderous pitches.

The regular Indian portage cutting off the bend of the river was so far away at this spot that we were compelled to go ashore and cut our own. Forcing our way through dense, knotty scrub spruce, plunging through muskeg and dense willows, stumbling and fighting over fractured rocks, we finally got the canoe and loads down to the foot of this long desperate stretch. John made but one comment: "When we see a portage, I guess maybe we would better believe the Indians." It was a sentiment so unusual for him that I could make no reply at the moment. I shall always think of these unnamed rapids as "John's Rapids."

The river twisting in an easterly direction brought us to a curious natural amphitheater enclosed by steep towering sand hills. Our experiences with the rapids and the end of a long day made us rather indifferent to our choice of a campsite, and it turned out to be the first poor one we had had. I saw one spruce hen here, the first of the entire trip.

The day of the twentieth of July was one of the loveliest of the summer. It was very cool, the air was crystal clear, and it seemed, instead of the middle of July, like one of those wonderful late October days in New England. But the river did not treat us with the same benignancy as the weather. Almost immediately a long rapid with falls necessitated a portage. At the end of this portage I saw goose droppings, the first sign of these birds we had seen. By midday we had come far up another lake, Sucker Lake, De-deli-ke-le-tu-eh, "The-place-we-get-suckers" Lake, and were forced ashore by a strong northwest wind. We now found that One-eyed Louis's map was incomprehensible; either he had left out a section of the river or we were on the wrong track.

Pushing on to the north, when the wind died down, we passed an old abandoned canoe on the shore and found the outlet of the lake almost turning back upon itself. It seemed we were constantly traveling in a series of jogs, which, coming back upon themselves, seemed to lead nowhere. The rocks along this shore were strikingly different from any we had seen. They were composed of layers or strata interbedded with brilliant white crystalline limestone. They were very erratic and often weathered into grotesque forms.

Turning south, we were soon involved in a long fast rapid which we ran with paddles. Somewhere near the end of it we shipped part of a wave, but the action was so fast that we did not notice it at the time. We struck once on a submerged rock, a glancing blow, and almost instantaneously slipped between two big boulders by the narrowest of margins. Dropping fast, we came into a small lake and then down another long rapid from which we spurted out into a quiet pool under a great high sand hill. Once more the river turned back upon itself, and we followed along an esker to the north. We heard a tremendous splashing far up the river, but it was so dark we could see nothing but a mass of spray. The disturbance was so great that I thought it must be a caribou or some other large animal, but to my surprise, after focusing the binoculars upon it, I found it to be a goose. They were evidently still in the stage of summer molt.

We camped in a fine, pleasant spot with the spruce widely spaced, giving it an agreeable appearance. There were two tiny abandoned log huts, Indians' shacks, scarcely five feet high, dark and windowless.

The next morning the peaceful, almost currentless water did not last long. Very shortly we were running down a rapid and then made a short portage around some falls. At this latter spot I saw a black poplar, the only one I had ever seen in this part of the North. It brought back to me memories of the Athabaska and Slave Rivers where this species of tree is very common. Once more we found ourselves twisting and darting through fast water, but the rapid was not difficult. Here one of the most unusual drainage phenomena presented itself. The river on which we were paddling seemed to be flowing as if on an embankment. A big esker hemmed it in on the left side, but on the right it fell away into another parallel channel somewhat lower than the river itself. In effect there were two rivers side by side. The water from ours spilled over the edge into the lower channel in a series of small cascades.

The roar of falls began to be heard, and soon we were at the lip of a goodly drop of some ten feet where the water poured over a ledge. This ledge, of light gray granite, was the first rock we had seen "in situ" for a long time and showed that we had passed out of the lense or zone of the softer complex rock of the previous miles.

We made a portage here of about half a mile which cut off a quite impassable bend of the river. While we rested at the end of it, we watched with some amusement two small terns pursuing a huge raven with great bravery and persistence. They dived and shrieked at it, and the larger, black bird drifted along on his wide wings croaking dismally.

Once more we found ourselves sliding down a long rapid. Unlike the others, we had made no effort to explore or preview it. It started innocently, and before we realized it we were in the clutch of the current. Instead of terminating, it became steeper, the current increased, and we found ourselves swept along willy-nilly. It became increasingly studded with rocks and boulders both above and below the surface. In frequent gasping moments it seemed impossible to find any passage through them. But it was too late for regrets. The rocks leaped up at us everywhere. It was like a horrible nightmare in which we were trapped with no place to turn or escape. As we shot down, fighting the rocks, twisting and dodging, the thread of the channel suddenly disappeared, split up by thousands of exposed boulders, but the pressure of the current hurtling us down into these savage waiting teeth did not relax. Looking wildly about me, I heard John shout from the stem, "The channel, that mark...there!" Down below us I could see something like a couple of sticks in the midst of the boiling water.

It seemed as if I had barely heard him scream his directions when we were bearing down upon it. In one blinding second I saw it was not a mark but a dead caribou pinned by the raging current against a sharp protruding rock, its horns pointing to the sky. We had run so directly for it that there seemed no escape but to crash. I reached over, put the paddle under the bow with the handle in my right hand, and as we partially struck, at the instant of contact, I pulled the handle upward. The blade and throat of the paddle took the grazing shock, and the leverage of the blade against the rock as I yanked on the handle flung us off and we shot down between it and another rock, just escaping both. The whole incident was instantaneous and we were immediately occupied with running the rest of the rapid, which seemed endless.

A short stretch of boulder-free water gave us an opportunity to collect our breath and wits. As we were rolling cigarettes I turned around to chide John a little on his "mark." He was looking back up the river and I heard him murmur, "My mark!…Phew! What a stink!"

We were not to rest long; almost immediately we were again embroiled in a long bouldery rapid. Much of this, having learned our lesson, we tackled more cautiously, poling down it, though we ran the lower end. It was about two miles long. Then, with the characteristic surprise of the North Country, we without warning shot out into an all sand-skirted lake without a rock in sight. The country was low and flat and covered with dense dwarf spruce and open patches of boggy muskeg.

This lake was extremely shoal. We passed through it to an opening to the east, and the violence of the headwind forced us ashore. Resuming our way after a few hours, we continued into another larger lake almost identical in character and shape. It was so shoal that we were forced well out into it. Again we turned north, and the river changed completely. It seemed nothing but a great marsh. There was a fine growth of coarse marsh grass. The current was almost imperceptible and the banks, barely above water, supported such a dense wall of small interlocking spruce that it was nearly impossible to force our way through them when we attempted to land.

Our good fortune was not to last; another violent rapid and then a falls interrupted us. We ran down to the falls and dragged the canoe over a ledge and then ran through the rest of the rapid until the light began to fade so badly that we were unable to go on. We camped without knowing whether the rapid would soon end or we would run it forever and forever to eternity.

During the day we had had glimpses of the strange distant escarpment. It still maintained its northeasterly trend, and it seemed as if somewhere we should be forced to cut through it. In the uncertain light of the campfire, I commented in my small brown diary: "I rather wonder about the return...just rapids, rapids, rapids."

Both of us agreed over our evening tea and dried meat that this was one of the worst rivers of our experience at a hellish thing to struggle through if one had a real load!

John could not quite bring himself to concede that this river was *the* worst, for I had already admitted that it was. In his years of solitary trapping and living, he had developed a degree of independence, which at times was very amusing. The frame and mold of his own judgments was so hardened that he could not bring himself to agree without reservation to anyone else's opinion. If I was sure a certain bay was the correct one to take, I could absolutely count on John's conviction that it was not. The only thing for me to do was to suggest what I thought was the wrong way to go, and John would then stoutly maintain that we should go in the direction I secretly approved. Several times John was quite aware of my subterfuge and yet even then could not bring himself to admit or change his ingrained habit. Things were really going remarkably smoothly. Neither personality grated upon the other. A certain mysterious personal equation had, been settled on the Kasmere Portage. Both of us had traveled long enough to develop a callousness of the inconvenience of the trail and a fatalism, which made us impervious to the irritating barbs of worry. We had a mutual "to-hell-with-it" acceptance of what came and what might come, which is a necessary and invaluable adjunct to this type of travel. And most important of all, at the time we wanted nothing more from the world than just what we were doing. Then, too, we could both talk endlessly and with enthusiasm about the North— about various technical matters indigenous to the country we were in, observations and experiences with various types of game, rivers, and rapids, Indians and white men, traders and trappers, methods and stratagems, all concerned with the struggle for survival against a common foe, the North.

The next day in a hard rain and a cold and penetrating wind from some still frozen lake in the Barrens, we commenced the descent of the last part of the rapid. "Set out and immediately ran down the second stretch of the long rapid, a very nasty one with big waves. We ran right over, a large rock, but a wave caught us just right and lifted the bow up and over. John had lost bottom with his pole. Either or both of our *puagans* are being very good to us. The country continues to be low and muskeg."

Coming out into a small lake with a northeast axis,[8] we fought and clawed along against the harsh wind until we found that our "opening" at this end of the lake was a blind bay. There was nothing to do but go back, and at last in the southeast corner we found the river again. Three more rapids followed in quick succession, and then the river quietly expanded into a narrow lake, Tu-ni-ni-li-tu-eh, Long Lake. Several broods of mergansers went scurrying up ahead of us, churning the water into fine foam. They were still too young to fly. There were thirty or forty in the group and they made a fine spectacle, the little birds wobbling and valiantly fleeing our approach until we came too near, when they would instantly sink out of sight like a stone while the old bird made off in a slow, apparently crippled condition. Imitating the peeping cries of the little ones, I could sometimes draw the mother near, but she would soon discover the ruse and make off again. The young birds always made for the banks where they could hide among the willows. After we had passed, when the mother believed she had decoyed us far enough away, she suddenly dropped her wounded disguise and rose up to circle back and regather her precious family.

Everywhere the land was still low, densely forested muskeg. In one spot we saw an outcrop of "high muskeg," a bluff of exposed, brown, peat-like, solid growth. This type of exposure is rather unusual in this country and consists of undercut cliffs of peat which is almost a lignite or brown coal in composition. Darkness was approaching and it seemed that for once there was no place to camp. The thick stunted spruces were so close-packed we would have had to chop a clearing and could not have laid a sleeping robe over the stumps. In the open muskeg, the ground was a soft yielding mat of spongy moss.

Crossing to the eastern side, we found a high, sloping, barren ridge. This too was solid organic growth, but we decided to camp here despite its dampness and lack of shelter and wood. We had been thoroughly chilled from the constant cold wind all day; it had, however, the virtue of keeping the mosquitoes at bay. There were a few knotty dwarf spruces with red beards of a fine reddish moss. The Indians had been here to collect moss for their babies' moss bags. Both the Crees and Chipewyans have a very convenient device for carrying and taking care of their babies. The little ones are laced into a bag, which are sometimes affixed to a board. These bags are often very ornately beaded, decorated with ribbons, and made of a brilliant plaid. The moss, which is very downy and soft, is dried and stuffed between the baby's legs as an absorbent. Since the baby is laced in so tightly that it cannot get out, the contraption may be hung on a branch or left about anywhere when the mother is engaged in any operation that demands her full attention. Furthermore, they can be conveniently portaged on the back.

We managed to get a fire going, burning green wood. It is surprising, but the farther north one goes the more resinous the stunted trees seem to be. The live, green wood burned fitfully but very fiercely, sending up dense clouds of acrid smoke. After a while, John said he could see a fine sandy beach down the river on the other side. It was so dark and the gloom was so deep from the low-hanging storm clouds, that I did not see how he could make out anything, but I gave in and we packed up and moved on. We paddled a long way. Soon his "sand beach" became a low white ground fog. The lake-river became more and more shoal. The mist was soon so impenetrable that we could not see where we were going, and black rocks would suddenly rear up right in front of us. We seemed to be moving, phantom-like, in a strange disembodied world of mist and rocks with no shore, no beginning, and no end. The current began to quicken, and through the fog we heard the dull muffled roar of rapids. We tried to make shore but it was impossible to get near it for the shoals and the masses of boulders. At last I suggested we go back to our original camp and my mild recommendation was silently acted upon. It was nearly midnight when we paddled the last weary upstream strokes and dragged ourselves up the hill to the spot we had left hours before. We were too tired to put up the silk tarpaulin, and when we had gone to sleep it rained hard for the rest of the night.

Awakening in the cold pouring rain, we set out, both of us feeling a little grimly that this could not last forever. Passing our shoals of the night before, we soon became involved in the longest rapid either of us had ever known.

It was simply mile after mile of fast water and boulders. At noon we were still in it. We boiled up the kettle at a spot, which showed some portage signs. We followed this on foot for a long way. It had been made some time in the past by a white man, for the trees showed white man's blazes. The portage was a very bad one; it twisted on endlessly and crossed several stretches of muskeg into which we sometimes plunged up to the knees in water before touching solid ice. At last it faded out into nothing but a big swamp.

Coming back to the smoldering fire hissing and spluttering in the downpour, we sat and watched the seething, rushing water for a long time. Both of us were reluctant to portage everything through the rain and the mosquitoes over such a quagmire. When John went into the bush to cut himself a new tamarack pole, he came back with the back of his black sweater a solid brown mass of wriggling, crawling mosquitoes. It gave his back an odd pulsating appearance.

Sitting by the fire and half suspended over it to envelop myself in the smoke and escape the mosquitoes, I wrote: "Both of us, I feel, are tired from the headwinds, rain, and constant strain of rapids, direction—finding, poor camps, and lack of sustaining heavy-work food." When I snapped the little diary shut, seventeen mosquitoes were caught between the pages.

After several draughts of good black tea from which the black flies and mosquitoes had been skimmed, our spirits felt stronger. For better or worse, we decided to see if we could make a successful descent with poles.

Down we went, twisting, dodging, sometimes retracing our course and dropping down a different channel as the way became hopelessly blocked with boulders. Sometimes I would get out and wade a little, leading the canoe down through the more impossible stretches. Hour after hour this went on until the river, as if exhausted in its endless struggle against the rocks, spread out into a delta-like fan and became a congested confusion of boulders with scarce four inches of water to be found. These gray boulders and shattered rocks ranged themselves more and more thickly until they coalesced into a solid wall. Where a trickle of water pierced the wall we slipped through, and then suddenly we came into a fine large lake full of islands.

On the map One-eyed Louis had drawn, he had laid great stress on a large lake near the end of the Kasmere River. He had said that the lake had two islands and we must pass between them to the east shore to pick up the river again. This, he had pointed out, was the last lake before Nueltin. The Crees call it Cross Lake, and the Idthen-eldeli call it both No-lake Lake—in the sense that the river does not end here but continues and the lake is really part of the river—and also the Water-goes-two-ways Lake, Nah-ili-tu-eh.

It stretched before us far away to the northwest and the southeast. We could see no end to it in either direction. Instead of two islands, we saw islands everywhere we looked. If this was the lake, what islands out of the dozens before us should we go between?

Setting our course due east, we crossed to a high, burned island and camped near a little tombolo strand of sand which connected this island with one to the east of it. It was a fine, protected, dry spot, and we reveled in the luxury of it after the muskeg and swamp country.

As I climbed to the high summit of the island, water and islands endlessly met my eye in every direction. I wondered whether this might not be Nueltin Lake itself.

There was nothing to indicate that it was not. All the information we had been able to gather had been so fragmentary and so indistinct that there was absolutely nothing defi-nite to go on. With these thoughts I wandered back to our camp, noting a fox and a Harris sparrow on the way.

The luxury of the location and the heavy northeast wind combined to keep us in the camp until the next day. I took the opportunity to sew up my pants, which were nearly falling from me. My shirt, too, was little more than a mass of rags, and I interwove these with some pieces of caribou skin. John thought I presented a very amusing and bizarre appearance, and I privately speculated on the delight of my pupils at home could they have seen me. With faithful regularity all the but-tons on my pants had given way, and I had been forced to sub-stitute small pegs of wood. We also filed the ax, oiled the gun, and went over the canoe carefully for any tears or rents in the canvas; fortunately, and to our great pride, there were none. We mended small rips in the mosquito netting with bits of string, shaved the canoe paddles smooth once more with frag-ments of quartz, and picked flies and mosquitoes out of the thick accumulation of fat in the frying pan. We shaved. I had shaved with comparative faithfulness anyway. Some years before when I had a beard, I had been mistaken by the Indians for a missionary and had later heard them comment that I looked like Jesus with glasses. I did not relish either of these confusions. We both felt almost gleeful in the thought that if this were not Nueltin, it must be Louis's lake, and that was not far from Nueltin.

On the afternoon of the third day, the wind moderated and we set out to the eastward. In time we came to the main shore and coasted down it to the south. To our joy we began to find good camping evidence.

These campsites and signs of Indian travel were very important, for we had picked our way along by them. When they disappeared for any real length of time, we could be fair-ly sure that we were getting off the track. It demanded end-less vigilance, acute observation, and the ability to distinguish between winter and summer camps. Winter routes often do not follow the watercourses, particularly running water, and they tend to cross the country from lake to lake. These signs are not obvious and at times consist only of a stick thrust into the ground, a small patch of ashes, or a few cuttings. If the small trees showed ax marks and had been cut off two or three feet above the ground, we could be sure that the camp had been a winter one, for the depth of the snow caused the tree to be cut at that height. The cuttings and stumps themselves were not obvious. They soon lost their identity as they weathered and became overgrown by the surrounding trees. One or two small stumps in the background of a dense forest of thousands of other trees do not stand out. Also, when an Indian cuts a small dead tree or two for his tiny fire, he usually bends it down and cuts close to the roots with his light ax, using one hand. The result is that the little trunk is half cut and half twisted off, giving the stump a very natural appearance. Nevertheless, it was by such slight indications as these that we had followed the trail. John was particularly skillful in spotting these evidences, and we would occasionally have long and friendly debates as to the various signs. Detecting them became almost a sport and a competition to see who could chalk one up before the other.

In our enthusiasm and joy, we ran up into an all-blind bay but came about and soon found the river where it left the lake parted by a small island. Here along the sandy shores, the banks were thick and almost matted with bleaching caribou antlers. And then, far away, we heard the deep, heavy, booming, throaty roar of falls, the last falls before Nueltin. This was reassuring, for we knew that the Kasmere discharged into Nueltin by just such a drop.

As we approached them, they had a low, hollow sound indicative of a goodly descent. We ran through a swift but deep rapid which was very pleasant. There were no rocks and the water moved along blackly and with a deceiving film wrinkled here and there by small, erratic, twisting whirlpools. We watched every foot of the bank on the right side for indications of the portage we had been informed would be found on that shore. So intent were we in this examination, that we did not realize how swiftly the beguiling river had swept us along, and suddenly found ourselves approaching the very lip of the falls. We turned frantically to the paddles and dug in furiously to make the other side. At the last moment John dropped his paddle, seized his pole, and gave us one last powerful thrust to the bank. On the left side we found the portage. It was a pleasantly short one with excellent footing.

The falls descended in two cascades over a ledge of coarse granite-gneiss, the strike or "grain" of which ran northeast. This rock, itself beautiful in pattern and flowing line, was cut across by dark bands of a material known as diabase, a later intrusive into the host rock. These black bands were in turn cut across by smaller bands of a yellowish pegmatite, and the entire display was very intricate and interesting. Like the orderly and precise interlocking of a wooden Chinese puzzle, they demonstrated the restricted steps and order of their formation.

Below the falls the river continued for a short space as it cut through the steep, seventy-foot reddish walls of a north-south running esker. High on the south side was a little group of cabins, deserted, but no doubt the permanent homes of some members of the Barren Land Band, if one can speak of anything of theirs as permanent.

The shores were everywhere littered with caribou horns and bones. Here and there were whole carcasses of animals, which had been killed in the winter or early spring. These rotting bodies on the shore and the tiny huts on the hill spoke the whole cycle of existence in the North—the death of the deer, the life of the Idthen-eldeli.

Then, turning to the north, a long narrow bay, and great Nueltin Lake, Nu-thel-tin-to-eh, Sleeping-Island Lake—one hundred and twenty miles of it lay before us. All the doubts, the rapids, the portages, the bad omens, the mournful predictions, the fearsome warning, all these were behind us now!

CHAPTER 8

Nueltin Lake

Nu-thel-tin-tu-eh, or as the maps have it, Nueltin Lake, has a very fragmentary though interesting history. Today, even with the wide use of the airplane in the North, it remains one of Canada's largest unmapped lakes and one of its least known.

The first white man to see it was an indomitable and courageous traveler, Samuel Hearne. Few annals of travel in all the great library of North American pioneer exploration are comparable in content or achievement with Hearne's great Odyssey. On his third attempt to reach the Coppermine River and the Polar Sea, Hearne, leaving Fort Prince of Wales with some Chipewyan Indians, arrived at the shores of the lake on the thirtieth of December, 1770. He called the lake Island Lake, a shortening of the full Chipewyan name. *

Hearne observed that the lake was about thirty-five miles

* This account is well worth anyone's reading who is interested in a heroic adventure and a remarkable picture of the North at the time of the first penetration by the white man: *A Journey from Prince of Wales's Fort in Hudson's Bay to the Northern Ocean. Undertaken by Order of the Hudson's Bay Company for the Discovery of Copper Mines, a North West Passage &c. in the Years 1769, 1770, 1771 & 1772*, by Samuel Hearne. London, A. Strahan and T. Cadell, 1795.

A later edition, edited with excellent addenda and a placing of geographical names in their present-day setting, was brought out by the Champlain Society, Toronto, 1911.

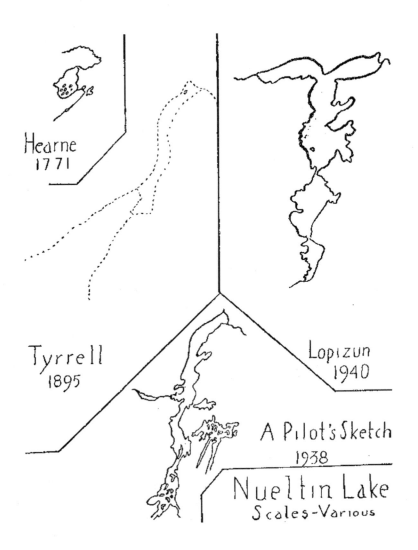

Hearne
1771

Tyrrell
1895

Lopizun
1940

A Pilot's Sketch
1938

Nueltin Lake
Scales-Various

wide where he crossed it, which was, he believed, at about the middle of the lake, which he placed at latitude 60 degrees, 45 minutes, and this is comparatively accurate. Later geographers questioned Hearne's estimate, without ever having been near the lake. They did not take into account the fact that, since it was winter, the approach to the lake from the east was made by the most easterly bay and the traverse across was to the longest bay on the other side, taking advantage of the unimpeded, frozen surface of the lake. Later this large bay was seen from the air, and Hearne's statement was corroborated.

Even in those days, Nueltin was an important gathering place for the Chipewyans, as witness Hearne's account: "At different parts of this Lake the most part of the wives and families of those Northern [Chipewyan, Idthen-eldeli] Indians who visit Prince of Wales Fort [modern Churchill, Manitoba] in October and November generally reside, and wait for their return; as there is little fear of their being in want of provisions, even without the assistance of gun and ammunition, which is a point of real consequence to them."

Hearne's description of the outstanding feature of the lake, which now met our eyes, was certainly to the point. "…from the North East to the South West it is much larger [than the thirty-five miles] and entirely full of islands, so near to each other as to make the whole lake resemble a jumble of serpentine rivers and creeks; and it is celebrated by the natives as abounding with great plenty of fine fish during the beginning of the Winter."

The lake was not again visited by any known white man from that December of 1770 until the summer of 1912. In that year, an American, Ernest C. Oberholtzer, in the company of an Indian named Billy Magee from Fort Frances, visited the lake and passed through it and its outlet which Hearne had called the Nemace-a-seepee-sish or Little Fish River down to Hudson Bay, until, continuing by canoe, he reached Winnipeg on the ninth of November. No record of this trip, an extremely laudable one, was ever published, but Oberholtzer was dimly remembered by a few of the really old residents of the country. On the top of a high hill to the east of the main narrows he left a friction-top tin can with a notation of his trip and his naming for the hill, Hawkes Summit. This can was found years later by a white trapper.*'

Tyrrell, in 1894, passed many miles to the west of the lake. Hearing about it from the Indians, he made various observations about it and changed its name to approximate the Chipewyan name of Nu-thel-tin-to-eh. On his map of the territory he drew in, entirely from hearsay, the outline of the lake and labeled it Nueltin Lake.

About ten years after Oberholtzer's remarkable journey, the first feelers of commercial penetration were extended by the Revillon Frères, who led the way by establishing a small outpost. Ten years later, the Hudson's Bay Company and some small private enterprises had begun to invade the general area. But, as I have previously pointed out, these efforts were very short-lived. At the time of our arrival, the lake and the routes to it had long been abandoned. Considering the nature and length of the approach, the portages and the difficulties of the Kasmere River, it is not hard to see why this was inevitable.

From our evening camp some six miles above the point of entrance, the lake stretched before us, a maze of islands and channels. Indeed, nowhere was there any really large open expanse of water. The west shore was bounded by a high esker so undercut by the waves that it stood out gleaming and yellow in the late twilight.

Whether we could ever find our way through this labyrinth of islands, whether we could find the Hudson's Bay post at the outlet of Windy Lake some ninety miles to the north of us, were problems we did not discuss. For the moment we reveled in the happiness of our arrival at this great lake, which we had been seeking since the late afternoon of July 6. Night found me writing the date "July 24" in my diary.

Throughout the trip I had harbored the conceit that I might map not only the route but also the shoreline at least of this vast lake, but this was to receive an abrupt answer the fol-

* Cecil ("Husky") Harris in company with I. H. Smith and William Varnson, 1924. Harris lost his life in Hudson Bay in the fall of 1940.

lowing day. That day I wrote: "We started out after the strong northwest wind moderated a bit. Our course was north and a bit west. We followed the main shore of high sand banks as we had been given to believe that the main west shore was moderately straight. We kept the islands on our right hand. We went along for some hours into a headwind, and at last it became apparent that we had run into a long dead-end bay. This was discouraging, as we seemed hemmed in everywhere by points and islands.

"We began to circle back, coming out on the east side of the islands we had previously passed on the west side; this of course making them practically unrecognizable. It was all very confusing and a little discouraging. This lake has been variously estimated from one hundred and twenty to one hundred and eighty miles long, and to be hopelessly trapped in the first three hours was not at all a good prospect.

"We at length found ourselves forced back to within sight of our own camp of this morning and last night!

"We climbed a hill. What a sight! Islands...bays ...channels...islands everywhere, every direction of the compass points, a vast maze as far as the eye could see. What was main shore, lakes, bays, islands, or points was all one endless confusion. Both of us wondered about either getting anywhere or back. It is not easy to paddle and map and get bearings all at the same time."

Somehow, somewhere, we had to break through to the north. As it was, it looked as if that way was entirely blocked by either islands or the mainland, we could not tell which. It was not feasible to follow every bay to its end to find out whether we were coasting a point of the mainland or an island.

As we had climbed down from the hill in our vain search for a break through to the north, John gave vent to his first really serious doubts of the trip. He shook his head slowly and his face had a bewildered look as if he had just seen something beyond human comprehension. "I dunno," he mused. "A man get himself caught up in that mess of islands and bays, he could spend a lifetime trying to get out. I dunno if we should try it; you can go on forever, but how about finding the way back?"[2]

We paddled along without direction for some time. Each of us was silent in the contemplation of the astounding confusion of sand and water we had seen. The enormity of it all seemed to rob us of any decision. Then on a reef we saw a tiny pile of stones, flat stones one upon the other. It looked like a miniature *inuitshuk*, those stone cairns the Eskimos erect in the Arctic. Grasping at this mute sign, we turned north and found ourselves involved in a winding narrows and soon completely hemmed in by islands.

Boiling up the teakettle on a low bare point, we happily discovered abundant camping evidence. Hearthstones and refuse from implement making were scattered about, and I found one very nice quartz knife. This was a fine spot for a caribou crossing. Someone some time must have gotten to this spot, and if they could get to it we must be able to get out from it.

Following through the twisting narrows to the north, we were forced ashore by the rising wind. All day it had been gray and cold and we had been paddling against a bitter headwind, but now the clouds became black and any further forward movement was impossible. Travel in the North is always subject to the will and whim of the winds, but one can usually count on good weather at least in July and into the middle of August. Whether the adverse weather conditions, which we had constantly faced, were characteristic of this particular region, comparatively close to ice-choked Hudson Bay, or whether it was an unusually bad year, we could not say. John cursed bitterly and vengefully about it. It was by far the worst traveling weather he had ever seen in summer, and one would not expect a very great difference in conditions between the country we had passed over and his own territory, Wollaston Lake.

Impatient at our wind bound state, we climbed the high hill back to our camp. We began to make a reconnaissance of the lake to the north and west. The top of the hill afforded an excellent vantage point. To our surprise and joy, we saw a large opening to the northwest. The distant western shore was a high sandy ridge and gave every appearance of being the main shore. To the north, a series of large overlapping islands ran obliquely northwest southeast. Northeast, another large opening extended indefinitely until at the horizon the water merged with some faint islands. Very far away and smoky blue was the suggestion of much higher hills.

Studying the western shore again with the binoculars, we could see a number of grayish-white objects. At that distance we could not see whether they were big, erratic boulders or not. I insisted that they were tents, but John would have none of it. His eyes were so infinitely superior to my own that I contented myself with a silent insistence that they *were* tents.

We went back to our camp very much cheered. The long opening to the northwest seemed to swing north, and at least we saw our way clear to advancing a good many miles. Also, it was reassuring to see the west shore. This, from our high point seemed to run down to the south in a long bay, which must have nearly connected with the blind bay we had run into in the morning. If that were so, it would explain a mysterious "x" Louis had drawn on his map of Nueltin. It must have indicated a portage at that spot connecting the two bays, and cutting off the maze through which we had been wandering.

We sat about the small fire alternately smoking and drinking tea. The black clouds were beginning to roll over us and the wind whined and whistled. I felt this was something of a special occasion, so we boiled up the last of the caribou delicacies Father Egernolf had given us, and far down in the grub box I found a small bag of damp and adhesive raisins which I had long hoarded for a real treat.

We were both thin; John's naturally deep sunken eyes had retreated further and his cheekbones stuck out in mosquito-scarred bumps. My hair formed a matted protective pad over the back of my neck. We both felt fine and strong for the rest of the journey. John grinned at me with his few broken teeth. "The old lake hasn't got us beat yet!" he said.

Our stock of flour had long been gone, eaten or given away. So too had a small bag of oatmeal which at the start of the trip we used to boil up in the frying pan. We still had sufficient tea; the real worry was that the tobacco supply was getting pretty thin. It never occurred to us that either wished anything more or different than what we had been eating. It never occurred to us to question the diet of the Chipewyans, who never have seen a vegetable in their lives, whose diet is still straight meat and fish, meat and fish. They seemed to survive and suffer no lack of vitamins; so had we. Sometimes, when we camped, I would pick a few of the wild cranberries, which grew everywhere. But I never felt any need of them. We were still too early for the blueberries; for a brief two weeks in late August they are very profuse. Despite the shrinkage of our commissary, our hopes were rising, for on this day we had seen a single fresh caribou track and also a wolf print. The deer were moving south!

In high expectation we set out the next day. We rounded our high point, which we both called "Observation Hill" and directed our course to the northwest. The wind was still very strong and had backed into the west so our progress was not very rapid. We seemed to have been paddling mechanically for a very long time before the white specks we had seen began to take form. Then we saw that they were tents, eight of them perched high on the sandy ridge of the western shore.

I shouted back to John, "*Tents*! See!"

But John was adamant. "Tents, yeh, but they're held down by *rocks*!"

The day was beautifully clear. The sun sparkled and danced on the waves of the great lake. The tents stood out white and clean against the brilliant yellow sand. We could even see the red silk handkerchiefs around the women's heads as they bustled about. They had evidently seen us approaching for there was much activity, people running about and coming down to the shore to look and then rushing back up to the tents to call others to the strange spectacle of a lone canoe approaching from the south.

When we came in to the shore, we saw only two other canoes there, heavy freighters at least twenty feet long. A rabble of tattered children, bright-eyed and staring came timidly down to look at us. Two young men followed. They were very ragged and their hair hung down in long, coarse, unkempt shocks. None of them could speak any English. The children, rather furtively at first, began to peep into our canoe like inquisitive and fidgety mice. This was the proof of Louis's prophecy;

we should find the *denee*, "the people," at Putahow River.

We climbed the steep bank and were met by an older, rather handsome man considerably better dressed than the young boys who had come down to meet us first. Though he refused to speak any English, I felt, from the look in his black eyes, he had an inkling of what we were trying to say.

We questioned him about the route and elicited the information that, if one knew the way, one could get to Windy Lake and the trading post in three days by leaving Nueltin Lake and going through a series of lakes to the northwest. If one followed the main shore of Nueltin, it would take at least seven to ten days and possibly more depending upon whether one could get through without being wind bound en route.

We asked him if one of the young fellows, a strong shaggy-manned youth who looked very powerful, would like to go along with us as we expected to be at the trading post in a week or possibly ten days. A long and rapid exchange of clicks and abdominal rumbles took place between the two of them and in the end the older man turned to us and said that the young chap would go.

Our going up to visit the camp caused a great commotion among the assembled people. They seemed, except for the older man and the young fellow, to be entirely women and children. The women were of all ages, from one or two immobile, ancient crones to more sprightly young ladies. When I stopped to take a photograph, there was a tremendous cackling and peals of laughter. Streams of clicking Chipewyan were howled at me and shrieked back and forth between the tents. I knew very well that the comments were not such as a like gathering of white women might have flung back and forth under similar circumstances.

There seemed to be plenty of food in the camp. Whitefish and even caribou meat were in evidence, though the latter was either dried or pemmican. There was no sign of any fresh meat; evidently the "deer" had not yet arrived. One necessity of life was lacking—tobacco. We had not the slightest difficulty in trading off all the tobacco we could produce. We were fairly swamped with beseeching hands crammed with pemmican and whitefish in various stages of decomposition. In one group of squatting women sat a single old creature. Her face was lined with a thousand wrinkles, and dressed in doleful black, she sat disconsolately alone sucking on a tremendous empty briar pipe. While the younger more nimble women were darting into their tents and rescuing meat and fish from dirty burlap bags to tempt us into a trade, she alone had nothing.

I walked up to her. She remained in her squatting position, her legs and toes tucked under her, and without looking at me bowed her gray head, opened her hands flat and upward upon her lap and murmured sadly. "*Doti*" (Nothing). I reached into my pocket and extracted a stick of black tobacco, "nigger twist," and put it into her hands. "*Zet-swoizi!*" I said, (My sweetheart!). The surrounding circle broke into shrieks and screams of surprise and laughter. The old lady looked up at me. Her old eyes twinkled from out the myriad wrinkles. She stuffed some of the tobacco into her great, black pipe and grinned up at me with a toothless smile.

It was a fine, brave, colorful spectacle. Apparently these were the families of the men we had met so many, many miles to the south. They had been left behind while their men went out to trade and to "Treaty." The two men had been delegated to hunt and in general supervise the camp. It brought back vividly to my mind Hearne's observation. Here was a wonderful illustration of the continuity of the North. Here the worm-eaten, faded pages of Hearne's narrative in my library so far away had come alive. In one hundred and fifty years, despite the white man and the airplane, the cycle of life was essentially just the same. Here was something which in a few short years was destined never to be repeated again: a strange people, a brave people, with a heritage and way of life stretching back through the mist of time to the bleak steppes of Siberia, dying, unable to change, disappearing into the timeless obscurity from whence they had come.

Behind the sand bank, really a high, even esker, I caught a glimpse of a winding river and a bay. Yes, One-eyed Louis's prediction had been right, for this was the Putahow River, or as it was known by the Crees, the Nipsa, "Willow" River.

The older man, our "interpreter," motioned that we

should go along in our canoe and meet him at his camp, which was some distance from the others. As we prepared to leave we were besieged by importunate females desiring to trade the last shred of anything resembling food in exchange for *zeltuey*, tobacco. As we were now confident that we would soon reach the trading post we did not hesitate to trade off all our tea and tobacco except for a couple of days' supply. Actually we had not received a great deal of food; our supply of tobacco and tea had been so small and we were about to be increased by one more—and this an Indian—appetite.

The pemmican is an important staple in this part of the North. It is made from caribou meat dried in thin strips in the sun. The meat, when it is completely sun-dried, is pounded up until it is almost as fine as meal. Caribou fat is then melted and mixed with the lean meat, and the resultant mass is cooled into a cement-like loaf or cake, sometimes twenty pounds or more in weight, and sewed up in a caribou hide from which the hair has been scraped. In this condition the pemmican will keep for an indefinite time, even years. It is the most delicious and sustaining food for the trail that exists. One is very fortunate to come upon some, for the parts of the North where it is still made are very obscure and limited and it is rarely or never made for other than personal use. There have been many types of pemmican. For instance, in the early days of the fur trade, the voyageurs existed almost solely on pemmican made from buffalo meat, but the caribou pemmican is much the finer flavored and the best. I never eat pemmican without remembering a story told to me by an old French-Cree voyageur. He would tell at rambling length about the ways of the fur brigades he knew when he was a very young man. He told me how at night they would take out a great block of buffalo pemmican and hack off pieces for the crew with a hatchet, and then he would sigh and say: "You know, sometimes they did not take much care how they made the pemmican, for once I remember when they cut down through a chunk with the little ax, they chopped right through an old moccasin."

Reaching our friend's camp we found not only the younger man but also the older one all ready to leave. We had not bargained for or wanted two of them, one was quite sufficient to find the way, but as they both evidently wished to go along, we did not object.

The fine-looking older one, whom John and I referred to as "Crooked Finger"—he had something the matter with the little finger of his right hand-paddled stern. John and I paddled amidships, and the other Indian, whom we called "Shaggy Head," took over the bow. He was an extremely powerful paddler. Both men brought as outfits their blankets and rifles, and Shaggy Head contributed two rather smelly whitefish. With all four of us at the paddles and the Indians seemingly bent on getting ahead with all possible speed, the canoe flew through the water.

True to our surmise, the west shore continued to the north in a long opening. The high sand bank, an enormous esker, persisted as such until we were to leave the lake. Not until we had traveled some miles did the true majesty of Nueltin reveal itself. We kept close to the straight shore and a chain of islands ran parallel to us at our right. Occasionally openings to the northeast would reveal vast stretches to a landless horizon. Becoming increasingly prominent, far to the north rose two distant, blue, very high hills, sharp and peaked in form.

As we tore along through the water a very ludicrous situation began to develop. We were so jammed into the seventeen-foot canoe, the paddles were so long, that an absolutely synchronized stroke had to be maintained. The two Indians set up a furious pace. John, who from years of lone traveling had adjusted himself to a much slower and deep-stroked motion, was unprepared to adapt himself to the mad haste either by habit or inclination. In consequence every once in a while he would be the cause of a shattering collision with the paddles of both Crooked Finger and Shaggy Head, who would say nothing but ply their blades all the more vigorously. When this happened, the canoe would lurch over and John would start raging at the elements, the Indians, and the world in general, and he would be forced, groaning and protesting, to pick up the beat whether he wished or not. I was more fortunate, for, when exhaustion approached, I had the semilegitimate excuse to stop and take bearings or sketch in the shoreline.

For some time a big canoe had been following us and now it began to draw near. As it came abreast, we saw that it contained a heterogenous assortment of women, babies, girls, and one young boy. All of them, except the babies, were paddling. As it approached it looked like some ridiculous, great water beetle with a hundred scrambling legs. The stern was in the capable hands of a very large powerful woman. How she could paddle! Despite our four-man power they kept alongside. The woman in the stern took great mile-eating, even strokes, keeping her arms rigid and extended and her back absolutely stiff and straight. The whole motion was from the hips, the power of her stroke being in the rhythmic swing of her body. Grinning and laughing, we went along together, sometimes bursting into sprints, which would always be returned in kind by the other canoe. One of the women would occasionally take time out to nurse her baby, but then she would pick up the stroke again.

At noon we all drew into the sandy beach and had dinner. It was the same for all of us; a cup of tea and white-fish roasted on a stick, the stick thrust through the fish from tail to mouth and the fish broiled over the coals. After these had been cooled a little they were attacked with the fingers, and the children plucked away the last of the firm sweet flesh until nothing but the backbones remained. I have eaten whitefish, far and away the finest eating fish in the North, from Reindeer Lake, Great Slave, Great Bear, salmon in Labrador, Arctic trout from Boothia Peninsula and Baffin Island, but in all these famous spots no fish I had eaten compared with the firm, delicious whitefish of Nueltin. While we were eating, the boy wandered off to a high hill. He had an ancient complicated rifle, like an old Russian Krag. The quest for the caribou was on.

The wind had now hauled around more favorably to us and John rigged up the sail. The Indians both protested that it was too big, but John would have none of it and went ahead and installed it in the canoe. The construction was very quick and simple; one of the poles was used for a mast and tied into the forward thwart. A smaller pole, notched at one end, was suspended through a loop to the mast and attached to the upper and outer corner of the tarpaulin, and the lower corners were fastened to the doubled tracking line that led back to the steersman who both controlled the sail and steered with his paddle. It billowed out in the wind and fairly dragged the canoe through the water.

The shoreline remained remarkably straight and not at all complicated by bays. It ran almost due north and throughout was bordered by the same uninterrupted, gleaming yellow esker. There were a few minor indentations and here and there I saw odd little sand hills, which had the form of alluvial cones such as I, had once seen at the foot of the Ellesmere Island ice cap. I could not get over the length and magnificence of the esker. Just as the ponderous and enormous dinosaurs of the Mesozoic Age have left their footprints as impressions and casts, so too these great eskers were the casts of the mighty and extinct rivers of the Ice Age.

Our course now began to bend to the east. Large and irregular bays made their appearance. The two high peaks to the north became more distinct; the islands to the east began to show far sparser vegetation. One very long island lay off some distance to the right. It was completely barren and very low, with a rounded back. It looked like some great animal in repose, a huge, sleeping island. It was from this island, I expected, that the lake had taken its name. As we rushed along in the sunlight, Crooked Finger alert and watchful in the stern, I wondered to myself whether this great lake was the scene of Mother Nonucho's last camp.

For, in the long ago, when the first Chipewyan came to the North, the first mother of all the Chipewyans, who had mated with a wolf or a wolf-dog, found nothing but ice. Everywhere she and her two small children traveled there was nothing but desolation. So she walked and walked to the south. Sometimes she would camp on some lake for a little while as, overcome with fatigue and despair, it seemed that she could go no farther. But then the wolves would leave her food and talking to them she was always told she must go farther to the south. So once more she would resume her way. Over the treeless Barrens she wandered. As the years went by she became older. Now when she saw the mighty, dark musk oxen she had to cry out with her full voice for she had become very feeble and they could not hear her. Her fingers, stiffened with the countless winter's cold, could barely make snares for rabbits. Now when she, in the extremity of want and hunger, heated a dried caribou shoulder blade over the coals, her tired old eyes could barely distinguish the cracks and burned spots, which told where the caribou were. The children had both grown up, and many times they begged her to stop, since now they were in a better land. But Mother Nonucho stumbled on for they were not yet in the land of the little trees.

Finally they came to a great lake, and as they traveled down its shore the children saw a line of green. By this time the old woman could no longer see. The children described to her these strange sticks, and the old woman smiled in happiness even though she could not see them. She knew that her quest and her duty were nearly over; she had brought her two children to the trees.

When they had traveled about halfway down this lake, they reached the trees and Mother Nonucho stopped. "Here, my children," she said, "here is our home, here is the home for all our people to come. Leave me for a little while for I am tired and old and the days are now all nights."

So the children left her. When they came back, she was gone. They knew that she was dead. She had gone into the ground. For they could hear her voice speaking as if from within the earth. And it said, "Here, my children, will I always be to help you."

And all through the North the old people knew that when they were sick or starving could they but get back to that lake, could they but camp on its shores, there, lying on the ground, the spirit of Mother Nonucho would come up through the earth and make them strong, make them well again; she would talk to the caribou and the musk oxen and call them near to her children. For Mother Nonucho had been strong. She had been faithful to the "older things." She had walked and led her children until even her feet were gone and she could walk no more. She had brought them safely to the land of the little trees.

For some time now our feminine escort had left us. Seeing two men on the shore, we veered from our course and ran in to the land. They were Indians who had just returned from Windy Lake. Crooked Finger and Shaggy Head engaged in a long and unintelligible conversation with them, and then we parted and paddled to the beach. Everything was portaged over this pebbly barrier into a small bay. Passing by the two islands, for just an instant great Nu-thel-tin-tu-eh could be seen in all its vastness—blue, tremendous, sparkling, its low islands, yellow and bare, the two hazy peaks to the north— and then it was all hidden as we went up into a still smaller bay and, running ashore, prepared to portage away from Nueltin on the way to Windy.

Our new companions, since they had brought only their guns and blankets, aided us greatly and we were able to take over everything including the canoe in one load. We trailed one after the other through a very boggy, wet, stretch of muskeg. With my head bent down by my load, I could just see the bottom of Crooked Finger's feet. They were large and moved very rapidly. The portage brought us out on a small lake, which soon expanded, into a much larger one as we progressed. The tops of the hills were now completely barren of trees though the growth on the lower slopes and at the water's edge was still fairly thick.

Another portage over an esker was completed. The country about us was the typical sandy, knobby, depression-sprinkled world with which we had become so familiar. With scant ceremony we had the tea pail boiling, and soon each sought his own particular spot of ground to sleep.

The two men were an interesting contrast. Crooked Finger was a tall, well-built man. His features were cleanly sculptured and pleasing. On the "outside" he would be considered a handsome man. His clothing was very clean. He talked with a low voice and was inclined to laugh softly and frequently. His black eyes were very expressive and he impressed me as being an unusually intelligent man. Without ostentation or conscious effort he had almost from the start taken over a silent domination and command of our group.

Shaggy Head, on the other hand, was short, squat, and

powerful. His clothing was in the last stages of disrepair and looked like my own. He had a long, heavy face with coarse features, very high oblique cheekbones, and deep-set eyes. He never said anything himself beyond deep, guttural, rasping monosyllables in reply to Crooked Finger. He never laughed. He wore constantly an ancient, heavy dark cap, invariably with the earflaps turned down. From beneath these the shaggy mane of his hair jutted out in jagged tufts. Sometimes he would turn his head and fasten his black, opaque eyes upon me and just look. Not the slightest expression crossed his face. It was as if he was examining some kind of an incomprehensible new animal or bug. Within him seemed to burn a constant feverish flame of impatience, restlessness, and search. Whenever we landed, and particularly when we camped, he was immediately and incessantly on the go. He would leave us with no word or comment and begin to range over the country like a wolf looking for a fresh track. He would disappear almost instantly, and then we would see him silently silhouetted on top of some hill, his head turning this way and that as he loped along. As he paddled in the bow—and it was he who set the fastest pace—I could see the big cords and muscles swell and subside through his thin shirt. All the while his eyes perpetually searched the shores and islands. It was always he who pointed out the way with a silent motion of his lifted paddle.

Through the day I had found it increasingly easy to talk with Crooked Finger. He did know a handful of English words and could also talk a little Cree. Once or twice I managed to convey some jokes, or at least some remarks calculated to tickle his fancy. He would translate them to Shaggy Head, and once I actually caught that somber one slyly grinning to himself.

I was glad to be traveling with Indians once more. Not the least of the pleasures of traveling with them is their immediate response to the country. Pointing out and commenting on the shapes of islands or hills, spotting ducks or birds, trying to imitate the cries of gulls and terns—all the hundreds of small things that make up the world about one they seemed to appreciate. This is a quality lacking in most white travelers. I had a particularly stimulating feeling that we were getting somewhere, getting on. There was no dallying or painful exploration of the portages; everything was rushed over, the onerous business done with once and for all and as quickly as back and legs could stand it. There was little respite in the paddling. We forged on and on.

In the intimacy of the evening campfire and the restful interim of a smoke, Crooked Finger informed me that his name was Lop-i-zun and Shaggy Head's was Zah-bah-deese. These were the equivalent, I later discovered, of Robertson and John Baptiste.

The next morning we made our start at a very early hour. We found ourselves moving up a long narrow lake called Thy-to-eh, "Sandy" Lake. A low esker formed the west shore. Once Zah-bah-deese hissed, "*Zsst!*" and pointed to the shore. As we turned in closer, I saw that it was a fresh caribou track. All morning long the two high peaks were in view but they gradually took on a more easterly bearing. The country to the east of us be-came increasingly higher, bolder, and more rugged. We passed a small stream coming in from the north and west. At the north end of this lake, which must have been some seven or eight miles in length, we entered a bay so shoal that John and Zah-bah-deese got out and followed on a sand ridge while Lop-i-zun and I worked the canoe through the shallows and a stretch of swamp. We then portaged over the esker into a small pond to the west. All along there had been scant evidence of this route ever having been used. It occurred to me that we were most fortunate in having the two Indians along, for without them it would have been nearly impossible to pick out the track.

The shore of the little pond was all a-bloom with arctic cotton, a species of flower very prevalent and common in the Barren Lands and the Arctic. I had not seen any signs of it until now. The flower resembles a high stalked dandelion in seed, but the tufts of silky, white cotton are much denser and longer.

Again we portaged and again we came out into a small lake, which rapidly enlarged into a much larger one and began to split up into long bays extending off to the southwest for undetermined distances. To the northeast was a very high green hill, a prominent landmark in a country remarkable for its lack of them. It seemed devoid of trees yet had an unusual and odd greenness.

By noon we had turned off through a narrows to the west and then doubled back to the northeast and come to the last portage before Windy Lake. Here my compass behaved in a strange and erratic fashion, and I made some errors in my sketch map. Whether this was caused by some local mineral attraction or my camera light meter I did not discover, for the error was not found until we had landed. The trees had now become infrequent and sparse and all exposed high slopes were bare.

The portage across to Windy Lake, though unobstructed by trees, was very stony and bad walking. The ground was littered with small boulders and fragments. Here we boiled up the kettle while I ascended a high hill to take a look at the surrounding country. From this point Windy Lake spread out far to the north. It was so cut up by islands and points that it was impossible to tell whether I was looking at one lake or a hundred. Two very long bays could be seen stretching and wriggling away to the southwest as far as the eye could see. Now the unusual green hill bore almost east. It was very warm and the black flies were very active and attentive.

Looking over the infinite complexity of the lake below me, once more I felt thankful for the companionship and guidance of the two Indians. The route had been so twisting, the point of departure from Nueltin Lake had been so obscure, and the prospect before me was so extraordinarily devious, that I was compelled to put down the happy circumstance of Lop-i-zun and Zah-bah-deese to the far-away conjuring of old Adam or propitious and benign *puagans*.

Embarking once more, we set out for the northeast and emerged into the larger part of the lake from the narrow little bay we had entered. Here, as we passed through another narrows, a tremendous single pyramidal rock rose up out of the channel. Not until we had passed close by it could I appreciate its truly immense size. It rose from the water sheer and majestic, brilliantly white and gleaming, composed of coarse light granite. It was difficult to visualize a power great enough to transport this gigantic, lone, proud sentinel.

Twisting through a narrow winding channel we came out into the main body of the lake. It stretched away to the far horizon toward the northwest where a few, dim islands could be seen apparently suspended above the water. It was the one hot day of the entire summer, and the more distant islands took on fantastic and wavering shapes in the heat mirage. We disregarded a very large open bay to the southwest and the big green hill began to fall behind us. A gentle breeze began to stir and we hoisted the sail, content to drift over the water in silence at scarcely paddle pace.

The sun became hotter. The glare of the water bound us all in torpor of heat and silence. John fell asleep beside me. For hours we drifted over the great, shining expanse of water. No one moved; no one spoke. It was very difficult for me to keep my eyes open. I could not see Zah-bah-deese, who was in the bow and hidden by the sail. Lop-i-zun stood like a bronze statue staring straight ahead with his hands gripping the steering paddle. The canoe did not seem to be moving except for a small ripple beside the bow. The shore and the islands drifted slowly by in the heat haze as in a dream. Now trees gathered only at the water's edge, and all the larger islands were bare. The more distant ones changed their purple, blurred shapes, elongating and shortening, rising above the water, and then disappearing. In this state of strange and distorted mental focus, this chimerical world of half-reality, half-delusion and mirage, we drifted on to the Barren Lands.

Late in the afternoon we approached and passed three islands almost identical in size, shape, and appearance. They were arranged parallel to each other. Identical triplets, they looked like great loaves of brown bread side by side in the water. Beyond them was an odd conical island of sand, like a giant's sombrero floating on the lake.

The lake stretched on endlessly to the northwest but we altered our course slightly and entered a little bay cut off from the rest of the lake by a long, wriggling, esker point. Hugging the esker, we turned to the west and the lake became like a river. To the north was a long high range of hills, rolling, barren, and of uniform height. Our southern shore was the esker, which, pierced by occasional openings, revealed that the lake continued on the other side of it. It was as if an engineer had constructed a long, low breakwater for us behind which we traveled in safety.

The dying sunset filled all the world, so silent, so vast, and so lone, with a reddish glow. Reflected by the barren range of hills, it gave them an unearthly tinge. Bathed in a haze of blood, the setting was unreal and strange.

Drifting, drifting silently, we all, except Lop-i-zun, had begun to drowse. The sail hung listlessly. The water gurgled in a small murmur around the bow. The sun dropped beneath the horizon. But still the red glow and the warmth persisted. We were close to the shore. Then, there were three tense whispered words from the stern:

"*Zsst! Idthen…attik…*deer!"

If ever three somnolent, quiet, drowsing beings sprang into violent action at a whispered word it was then. Four meat-starved men sat bolt upright. Lop-i-zun's .30-.30 crashed. From the bow, almost simultaneously, Zah-bah-deese's gun roared and flamed and kept on roaring. In between came the thunderous explosions of my Mannlicher.

As my gun spoke over the top of Zah-bah-deese's black cap, he dropped his own, which he had fired straight up in the air, and stuck his fingers in his ears. On the low bank, a single bewildered and reproachful caribou staggered a trifle, looked about slowly, and walked quietly and deliberately over a small hill.

Jumping out of the canoe into the water and running up the bank, I dropped the unfortunate animal. I heard the canoe ground on the shore. Lop-i-zun came up the hill running, with his knife in his hand. Some one was already gathering twigs. In less time than one could tell it, the head was cut off, the under-muzzle slit, the tongue extracted, the side slashed, the entrails dragged out and then the choice liver and kidneys.

We returned to the fire and spitted the tongue on a stick, put the kidneys and liver into the frying pan, wiped some of the blood from our hands and, this gesture to civilization accomplished, each seized a piece of meat and began gnawing on it without a word but all grinning at one another.

When we had gorged ourselves, we went back and cut up the quarters and brisket and returned with them to the canoe. It was a scene of sheer atavism in which all of us, regardless of blood and station, had acted completely as one and as our ancestors in the dim past had always done.

In the thunderous barrage of shots, Lop-i-zun's first one had crippled the caribou. He hit it in the back leg. None of the other shots had struck it until I went ashore. When Lop-i-zun first went to the dying animal, he searched all over it. Then he looked up at me with a strange, puzzled, and rather frightened expression. There was no other wound on the animal but the one in the leg. When he cut out the tongue, he again looked at me and gave a relieved short laugh. My shot had struck the animal below the horns and passed, oddly enough, out through its mouth.

Before we put the quarters into the canoe, Lop-i-zun examined the lower part of the legs very carefully, feeling with his long thin fingers for mosquito bites. He continued his minute exploration to the bottoms of the hoofs. He explained to me that, as this was the first caribou we had seen, we could get an indication of their movements from the following evidence. If the ankles were badly bitten and swollen, it proved that the caribou were down very recently from the Barrens and were moving toward the trees. Thus, they would be met on the edge of the Barrens moving south. But, if there was little sign of this, it showed that they were already to be found within the tree line; by walking through the shrubs and brush they kept the mosquitoes from them. And if the hoofs showed the outer, hard edges worn down flat, they were recently in the Barrens and had not yet reached the woods, the wearing down being caused by the lack of heavy moss and the prevalence of rock and hard sand.

According to Lop-i-zun, the spot where we had killed the caribou was right across from where the Revillon Post had stood long ago. There was no sign of it as we passed, but there was indication that some one had camped there rather recently and put up a tent. On a high hill back of the spot was a large stone cairn, and back of this the range of rolling hills continued, their bare summits and slopes clustered with a profusion of boulders of all sizes and shapes.

The river-lake character of our route persisted for a long time, and the sun had been down for some hours when we came into an all expansion and Lop-i-zun steered the canoe toward the shore. As it was now dark, he suggested that we camp here, a nice sandy spot swept by the breeze. John, however, with his characteristic and well-earned independence of spirit, demanded that we go on. It was a delicate matter and I took no hand in it. It had always been my own custom to follow Indians implicitly in matters such as this, but I was quite aware of the strength of John's determination once it was aroused. The two Indians said nothing more but silently turned the canoe from the shore to the north.

It became dark rapidly. Black, ominous clouds, which had gathered, to crouch on the horizon at sundown now spread over the sky. Soon the lake began to contract into a true river. We could feel signs of current plucking at the canoe. The shores disappeared in the blackness, but close to the canoe reefs and black rocks stealthily began to show themselves. We still had the sail erect but the Indians would not stop to take it down. Zah-bah-deese began to rumble and mutter directions from the bow. Neither Lop-i-zun nor we could see him for the sail. Furthermore, Lop-i-zun could see nothing ahead of the canoe because of the sail and the darkness. The canoe began to gather a speed of its own. The low snarling and roaring of a rapid explained its quickened motion.

John moved forward to take down the sail. It was too late. Even in the darkness we could see the white water and the riffles hissing and gleaming next to the canoe. The canoe had become so uneasy as it began to enter the waves of the rapid that it was impossible for John to go through with the complicated business of getting the sail down, and he sat back and silently watched the water. Zah-bah-deese now took command of the situation, and with strong, rough gutturals thrown back at Lop-i-zun fended off the boulders and swung the bow about with his powerful paddle. I sat helpless and waited for the first, ripping, tearing sound of the canoe bottom being torn to shreds. A black, white-fringed wave rose up out of the dark at John's side and the spray swished over us. The canoe bucked and twisted as Zah-bah-deese shoved and pulled it this way and that. The sail, half dragging in the water, slapped and flapped against us half enveloping us both in its clinging damp folds. With a great lunge the canoe shot out into quiet water.

We all sat motionless for a moment. The canoe joggled quietly up and down. John crawled painfully forward and slowly took down the sail. "By Jesus!" he murmured, "I never shot a rapid in the night-time before and I never shot a rapid under full sail and, by Jesus, I'm never going to shoot one with both!"[3]

Everyone started paddling furiously. The river was sluggish and twisted about in what seemed to be a swamp. Several times in the blackness, rushing on with all our power, we ran abruptly upon sandbars. At this the canoe would come to such a sudden and unexpected halt that we would all be pitched forward. Everyone would burst out laughing. All of us seemed to feel better now that the little lesson of disregarding intelligent people's advice had been learned.

Once I saw, drifting close to the canoe, what seemed to be evidence of beaver cuttings. Lop-i-zun agreed with me. It seemed to me remarkable to find any beaver evidence so near the last limit of the trees. However, the original name for Windy Lake had been Beaver-Lodge Lake, and not until the coming of a white trader named "Slim" Carlson had it become known by its present name. The Chipewyans had now taken the name Windy Lake and translated it back into their own language, Chaun-li-to-eh. From its size and position, I had no doubt in my own mind that Windy was the mysterious "Fatt Lake" of Hearne's narrative. It is the largest lake between Nueltin and Kasba Lakes, and, from his course, Hearne must have crossed it. It had not previously been identified as such, but the conclusion seems justified.

On and on we went in the night. The river split and passed on either side of a small island. We came out into a larger stream. Across the river we could barely see, ghostly and silent, the outlines of two small shacks and the dim forms of two tents on the shore—at last—the trading post.[4]

As we crept nearer and drifted into the landing, we heard talking in one of the tents. It was a strange language. We stopped paddling and listened. Lop-i-zun touched my arm lightly with his paddle. I could not see his face as he leaned forward and whispered to me, but in his voice was a little suggestion of the age-old feeling, the fear, the contempt, and the hatred, of his people for those of the language we heard.

"*T'enna!*" Eskimos.

CHAPTER 9

Windy

Neither of the Indians would get out of the canoe until John and I had gone up on the shore. They let the canoe drift back a little way and waited to see what kind of reception we would get. Two of the Eskimos came out of their tent when they heard John and me talking. I thrust out my hand and greeted one of them in Eskimo saying, "*Tyma.*" He grasped my hand and repeated the greeting over and over again. By this time a lantern had been lighted in the other tent and we heard a muffled voice call out in English, "Hello? Hello? What's all the row?"

We threw the flaps of the tent back and went in to find the post manager and his son blinking at us from a pile of blankets and caribou skins. They were glad to see us, though they had the incredulous expressions of people seeing beings from another planet. Over our protestations, they got up and we all went up to the dwelling house, turning their tent over to the Indians.

The post manager[1] was a veteran trader in the North, not only here but in posts to the south. Many years before, he had married a Cree from the south end of Reindeer, and he had a number of children of whom one, Charles, a boy of fourteen, was here with him. The rest of his family was "outside" in Winnipeg. We were the first white people he had seen since the

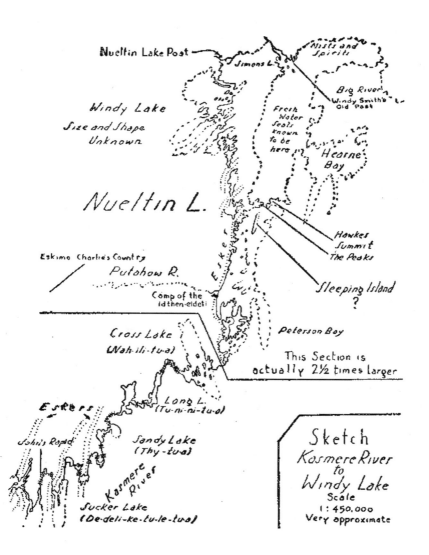

Nueltin Lake Post

Simons L.

Mists and Spirits

Windy Lake
Size and Shape
Unknown

Big River
Windy Smith's
Old Post

Fresh
Water
Seals
known
to be
here

Hearne
Bay

Nueltin L.

Hawkes
Summit
The Peaks

Eskimo Charlie's Country

Putahow R.

Sleeping Island
?

Camp of the
Id then-eldeti

Cross Lake
(Nah-ili-tu-a)

Peterson Bay

This Section is
actually 2½ times larger

Long L.
(Tu-ni-ni-tu-a)

Eskers

Sandy Lake
(Thy-tu-a)

John's Rapid

Kasmere River

Sucker Lake
(De-deli-ke-tu-le-tu-a)

Sketch
Kasmere River
to
Windy Lake
Scale
1 : 450,000
Very approximate

police patrol of the preceding winter, and a very welcome sight.

It was well after midnight, but true to the excellent northern custom we were soon sitting down for a cup of tea and something to eat. While we ate ravenously, Fred, the post manager, boomed out questions at us that we answered in mumbles between bites. He was particularly glad to see John, for they were men of the same birth, and it was a pleasure for both of them to hear and speak their native tongue again. Fred was a big, raw-boned man and his voice had a booming ring that was startling after the subdued voices of the Indians and ourselves. His son Charles was very shy. He said nothing but his face, strongly Indian, spoke silent curiosity. He disappeared very shortly and the tempo of discourse increased as we finished the meal.

Our conversation ranged over a number of topics. Our first question had been about the supply of tobacco. In this matter we experienced the first real catastrophe of the trip. The trading post was totally bare of any kind of tobacco. This calamitous and unheard-of situation for a trading post demonstrated better than anything else its extreme isolation. We talked the night away, and the last thing I heard as I unrolled my sleeping robe on a pile of caribou skins in the early morning light was John and Fred going at it with unabated enthusiasm in their mother tongue.

As is often the custom when travelers arrive at a destination like this, the next day was devoted solely to eating and conversation. Fred was most upset that we had brought in no mail for him. Well he might be, for he had been seven months without any word from the outside. Though he had a radio, as does practically every post in the North now, he had received no information, though his district manager was operating up and down the coast of Hudson Bay on a schooner and periodically sending messages to the other posts.

When Fred had first arrived here, some years previously, he had come in with his family to find the store burned to the ground. He was forced to set to work and rebuild it with his own hands using the small and scant timber of the locality. This was no easy task, particularly with the added complication of a family to provide for against the imminent approach of winter. At the present time he was forced to go a good five miles for his winter supply of wood.

The trade of the post was primarily with the Eskimos. Of the Inland or Caribou Eskimo group, they were a branch of the Padlimiut, "People of the Willows." Their country lies off to the north and northwest of Windy, centering around the Kazan River and ranging up and down it from Hicoliqjuak—Yathkyed or Frozen Lake—to Ennadai Lake. They are remnants of the people Tyrrell met in 1894 when he first explored the Kazan, and indeed one, Kakoot, who guided him and his party part of the way, was accustomed to trade here at Windy. The post itself had first been established in 1922 by Revillon Frères.

The present position of the buildings was the most recent of a number of shifts and trading movements in this section. At one time the post had been at the mouth of the Putahow, then on Windy Lake, at the spot Lop-i-zun had indicated, and finally here at the confluence of Windy River and a small stream called Red River. The competing free traders and the Hudson's Bay Company had dictated various strategic shifts calculated to intercept the Eskimos coming down from the northwest before they should reach other opposition posts. With the dissolution of the Revillon holdings, the post had been added to the Hudson's Bay Company chain.

The establishment consisted of three buildings. The dwelling house, of logs, stood twenty feet or so above the river. A few hundred yards to the west and farther back from the river was a very small box-like log store, scarcely more than twenty feet square inside. Some distance from this was a desolate shack with dried fox skeletons on the roof, which was the visiting guest hall of trappers who came in to trade. In back of the house was an insignificant upright coffin affair built of packing-box boards and bur lap. This strange creation sufficed for the humbler functions. Except for the visitor's shack, covered with sod, all the roofs were sheathed in a tarpaper held down with large boulders. All the buildings were completely exposed, the only trees being small copses of stunted spruce some distance away in the hollows. The buildings were so weather-beaten and insignificant that at a short distance they were scarcely distinguishable from the surrounding tremendous boulders, some of which were as large as the buildings themselves. The house was very comfortable. The logs were well chinked with mud and moss and it consisted of one general room with a large stove, a small cupboard large enough for a single bed, and a storeroom.

Fred had found the Eskimos admirable people with whom to deal. To nearly all traders in the North who have had experience with both Indians and Eskimos, there is no comparison between the two as far as trading and trading ethics are concerned. As a general thing, the Eskimo waits until he has an accumulation of fur and then comes in to the trading post with a very definite idea of what he wants. He barters for these desired articles quickly with a minimum of waste and then departs. The Indian is more often quite the opposite. He may make many trips, sometimes with quantities of fur, sometimes with a single pelt, sometimes with nothing. By the time he is ready to trade he has usually forgotten what his original want was, or the confusion of tempting articles he sees puts him into a state of indecision, which takes hours to solve. Then he starts with the primary assumption that he is being cheated on the price at which his fur is assessed. He delights to wrangle and haggle, and is inclined to do it purely as a matter of form. At the conclusion of his deal he embarks upon a campaign to secure more goods in return for optimistic promises for the future.

These cousins of the Padlimiut are an extremely interesting people. Inhabiting as they do the deep interior of the Barrens, their culture is in many ways quite different from their coastal relatives. Their life revolved entirely around the caribou, and all the marine features that one associates as synonymous with the Eskimo are of course entirely lacking. Their complete isolation had protected them from the inroads of the missionaries, and so they pursued their independent primitive life and thoughts happily and without confusion and improvement.

They were very honest and quick in their trading. They arrived, usually at night, brought in their piles of foxes, and took their goods to the amount of the trader's estimate without quibbling or begging. They cleared their debts with punctuality and dispatch. They preferred, oddly, the old .44 rifle and insisted on casting their own bullets and loading their own cartridges. This was not a matter of lack of knowledge or acquaintance with more modern arms, it was simply a preference founded no doubt on very reasonable and sensible grounds.

They rarely if ever brought with them either their women or children but appeared in small groups of three or four men and were often gone within a few hours. Unlike the Indian who loves to buy as often as possible, and so will prefer to make a multitude of infinitesimal small purchases well strung out in time and quantity, these people bought in bulk. It was nothing for them to come in and take away a case of tea or many pounds of lead and powder. Their currency was almost exclusively white or Arctic foxes, which they would lay down upon the counter and for which they would be proffered a number of wooden sticks to the estimated value of the catch. These were then returned to the amount of the purchase they might make.

When they occasionally came in summer, they would arrive on foot. In winter, of course, they drove in with their dogs and big wooden ice-shod sleds. The three who were here right now had come in expectation of the annual plane and a restocking of the trading post, which was very low in practically everything. The dearth of tobacco was painful evidence in point.

They were enormously fond of smoking tiny little black pipes of their own manufacture. These pipes, curiously oriental in shape, were made of a soft slate material or of bone and, as in the case of one I had been given, were often very ingeniously ornamented with strips of brass from cartridge cases.

I went out in the afternoon to photograph the three who were living in one of the tents. They looked very much like hundreds of other Eskimos I had seen. They were the same small, powerfully built, smiling, agreeable people with the broad faces of pronounced Mongolian cast which one finds from Greenland to Siberia. Standing in their overalls with mosquito nets swathed around their hats, it is hard to believe that they were probably as untouched, unspoiled natives as live today on the North American continent. Their boots or kamiks were of caribou skin with the hair scraped off and were very thin, yellow, and parchment-like, beautifully sewed, and by some process of the Eskimos quite waterproof. The Eskimos spent most of their time on the high hill back of the post, where, squatting and leaning their backs against the flagpole, they would sit motionless for hours watching the hills for tuktu, "caribou."

Like the Idthen-eldeli, they had experienced a bad winter. Fred reported they had brought the news that six of the band had died in the winter. It is difficult to estimate the numbers of these people. They do not resort regularly to the same post and may not appear for several years. This custom, as well as that of leaving their families behind, makes judgment of their total numbers problematical. Suffice it to say that today the band is not a large one. The rate of increase is very low, and the Kazan is said to be lined with their graves. Like all living, nomadic things in the North, they are subject continually to the whims and fancies of nature. Like the wandering Chipewyan, theirs is a land of starvation and plenty. During the winter of 1925–1926 the caribou migration passed in a blinding blizzard and many of them were unable to lay up their winter supply of meat; that winter forty-two of them are known to have died from starvation. And now with mining and airplanes penetrating ever farther into the North, bringing the white man's diseases against which they, like the Chipewyans, have little natural resistance, their days are surely numbered.

The Chipewyans, even the band camped at the mouth of the Putahow, did not frequent this post in large numbers. Occasional stragglers would come in, or one or two might appear if particularly hard pressed. Having absolutely nothing to do with Eskimos, there being not the slightest linguistic or ethnic bond and no doubt still a heavy undercurrent of the fear and animosity which has always characterized these two peoples, the Chipewyans preferred to do their trading at Brochet many weary miles to the south.

The extreme isolation of this post and the freight rate by

plane or water made the price of goods very high. The rate was something like thirty-seven cents a pound, an initial charge on any article whether nails or tea. A gallon of gasoline sold for six dollars, and the other prices were in like proportion.

The whole matter of the geographical distribution of the native people in this area is perplexing and interesting. Certainly since the coming of the white man there have been great changes. When Hearne made his famous trips in 1769–1772, much of the area now occupied by the Inland Eskimos was definitely not in their possession and the Chipewyans were accustomed to range far north of their present hunting grounds. In these trips, which by their indirection covered an enormous area, Hearne seems to have found much of the central portion and indeed the entire Kazan watershed, at least as far as Yathkyed Lake, absolutely destitute of Eskimos.

By 1894, the time of Tyrrell's trip, the Eskimos had moved into this region, and the Chipewyans no longer went much farther than Ennadai Lake. Now they have withdrawn even farther south. From their own account it seems that the Idthen-eldeli ranged in an annual circuit over a tremendous territory, the focus of it Nueltin Lake and the axis a north and northwesterly direction. Following the caribou north from Nueltin in the spring, they, like the wolves, stayed on the heels of the movement up to the edge of the Barrens. As summer came on, they pursued the caribou out into the Barrens and moved northwest across the watercourses and by means of the big lakes, where there was abundant fish, until they reached Dubawnt Lake, "Water-around-the-Shore" Lake. They then began to turn back, traveling slowly, and made their way in an elliptical course nearer the limit of the trees and at their edge waited for the fall migration. As this came on and the caribou began to return to the forests, they followed them back to Nueltin Lake, where they stopped and made a semi-permanent residence until the spring cycle set them off again. Though it is obvious that the Chipewyans in the remote yet historical past did make these repeated and perhaps annual forays out in the Barrens, it is also obvious from their lack of adaptability to the unhospitable tundra, an adaptation in which the Inland Eskimos are infinitely superior, that the former have always been primarily a people of the forest and the real centers of their life and culture have always been within the tree line.

From various Chipewyan accounts and place names, there would seem to be indication, too, that the Crees ranged far north of what we think of as their country now. There is a point on the Cochrane River with a name meaning "Many Crees used to camp here," and one on Ennadai Lake on the edge of the Barrens called in Chipewyan, "The place we speared the Crees when crossing."[2] However, for permanent residence and acknowledged hunting territory, the Crees do not seem to have moved north of the Churchill River. In their own accounts are repeated legends, which suggest their migrating from the east.

The Chipewyans occupying this strip of forest country were not particularly happy in their neighbors. Directly to the south of them were the Crees, whom they term "*Enna*," which means "enemy" and is synonymous with "bad" or "hostile" people, and to the north were the Eskimos whom they term "*T'enna*" or "enemy of the flat country." These three peoples all had a mutual dislike and contempt for each other, but the animosity between the Chipewyans and the Eskimos seems to have been the most ill tempered and violent. The feeling, though not expressed in action, still persists. I have often heard Crees dismiss the Chipewyans as a miserable people, "foam eaters"—that is people who are not really men and hunters but fish eaters—who "talk with a voice like frogs." The Chipewyans, when things go wrong, often are sure that it is some unmentionable Cree who has sent a bad wish. Both of them suspect and avoid Eskimos. What the Eskimo feeling is today I am not aware, but their opinion of either of these peoples is probably lower than their estimation of white men, whom they frequently class as selfish people with the minds and tempers of small children, and as such to be humored.

What the thoughts of these Eskimos at Windy might have been, I was unable to ascertain, but I suspect they were consistent with the judgments others of their kind held in regard to the white man. I knew of a man who has since made a famous name for himself from his residence among them..[3] Him they considered a dirty and disgusting creature for they had seen him micturate and eat a piece of meat at the same time. Another group was positive that the white man had, if any brain at all, a very feeble one, for he was known to be always writing things down in a little book. Obviously the man had so insufficient a memory that he had to write everything down for future reference. In regard to the Mounted Police, another group confided that they were all right for they had the minds of children so they treated them as such and would take good care of them. They were sure of this because only the white man lost his temper and shouted and roared, a habit unthinkable in a grown man, but pardonable and characteristic in children. Another band was sure that the white man was not only disgusting but also avaricious and extraordinarily selfish; otherwise why did he build a little house and save his excrement in it? Also, all white men were unquestionably fools to trade such beautiful and useful articles as rifles and canoes for such worthless things as white fox pelts for which one could find no other use whatsoever. The various "wonders" of the white man were dismissed as merely incidental, for everyone had at least one old relative who in various states of frenzy and trance had made a trip or two to the moon.

Fred had heard nothing about any Chipewyans coming from Churchill with freight. There was, however, an airplane supposedly arriving with supplies some time before "freeze-up." It was now long overdue. This possibility of transport threw an entirely new light upon my length of stay and my potential method and route of return "outside."

The view from the post, or more particularly from the high hill back of the post, was an interesting one. To the north stretched the high escarpment of hills, perfectly tree-less, which our route had followed the previous day. These ran roughly northeast southwest. Windy River could be seen winding away to the north and east where it finally disappeared as it broke through these hills. To the north-west the country was endless and undulating with here and there a few small trees in the hollows. The same type of topography was visible to the south, and the southwest revealed a vast, meadowy, flat land and far away the silvery sheen of Windy Lake sparkling in the sun.

Patches of snow could be seen here and there in the deeper valleys and depressions. We were informed that the ice had not broken up on Windy Lake until July 4, and the weather had been unusually bad. In fact, the first real day of summer at the post had been the day of our arrival. Ever since early spring, really a nonexistent season here, there had been a steady succession of cold winds, sleet, snow, rain, and general unpleasantness. The caribou had last been seen on their spring migration—moving north, although a few stragglers had held over until June. They had not yet begun to return in any large numbers.

Fred's son Charles was an interesting boy. Only fourteen, he was tall and husky. He had enjoyed considerable success with his own trap-line the preceding winter, had caught seventy foxes and ten wolves. He was dark and the Cree blood dominated his features. He was very quiet and only the greatest effort could extract more than a monosyllable or two from him. He was unobtrusively capable and efficient about the house and spent a great deal of time with his excellent team of dogs.

For the most part Fred and Charles were left strictly by themselves. The trading trips of the Eskimos were matters of but a few hours, and neither of them was sufficiently versed in Eskimo to hold more than the crudest of conversations in the trading jargon. The Indians rarely appeared and did not hang around the store for days, as is their custom farther south. Constable Chappious of the Royal Canadian Mounted Police had stopped briefly on one of his indefatigable patrols during the winter. Beyond these brief contacts with other human beings, their world was their own. But Fred was too much of a veteran of the North and Charles was too much of it for them to find the time dull or irksome. There were a thousand duties to be attended to. There were dogs to be fed, nets to be set and lifted, meat and firewood to be obtained, a thousand other constant necessities demanding rigorous attention if the struggle for survival is to be successful and bearable. There was of course the radio, but they did not listen to it very often. There was nothing from the "outside" that was applicable or of interest to life at Windy.

Late in the afternoon, Zah-bah-deese came to the door and announced, "Idthen!" We went out; a lone caribou could be seen far off in a broad patch of muskeg. I went down the river with the two Indians and Charles, and we began to stalk the animal. Soon it moved away and we could not get near enough to it either for the Indians to do any damage or for me to get a photograph. At least it was an indication that the "deer" were on the move, and we might now expect them any time and in any quantity. The preceding fall they had been particularly abundant, and as they passed the house during the night Fred and Charles had heard the clashing of their horns as they crowded by and the rumble of the thousands of hoofs like thunder. I was anxious to turn over some of our fresh meat to the Eskimos for I had noticed they had nothing. Neither Lop-i-zun nor Zah-bah-deese would consent to take it from the canoe and give it to them so I had to perform the small office myself.

Since our first meeting with the two Indians, the matter of Lop-i-zun's finger had been on my mind. The little finger of his right hand had been injured, as he explained to me, in a fall. The joint was badly swollen and the swelling had extended well up the hand. It was apparently extremely painful and he was unable to use the finger at all. From his description of the way it had been bent, I thought that it had been dislocated. The swelling was so bad and it was so puffed up that I could not feel whether there was any dislocation or not. He had asked me repeatedly to fix it, but we had put it off until our arrival at the post.

Acting on the theory of dislocation, John attempted to pull it out and slip the bone back into place. John was a strong man but all his tugging seemed to cause only increased, restrained agony on the part of his unhappy victim. This technique proving of no avail, we reversed the diagnosis and decided that it must be a bad sprain. Consequently I manufactured a splint and advised Lop-i-zun to soak the finger in hot water. He was willing to do this but he objected to the fact that we had not put any medicine on it. When I painted it with iodine he seemed greatly relieved. He followed my instructions for an hour or so, but finding that the medicine was washed off by this treatment he desisted and came back for more. Though he removed the splint, he kept it faithfully in his pocket, for I had painted that also. A year later I was to pass a canoe-load of Chipewyan Indians. Among them was a man who, when we drew alongside, held something high in the air. It was Lop-i-zun and the splint.

The lack of tobacco was more than annoying. It was a loss of comfort that we felt as a real hardship. How pockets and exhausted packages were scraped for the smallest shreds! It was almost unheard of—a trading post out of its primary trade article. But the spring barter had been heavy, the Eskimo demands large, and supplies were long overdue. There was nothing to do but sniff hungrily when one or the other managed to scratch up sufficient particles to make a thin cigarette. Whenever one of us manufactured one of these limp and drooping little affairs, he felt guilty smoking it.

The following day, July 29, the weather turned back to its more usual state. It was cold and a raw northeast wind was blowing, herding low, heavy gray clouds across the Barrens.

One caribou does not last very long among eight men, particularly when this is almost all they have to eat, so it seemed advisable to go on a hunt. John and Fred were far too engrossed in the delights of chatting in their own tongue to go, and the three Eskimos had resumed their vigil on the hill. It afforded them the double advantage of a position to spot caribou and the first appearance of the long-awaited plane. Charles, Zah-bah-deese, Lop-i-zun, and I set out from the post in the canoe.

We dropped down river about two miles to where it begins to expand into a small lake. On the southwest shore were two buildings, the deserted relics of a former trading venture undertaken some years back by a storied and famous north- ern traveler, "Del" Simons. Northeast of this spot was a high hill called Simons Hill, which we climbed. Sitting on its bar- ren windswept top we began to search the country in every direction for caribou.

Far away to the north stretched the endless Barrens. Not a tree, not a shrub was to be seen except close to the river's edge immediately below us. The gray skyline was bounded by the distant rolling hills. So far away were they that they had lost their individual contours and lineaments and seemed like great immobile swells of earth.

Reaching from the foreground to these hills was a vast plain dotted with lakes. They stretched away to the north in endless repetition, and the more distant ones seemed squeezed horizontally into lines. In all this world of dull brown and darker green, not a moving thing, not a bird, not a creature was to be seen.

Charles and I both had binoculars, but the Indians used just their own marvelous eyes. It was interesting and instructive to see the manner in which they searched. They did not sweep the tremendous expanse but took one section and stared very intently at it for a long time. Then, satisfied that nothing was stirring in this restricted spot, they would pick out another zone and study that for an equally long while.

What an Indian looks for in such a search as this is not a caribou, not anything which looks like an animal either in shape or size or color; he looks for something that moves or has moved from the spot where he has first seen it. The keen power of his eyes and their wonderful recognition and reception of the least movement of living animals is something at which I have never ceased to marvel. Long before either Charles or I had begun to see any game with the binoculars, they had already spotted caribou.

At that great distance, they bore no resemblance to animals at all. Indeed, when they were still, it was impossible to tell them from a thousand other dots, the boulders and rocks, which covered the distant landscape. However, if one were fortunate enough to have been looking at the right spot for a long time, apparently a small rock would detach itself and move over a little way. This was a caribou.

It was astonishing how they gradually began to appear. Tracts we had futilely studied many times would begin to show caribou. Once locating them, the eye seemed to go through an adjustment, disregarding the barren areas and focusing on the limited spots where the deer had been seen, and in that process gradually picking out the animals.

It was an uncanny thing. The caribou seemed, in a way, to sprout gradually and mysteriously out of the ground. You would study an open, frankly bare, exposed slope and see nothing on it, then, coming back to it a few seconds later, some shift, some new shadow would reveal a small black dot that somehow looked different from the other dots. Then it would melt from sight as you watched it. It would dissolve as if into the ground. For a moment you would think it was nothing, a wish, or a flick of the eyelid, but, there, it would reappear. In practically no instance could the shape or form of the caribou be distinguished, and it was never their color that identified and revealed them.

I go to such length because it is an important thing and also an interesting mental complexity. Probably one reason it is so difficult for the novice is that he expects to see caribou. His brain refuses to register or recognize anything but what he has predetermined in his own mind's eye, something already established as an animal with four legs and horns—and this never appears.

From our hill, the deer, and there now had been located twenty or more at widely separated intervals, seemed to be feeding and gradually moving west. To head them off, we decided to drop down river in the canoe. As we slipped along, a tense and expectant excitement gripped everyone. It matters not with Indians whether they have hunted caribou all their lives, when the hunt is on they are always tremendously eager and keyed up.'

We had not gone more than a quarter of a mile when there was a low rumble from Zah-bah-deese. Lop-i-zun indicated that there were caribou in the muskeg close to the left bank of the river. Charles swung the canoe to the bank and we disembarked as quietly as we could. A low fringing scrub of willows and small spruce partially hid us from view. The deer were feeding out in the open muskeg and moving slowly and deliberately across our front. Very swiftly and silently the two Indians worked ahead along the barrier of scrub. They went in jerky, quick, darting movements, which would suddenly be suspended almost in mid-air as they froze into immobility. They got well ahead of us, and Charles and I squatted down in a small thicket. We now saw that there were six or seven big bucks, and they were moving diagonally toward us. Two of them were less than a hundred yards away. They approached slowly, grunting contentedly, lowering their heads to crop the succulent ground plants, snuffing and shaking their heads at the attacks of the flies. Sometimes one would stop and stare moodily about him. From where we crouched, close to the ground, they looked enormous; actually they are not large animals. Their huge ungainly horns still clubbed and in the velvet, looked like awkward branches of some grotesque tree. They were fat and their coats were already beginning to turn brown, though one of the older bucks was still mostly in a yellowish winter white. Their large protruding eyes seemed to stare right at us but they moved on closer with no sign of recognition.

As Charles and I waited quietly for the more distant ones to move in, with startling unexpectedness and for no apparent reason, Zah-bah-deese, and immediately thereafter Lop-i-zun, opened fire. Their guns roared and flamed until they had exhausted the magazines. Charles made a fine shot at a big buck well over a hundred and fifty paces away. It was standing on a ridge and was beautifully silhouetted against the skyline. Without protest or struggle several of the animals sank down into the soft moss. One of them made a long groaning sigh and then all was quiet. Death on the Barrens—now there was no sign; the gray clouds rolled on as ever, but soon would come from the leaden sky the gulls and the ravens, the endless cycle of death and life.

The butchering of caribou is not greatly different from the dressing of any large game. With the Chipewyans, however, the process is an extremely swift and sure one. No false stroke of the knife is made and they seem to have a surgeon's uncanny skill in their precision in separating joints and organs. The first operation consisted of pulling the head forward by the horns. The head was severed neatly at the back of the neck. It was then reversed and the under jaw slit up from the throat.

A hand was plunged into this opening and the tongue extracted and cut off near its roots. From here on the gutting and quartering follow conventional lines.

While we were busy quartering the meat, Lop-i-zun called to me to come over to the farthest animal. He seemed greatly excited. I could not imagine what it was all about until he pointed out to me the very unusual formation of the horns. The caribou horns usually extend as a smooth limb from the base of the skull to their ends where they flatten out into a more palmated form bearing the points. Jutting out from the forehead but connected to the base of the horns, are two flattened, shovel-like prongs. On this animal, there was a single long spike-like point running backward and out from about the middle of the bend of the main limb of each antler. It was a freak apparently unfamiliar to Lop-i-zun. He was very excited about it and demanded that I take a picture.

Of all the members of the deer family, the Barren Ground caribou has antlers most disproportionate to its size. The caribou itself does not weigh much more than a good-sized buck of our own deer species, but his forward-curving horns may be as much as four feet in height from base to tip. Unlike our native or Virginia whitetails, both sexes of the caribou bear antlers. One wonders at these strange provisions of nature, their use is so limited and out of proportion to their enormous size. Even in rutting season the bulls do not fight much beyond a desultory pushing match. Their real defense is their hoofs and their speed, and yet they have been endowed with these gigantic and cumbersome burdens.

As far as I could determine, the caribou seemed to have been browsing principally on a type of dwarf birch, at least a ground-hugging small plant with leaves resembling the birch. They were moderately fat, more so than we had expected as the season was not sufficiently advanced for them to begin to put on their heavy back fat, the, "*de-pouille*" of the French voyageurs. The best criterion of the fatness of the caribou is the apparent length of his short stub of a tail. When he is very fat the tail hardly sticks out at all. Usually at this time of year they are inclined to be very lean from their constant movement and running away from the flies. The unusually wet spring and cold summer may have accounted for their good condition.

We turned the four carcasses over and covered the vents with the severed heads. We expected to come back and get the rest of the meat, and we knew that unless we did this, the seagulls, which are everywhere in the Barrens, would enter the insides of the bodies and destroy all the remaining meat. This insatiable, carnivorous appetite of seagulls, like that of ravens, is very marked in the country.

When we returned to the post, we found that the Eskimos had left for their camps somewhere to the north near Ennadai Lake. The fact that the caribou were now definitely migrating and coming down from the Barrens toward the trees no doubt had prompted them to depart before they should miss the big migration.

That evening we had a long discussion as to just what our next move would be. I felt very strongly that the two Indians were anxious to get back to their families, particularly as there was no tobacco at the post and also because the deer were moving. There was really nothing for them to do here. They had performed their share of the bargain admirably, and I felt guilty to keep them longer. At the same time, now that I was here, I was very reluctant to turn back so soon. I wished to spend more time and go farther north into the Barrens. I particularly wished to wander farther afield and make observations on the abundant glacial phenomena. Added to this was the fact that the really big migration was not yet under way, and though we had seen some caribou, the great multitudes and herds had not yet come before the lens of my camera. As we had but the single canoe, if I were to go back by canoe, I must leave with John and the Indians in another day at least. There was the possibility of letting John and the Indians go back and staying on in the hope that, despite the lateness of the season, the plane, of which no word had been heard, would come in and I might be able to get outside on it. However, that would mean that John would have to go back, after leaving the Indians at Putahow, alone to Brochet. I did not like the idea of that even though he had been so recently over the route, and I had constructed a map sufficiently accurate and detailed, being a mile to the inch, for him to travel on. The trip would of course not be so arduous and it would take far less time as he would know the way and also would be going downstream on the Cochrane. Most important, he would have no load at all. This latter possibility was one we had thoroughly envisaged and agreed upon before we had left Brochet. Nevertheless, I could not bring my heart to it. We came to no decision, but I thought about the matter for a good part of the night.

The next morning it was still overcast and the wind had a damp, cold bite. Charles and I set out on an excursion to the country north of the post. His father had rigged up a very useful and ingenious affair, which I had never before seen, used in the North. The principle was that of the old "travois" used on the plains, two long poles connected with a collar and spreading out behind. In this case, the collar was worn by one of the sled dogs. On the two widespread poles behind the dog were nailed a few connecting flat boards which acted as a carrying platform. The poles were shaved flat on their bottom ends and slipped over the ground with little friction. They were sufficiently widespread so that the load did not overturn when the going was rough or bouldery. On the treeless, moss-covered Barrens the arrangement worked very effectively. The load a dog can drag in this fashion is surprising; the method has great advantage over the saddlebag type of packing, which is the conventional method of summer travel with dogs. The load that can be transported is greater and there is less danger of the dog working it off. Further, a wooden box can be carried this way and there is less hazard of breakage. Charles used his lead dog for this work. He was a large, perfectly white, pure-strain Eskimo dog that he had secured from the Padlimiuts. He was unusually shy and wary and refused to budge when I was behind him where he could not observe my every move. He obeyed no one but Charles.

The ordinary lot of dogs in the North, despite their great service, is not a pleasant or happy one. Their only caress is that of the club and the lash. Their only reward as they grow old is abandonment and starvation or death at the jaws of their own kind when they become unable to defend themselves. Although in the winter when they are in constant use they are fed and bedded with something approaching care and certainty, in the summer they are not always treated with the same consideration. Some Indians go as far as to leave dogs on islands and allow them to fend for themselves. Whether it is summer or winter they are the complaining recipients of constant and countless blows and beatings. There are many portage trails in the North, which are littered with hundreds of small billets and clubs of wood, which have been flung at and crashed down upon the dogs of teams that have passed over the trail in winter. Some drivers, both white and Indian, in fits of desperation and exasperation with recalcitrant dogs, are wont to seize the animal and bite its ears, but this practice is not as common as the desire, for it is hard on the teeth. In the North it is a saying that the only people harder on dogs than Indians are missionaries.

After the big hill back of the post the land became a series of ridges composed of masses of irregular angular rocks. They had all the characteristics of a moraine or glacial dump. The going was very rough. After crossing them we passed over a broad, flat muskeg meadow—the bottom of a lake no longer in existence. We saw one caribou restlessly charging this way and that across the boggy meadow as he tried to elude the flies. The wide, flexible, and spreading hoofs of the caribou are wonderfully adapted to this type of country. Here and there in the protected hollows were small oases of scrubby, tough, stunted spruce. Such outcrops of rock as we passed were gray quartzite so smoothed and polished by the passage of the extinct ice that they seemed almost like the shelled backs of some strange burrowing creatures just barely exposed above the ground. In the case of some more protuberant exposures the violent effect of the winter frosts was very evident. The cold had been so vicious the solid rock was almost completely disintegrated. It was seamed and split by a thousand minute fissures, and the shattered fragments had been reduced to coarse sand lying in small cone-like scree at the base of the parent rock.

Our travels—our pace had been a rapid one—eventually brought us to a country much more broken and rough.

Charles led the way into a long ravine. Some ancient earth movement had opened up a narrow, canyon-like gash. Here, next to a small hidden pond, were some very unusual spruces. Though well out in the Barrens, this deep concealed hollow supported several spruce with trunks at least eighteen inches in diameter. The trees were not very high, the tops refusing to grow above the protecting walls of the depression. Some looked like inverted carrots. It was difficult to judge how old these ancient warriors against the elements were. Isolated in islands such as this, they have never been attacked by fire and so must live to a tremendous age to attain the thickness they do. I had previously examined some spruce trunks, which were about six inches across at the butt, and the annual rings were almost microscopic in their separation. Those were approximately ninety years old.

Following the ravine, which ran roughly northeast, we came upon a beautiful spectacle. Hidden within the overhanging and precipitous walls of gray quartzite which were everywhere streaked and splashed with lurid and variegated growths of lichens, was a miniature glacier. From Charles's account, it never thawed out or became any smaller. The ice, where it was undercut, was translucent and glowed with an indescribable greenish blue. It was as if some strange opalescent fire burned within it. In my imagination, it was not difficult to picture this mass as a dying remnant of the mighty continental ice sheet of twenty-five thousand years ago, which had for so long buried this land in a silence even more profound than now gripped it.

The colors, down there in the depth of the ravine, were spectacular; the gleaming white ice, its green and blue underbody, the gray crumbling cliffs on either side, splotched with vivid crimson and startling yellow and orange, and the walls further enhanced with streaks and slashes of a pink, volcanic intrusive called rhyolite.

I was very reluctant to leave. But while I clambered about, took pictures, and collected specimens, Charles showed silent but increasing impatience. Finally he explained that he was afraid of big rocks rolling down upon us from the grim, frost-shattered heights above. I knew that this was not the true reason. In this weird and awe-inspiring spot, the blood of his Cree ancestors was making him uneasy.

As we traveled north again, I noticed another peculiar feature. The ground everywhere was littered with large, pinkish granite boulders. These had all been weathered in a singular manner. Technically the term is "exfoliation"; the rock literally unpeels large curved layers of rock split off by the frost action so that the rock itself in time becomes spherical. These boulders lay about on the surface of the ground each a nearly perfect ball, and around the base of each lay the spalled-off layers of rock like the skins of an onion, giving the rocks the appearance of huge pink cabbage-like plants embraced in their protecting pink leaves or calyx.

This violent and penetrating action of the severe winter frost is evident everywhere and has its effect both upon nature and the articles of man's manufacture. An ax of hard and highly tempered steel will shatter to bits on a really cold day. The least trace of oil and grease must be removed from any mechanism such as a gun. Trees sometimes literally explode from the freezing and pressure of the sap. The steel runners of toboggans and sleds will not travel over the snow, which has become as gritty as sand. Ice runners are substituted. The very ground arranges itself into curious almost geometrical patterns due to the frost heaving of the thin topsoil. A foot or so below the surface the ground is permanently frozen. To what depth is dependent on the location, but I recall a mine I went down where the evidence indicated permanent frost down to the 180-foot level. When the topsoil melts in the summer another odd phenomenon takes place, which is particularly revealed, in the Barrens. The top layer, becoming warmed and thawed to a depth of eight inches or so by the long hours of sunlight, begins to slide, wherever there is any grade, and flow upon its still frozen sub-surface. In this slow and creeping flowage it has the characteristic of an infinitely retarded river for it carries all on the surface, loose rocks and such, along with it in its endless and inexorable creep to lower levels.

We wandered on after boiling our small tea pail in a little copse of spruce. The sky had now become more lowering, and it began to rain a fine, cold, stinging drizzle. We saw but one caribou. It was far away and feeding on top of a hill which Charles called "Jo's Hill." It moved off so that its body was hidden from us, but for a long time we could see its horns outlined against the gray sky moving along in silhouette on the top of the ridge quite without body and substance. Charles called it Jo's Hill from an event connected with an Indian named Jo Highway, who had come up from Brochet one year and spent the winter near the post. That year the deer failed to pass the post in their migration, and Jo could be found day after day sitting immovable on the crest of this hill watching and waiting with anxious and hungry eyes to the north.

Probably fewer phrases in the North mean more misery, starvation, and distress than: "The year the deer didn't come." It is death and tragedy to the people, the Padlimiut and the Idthen-eldeli, whose lives are lives only in the death of the caribou. Sometimes, but very rarely, the white man too is a victim. Far away to the northwest of us on the banks of the Thelon River were three lonely graves—a boy nineteen, a young man, and the last of the great pioneer roamers of the North. White men—for them too, "the deer didn't come."* [5]

We had now gone as far as it seemed the day would allow. We began to work back toward the post taking a different course than the one we had pursued on our trip out. On the way I saw the first ptarmigan of the trip. It was in summer plumage and very striking in its mottled coloration as it flew off into the willows. The year that the caribou failed here, it was estimated that about two thousands of these birds were killed during the winter. In the winter, when their plumage is almost entirely white, the birds arrive from the north in tremendous numbers. They are very unwary, relying on their protective coloring, and are caught easily. Occasionally the Indians catch them with snares and even spread fishnets in the willows to trap them.

Charles, though he had been so shy and silent that he

* For a heroic and gripping true account, the diary of one of these victims should be read: *Unflinching*, by Edgar Christian. Funk & Wagnalls Co., New York, 1938.

rarely said a word and disappeared like a shadow when we were in the house, during our wanderings was much more approachable, though hardly communicative. Out here on the Barrens it was quickly obvious that he had a very keen eye for the world about him. I had given him the only book I had carried with me, Peterson's *A Field Guide to the Birds*. He was very pleased with it. In his every spare moment around the post I had seen him poring through the pages and studying the illustrations. He also had a clear and accurate hand at mapping, and we compared local notes with much interest. His reticence was not to be wondered at. All his life he had known no white men but the casual traders and trappers whose dealings had been entirely with his father. I am sure too that Charles felt the burden of difference, which all native-white unions entail. Though ordinarily it made no complications, in the presence of a new acquaintance and contact, it imposed upon him a certain indefiniteness of standing which was embarrassing to him. As we walked along and I chatted with him, the estrangement and reserve began to thaw, but once back at the post he was again the lean and quiet wraith.

After some distance, we had an exhibition by a lone bull caribou, which is characteristic of them at certain times. We had come around a slight knoll and to our mutual surprise found ourselves face to face with a caribou not more than thirty yards away. He was walking directly toward us. Then he saw us, wheeled, and went off at a gallop. I could not but laugh. From the rear his gallop was the most ridiculous looking business. His front feet splayed out, and he was so loose-jointed that his hoofs seem to flap up at us in the air. At the same time his long legs were rigid and gave him an ungainly, camel-like, rocking-chair motion. In an astonishingly short time, despite his awkward appearance, he was far away. After he had reached a safe distance, we could see him slow down and then swing about to quarter us. He made a loping semi-circle, watching us constantly with the greatest of curiosity. Not content with his escape he continued to circle us, moving nearer each time. We altered our course while he was hidden from us. Then, to our amusement, rounding another knoll, we saw him again coming straight for us. This time I fired at him with no serious intent. Startled and aggrieved, he stopped, wheeled, and rushed off again with more directness of purpose than he had previously shown.

We reached the post with no more adventures and after a fine supper of caribou meat, John, Fred, and I talked until three-thirty in the morning. There was little else to eat; the post was even out of salt. Like the conversations at Brochet, our talk spun on with the past and present, reminiscence and surmise, so interwoven that there was no time continuity.

The next morning, the last day of July, the wind was howling about the post and sheets of rain came slanting down from the northeast with such violence that everyone stayed within doors. It was a good opportunity for me to bring my notes up to date. The Indians came up from their tent near the shore and sat about although it was an almost impossible ordeal for Zah-bah-deese, who kept creeping out to see if it was still raining. They were both becoming increasingly restless. Lop-i-zun explained to me that there was no one back at Putahow to hunt the deer when they should arrive there. I was completely sympathetic with him and determined that they should leave the next day whether I went with them or not. I had some amusement with Lop-i-zun joking about playing "udzi."

The Chipewyans like most of the northern Indians are inveterate and insatiable gamblers. The more southern Crees are familiar with the white man's poker, but the real gambling game of the Chipewyans is udzi, or as some of them call it u-chee. This game has existed from time immemorial and despite the stern efforts of missionaries is still played with an abandon bordering on madness. The simplest form of the game consists of two players sitting opposite each other in a cross-legged crouch. One player has a blanket or hide draped over his knees and lap. As the game commences he puts his hands under the blanket and shuffles about a small stone or piece of bone about an inch long. He sways back and forth to the beat of a drum. His opponent taking up the rhythm of the drum likewise sways back and forth and then claps his hands. The other player lifts his two hands from beneath the blanket with the fists clenched and extended. The person who has clapped then points to the hand or the blanket indicating that he believes the button or bone is in either hand or left under the blanket. A score is kept with sticks. If the guesser is correct, the bone is surrendered to him and the play is reversed. If his guess is incorrect, the first player keeps the bone and chalks up one stick. The first person to win all six sticks then takes whatever the stake may be,

A technical description such as this does not convey at all the pace and mounting excitement of the contest. As the game progresses the rate becomes faster, the drum beats louder, and the players' movement so rapid that the eye can hardly follow them. The stakes become larger; furs, dogs, rifle, everything may be thrown into the pile as one player finds the tide of fortune going against him. Sometimes four or six men will engage in a sort of mass combat. The greatest battles have been waged between different bands and peoples. On the edge of the tree line old Kasmere was wont to engage Eskimos; on the shores of Wollaston, Crees have played Chipewyans. In those unrecorded struggles, the booming drums, the darting hands, the inflamed dark eyes have waged great udzi struggles in which not only wealth and gain but also prestige and glory were the stakes. The story is still told of two Crees and two Chipewyans who played at Cree Lake many years ago for four days and nights without stopping; two were always awake to carry on the contest.

My only active experience with the game was with an Indian with whom I had happened to share a tent many years before. He was in custody of the police and was about to be taken out to jail. We whiled away many ex-citing hours at udzi, but my interest was primarily in the technique and method of the game, and so our stakes were inconsequential. He was very envious of me for I happened to have a small silver football, a watch charm. This, he opined, was the finest thing to play udzi with that had ever come into the country. Added to that, he explained: "You have such a strange face and your eyes are behind glass so that I never know what you are going to do!"

As the rain continued to roar down upon the roof, we each settled down to the enjoyments of an indoor day. Charles secreted himself in the little room and pored over the book on birds. The Indians settled themselves near the stove and spit on the floor at regular intervals while they watched me writing. John and Fred carried on their native tongue dialogue.

From Fred I gathered that twenty-five miles north of here, the trees, even the struggling, gnarled little midgets, die out completely. At Padlei, the Eskimo post some distance to the north; however, they reappear in the form of a small oasis. Evidence in this region, as in many other observed parts of the Barrens, seems to point to the tree line having receded. I have noticed signs of this several times, but the criteria are too uncontrolled for one to do more than hazard it as a possibility. The post itself, here on Windy River, was supposed to be about fifteen miles west of Nueltin Lake, though Fred in all his years here had never been down to the mouth of the river. The Indians reported it to him as being very rough and full of rapids with one falls near the mouth. A long re-entrant from the lake running northwest southeast embraced the mouth of the river. A little river coming in at this spot from the northwest was an important feature, though in significant in itself, for it had been, and was to be, very misleading in approaching the post by air.

In Fred's experience, July was the only real summer month. In August it began to get cold again, and by the latter part of that month snow flurries were not infrequent. The small lakes started to freeze by the middle of September. It was his and Charles's tent poles we had seen at the old Revillon site. They had been fishing there and although it was in the first week of July, they could see that the main body of Windy Lake was still covered with ice.

Once again we discussed the matter of return. Both John and Fred urged me to stay and chance going out by plane. I was very eager to do this, particularly with the caribou coming in and the opportunities for some good pictures. There was so much to do and so little time to do it in. However, the thought of John's going back over the portages and rapids of the Kasmere still persisted and still made the decision of our parting a difficult one. All night I had lain and tossed in the caribou skins on the floor de-bating the ethics of the matter. In my diary I had tried to outline the dilemma to help me arrive at some solution:

"I have been in a great quandary and turned the matter over in my mind all night. It is obviously the thing to do for me [to stay], and there is no point in retracing the old route. At the same time, it gives me a marvelous opportunity to see the unknown country between here and Churchill from the air and also to obtain a fine picture of Nueltin Lake as a whole. Furthermore, it assures my getting to 'steel,' and I would not have to go through the business of trying to get out from Brochet, four hundred miles from the railway, late in the season.

"This may be the only time I will be in this part of the country, and so I should take full advantage of it.

"On the other side of the ledger is the trip back with John, who is an admirable fellow traveler, and the opportunity to check my map for distance. Also, it is very much on my conscience his going back alone. However, he is a very experienced traveler in the North, and he would have a good outfit for I shall lend him my gun and plenty of shells. The Indians will take him over the only part of the route, which is difficult to follow, and he will have the Cochrane going downstream. We made this possibility a matter of agreement before starting out. Yet, it is a little like desertion in my mind, and that is no doubt why I feel so badly about it.

"I also have made him a copy of the map (the map which traces our course from the Cochrane to the post here), so he is not unprepared in that detail...also a map of the Cochrane River.

"There is of course the question of whether the plane is coming in here or not; further, if it does, can it find the post this time? However, I am willing to take a chance on that.

"I should have opportunity to get some good pictures of the deer. I hope that John gets through O.K. There is absolutely no reason why he should not. He will be meeting Indians all along the road coming north from Brochet and 'Treaty,' and I expect that he will travel very fast now. In a day or two I may feel better about it all, but I confess I feel lousy now."

The next morning, John laughed away my fears and doubts. He said that after trapping and traveling in the

Wollaston Lake country alone for nine years, there was no reason to worry about him. He thought he would make Brochet in about fifteen days as he would be traveling very light and would not have to waste any time searching for the route, and of course the Indians would be with him through the long intricate trip down to the mouth of the Putahow. Fred very forcibly backed up John's arguments.

I admitted it was rather ridiculous for me for a minute to have the conceit that I in any way would abet his safety and the surety of his successful return to Brochet. It is hard in the North, though, to part with those with whom you have happily traveled so many miles. The decision was at last made. We talked for a little while about the year to come; there were still more places in the North we both wished to see, and we both wished to see them together.

We all went over to the store, and I outfitted everyone for the return trip. To Lop-i-zun and Zah-bah-deese went another box of cartridges, which here cost three dollars and a half a box. To this was added tea, which sold for one dollar a half a pound, new cigarette lighters, and to Zah-bah-deese, the inscrutable, a new pair of rubbers.

To John went a shotgun and sundry other articles and a letter to Alec at Brochet, which among other things guaranteed him some assistance in getting much of his fall trapping outfit together.

Lop-i-zun, as a parting gesture, drew me his interpretation of the shape of Nueltin. Then he wrote out a letter in the syllabic characters with which all the Northern people are familiar, though many of them cannot use them, to a friend in Churchill named John Thu-i-aze, John "Lit-tle-Milk." He then handed over to me a cartridge pouch, which, though black with use, was very beautiful. It was beaded in a very odd and unusual style with multi-colored wheels of geometric design which a few Chipewyans and the Inland Eskimos favor and which is now fast disappearing.

We all went down to the little dock together. The Indians were jubilant and fairly jumping to be off. The sun was shining and a fine fair wind swept across the Barrens. At the last moment I gave Lop-i-zun a little rubber dog, which squeaked when, pressed and exuded a pink rubber tongue. This, I explained, was meant as a present for his little child. Lop-i-zun's delight with the toy was so great that I suspected his child-like Bacheese's grandson-would not have much chance to play with it. He tucked it carefully into his shirt, and every time he leaned over a high "peep" would come out of his chest. For the first time, Zah-bah-deese broke into a deep, rumbling laugh. It seemed very painful to him.

They climbed into the canoe. Lop-i-zun took the stern, then before him John, then Zah-bah-deese in the bow. I leaned down to each and made that sharp, embarrassed, brief handshake everywhere used in the North.

Like true Northern men, they never looked back. I watched as long as I could see them. They moved very fast. Their paddles flashed in the sun. The faithful sleek gray canoe and John's faded and familiar blue shirt were hidden at last by a bend in the river. Then I turned my back and watched the low bank of clouds on the horizon, stealing up over the Barrens, north.[7]

The same old feeling rushed over me. It was always the same: "See you somewhere, next year maybe…see you some time…at Pelican, Brochet, Athabaska, Cree Lake, the Slave, the Grease, the Fond du Lac… lakes, lakes, rivers, rivers… the Barrens."

It was the same feeling I had experienced so many years before; the sun was shining then, too. Far away the buzzing of a plane came nearer. It was time to leave. Solomon, my Cree friend and companion, stood with me, shading his eyes to see the plane and he said more to himself than to me: "You will come back… maybe not nex' year, maybe not year nex'. But you will come back, and then we make long trip. Then some-time we make a trip again. We stronger. We tough, and then, we make the long trip an' never come back."

Somehow I did not feel like doing a great deal for the rest of the day. Charles and I decided that we would take two dogs and go down to the mouth of Windy River the next day. Late in the afternoon furious rain squalls began to lash about the log house. All summer the winds had been northeast and northwest. From my diary I counted but three days which had been bright and sunny since we had left Brochet in the first week of July.

That night I thought of John, Lop-i-zun, and Zah-bah-deese for a long time. At last I went to sleep. Fortunately for my peace of mind I did not have a peculiar dream which I have experienced several times in the North and which has always been followed by some particularly vicious thrust of Nature.

At last I had found what I wanted. Together John and I had found great Nu-thel-tin-tu-eh, the lake of the Sleeping Island; I had camped on its shores, felt and seen its majesty, captured with my pencil and compass an ancient route. Once more I had glimpsed for a moment some of the fast fading life of the North, captured it in fragments before it was lost. Once more I was back in the Barrens. Here I was free, here there was no time, here was a world that to myself I could call my own for just a little while for no one could get to it unless they had the desire that had been mine. Here was the world as it had always been, untrammeled, undefeated, a true frontier, one of the last on the continent going but not yet gone.

CHAPTER 10

Days in the Barrens

With the departure of John and the Indians, it turned black and ugly. All the next day the wind howled down from the northwest bringing dark, heavy, low clouds. Our proposed trip to the mouth of Windy River was postponed at least until some improvement in the weather. The lashing, screaming wind and the sudden vengeful bursts of cold rain mocked and intensified a consuming restlessness with which everyone in the North seems sooner or later to become obsessed. It is as if he were in self-protection forced to share the unseen movement and the rhythm of the natural world about him. It is almost as if he felt that should he remain inactive for even a few hours the deadening, gray impact of the world of raw nature would crush him. He is constantly fleeing an unknown, a subconscious enemy. Once he surrenders, he is lost; he is engulfed in a gripping prison of apathy, the space, the crushing power of a world of nature too big to struggle against; it breaks the spirit, it leaves his body to be swallowed up in the immensity. This world of insatiable relentless movement seems to possess everything in the Barrens and lastly it is communicated to man himself. The living world, the animals, the birds, the very winds, storms, and lastly the ground itself, seems in a constant state of flux and movement. The caribou are ever wandering over the country, day and night. The wolves, the foxes, even the tiny lemming roam and migrate and pass, it seems, never resting. The birds migrate and change, are here today and silently gone tomorrow. The fish appear and disappear, ever migrating, moving from the lakes up the rivers and back again. The weather is never constant for day—sunshine, storms, and always the winds are blowing and herding the distraught clouds across the sky. The gray rocks crack and crumble; the land flows and creeps; the greater the depth into the earth the slower the rhythm and the movement but always it is there, inexorable, mighty and timeless. The coasts are slowly emerging from the sea, but the evidence is perceptible; the great glaciers far to the north grind down to the ocean. The lakes are retreating, and the trees and muskeg follow them. The rivers eat and groan in their labors as they devour the banks and with their moving boulders grind away at their rapids and falls. In this macrocosm of change and flux is man. He too must catch the strange beat or perish; the Idthen-eldeli wandering, wandering, hunting, pursuing, migrating north in the fall, south in the summer; the Padlimiut endlessly traveling, changing their camps here and there from lake to lake, river to river, caribou-crossing to caribou-crossing, hunting, fishing, searching.

In this world of frenetic energy at first dimly seen and scarcely felt, the white man does not always fit with impunity. The white trapper and the prospector, by the nature of their calling may adapt themselves, if they survive at all, unconsciously to the primitive and all demanding pace. The trapper is always on the move seeking new areas, absorbed in a thousand tasks. So too is the prospector. His is a never-ending search; like the roving animals he too is ever seeking and never satisfied. These men, after the unfit have been remorselessly weeded out, manage to stick it. The trader is less adapted by vocation. Yet it is always noticeable that the old-time trader, the veteran, has been absorbed completely by the demands of the northern tempo. He is always busy, endlessly busy, going back and forth to the store, checking goods, supervising his wood supply, off on freight trips, repairing, doing book work, a thousand details, with a haste and hurry seemingly ridiculous in a world where there is no time. But it is the maintenance of this effort that keeps him mentally sound and happy. There is no let-up and though he may sigh for one, if it is presented to him, he is lost. It is always the same story. When an old trader goes "outside" for the long dreamed-of furlough, the inactivity is soon irksome. He wants to get back, for "outside," as he says, there is nothing to do.

For those who try to escape this strange tempo, who try to face the monotony without activity, an unpleasant fate is in store. If they do it for a long time the crushing weight of the world of nature presses down upon them with a hard hand. They seem to sink into an initiative—and activity-erasing blankness. The burden, which they will not remove by a thousand daily small duties and activities piles up until it, becomes too formidable for the mind to handle. They are the ones who become vague and indefinite; responsibility, action, directness of purpose fade and with them discrimination and keenness of mind. Their sensibilities are dulled. In the cloudiness and inadequacy of their thought, they rally sufficiently to become morose and hypersensitive to other people. Their grip on life has slipped for they have lost the drive to follow the life-demands, which surround them. They become alarmed and truculent that others may notice it. In the parlance of the North, they have become "bushed." These cases are not unusual or infrequent. Anyone who has traveled in the North at all extensively has come upon these unfortunate, burned-out human fragments. The escape from the monotony, the immensity, the crushing mightiness, the haunting fears of death at every turn, is only in moving like the animals, a constant doing.

In the afternoon, Charles and I went down the river to Simons Hill to see what the caribou might be doing. After a long while we began to pick out the animals but we could only spot twelve and they were all moving away from us, upwind and to the north.

Coming back up the river, we stopped to lift the net and gathered in an assortment of fine big whitefish, some large lake trout, and the usual suckers. Grayling were abundant here, but the four-and-one-half-inch mesh of the net was too large to capture them. Very large whitefish and lake trout ascend this river from Nueltin Lake.

During the night the strong northwest wind swept away the storm clouds and the morning found the day crystal clear and cold. It was more like a crisp November day than the first week in August. After some discussion it was decided to hold off on the river trip. We were afraid that in our absence the plane might come in. Though Fred had heard no word, the season was fast drawing to a close and the plane, if it was to come at all, must come soon. Every night we had faithfully listened to his small radio for some word. We could hear the Nelson River Manager giving instructions to various trading posts. He was moving up and down the coast of Hudson Bay on the Company schooner, the Fort Severn, inspecting the posts and superintending the shipment of freight to them. But despite the fact that every other post in his district seemed to be advised and instructed on some detail of his progress and movements, we heard no reference at all to Nueltin Lake. Fred would turn on the radio religiously each night at the appointed time. He would fairly bury one large red ear in the small speaker of the machine. We would all sit with bated breath while his face, which had at first been full of anticipation gradually changed. His expectant blue eyes would narrow. As the crackling and muffled words came to an end, he would growl expletives at the brown box and then glare at Charles and me as if we had just insulted him. He would shake his massive, domed head like an irritated and baffled Saint Bernard and roar at us: "I can't understand it! Seven months! Not a word! Are they crazy? We've got no tobacco, no salt, what are they doing?" Over and over again the same words would climax the stuttering silence of the radio. Curiously, the word order and refrain were always exactly the same. Charles never said anything to these outbursts. I reflected that he must have heard the same sequence hundreds of times. My own thoughts were too engaged with the new complications that the silence of the broadcaster suggested. It would mean waiting until December and going out with dogs, for there was no extra canoe here at the post.

In the afternoon we all went together down the river to search for caribou once more. It was very pleasant in the cold clear air. From the top of the hill we scanned the Barrens far and wide, but only a scattering of animals could be seen and they were very far away. The small blue berries, which grew close to the ground, were beginning to ripen. Between our searching with the binoculars we wandered about and picked these berries. They were excellent. From the top of the hill we could see the gray dilapidated buildings of the long defunct "Simons Ltd." Their builder and former owner was the subject of much of Fred's and my random chatting. He was a storied figure in this part of the North and something of a Paul Bunyan legend was already beginning to grow up about him. He was a big and powerful man and in his day a hard and wide traveler. His feats were many and had taken on greater color with time. Among many other things he was renowned through the country as a particularly fortunate hand when it came to any game of chance, even udzi. The story is still told of the year he passed through Brochet. When he stopped he was asked what he was out to do during the coming fur season and he replied, "Trapping!" and slapping his pocket he continued, "Yes, sir, and I got all my traps right here, fifty-two of them." When he came down to Brochet at the end of the winter hunt, he had a larger pack of furs than any trapper, white or red, in the country.

When the slight breeze dropped we were forced to abandon our watch since the flies became too thick for anything but movement. We all went back to the post and occupied ourselves with various small tasks. Fred made some doughnuts and I sewed up my clothing again with skins.

The night was a beautiful one. By this time the stars had begun to appear and they sparkled with glittering brilliance. Over all the sky glowed and wavered a beautiful golden aurora borealis. The summer had not been a particularly notable one for such displays, and this was the most spectacular one I had seen to date. I have never ceased to wonder at the mystery and beauty of it. It too seems to have caught the wavering, restless rhythm of the North. Some of the Indians, and a few white men, say that when it is most brilliant in winter, when all the sky seems on fire, they can hear it making a slight noise, a faint rustling and swishing like the rippling of a silk flag.

One exhibition stands out in my mind with particular vividness. Late in September one year a Cree and I were crossing Reindeer Lake. It was near midnight and the night was very dark. It was so dark that we could see no shore or islands and it seemed as if we were floating in a black void. As we silently slipped along in the Stygian darkness a long plume of light uncoiled in the northeast and spread over the zenith. Great fingers of golden light shot up to the heavens where they beckoned and wavered only to be reinforced by more swaying columns that had a greenish tinge. Soon the whole sky was aflame with the cold pulsating streamers and banners of light. It was incredibly brilliant, and strangely some of the light seemed to detach itself from the zenith and pour down upon us to remain hanging and trembling like a curtain above us. The black water was all glittering with the reflection of the light. I looked back at my companion. He was dimly outlined, monstrous and misshapen in the strange glow. "What do you call these?" I asked. From out of the night his voice come low but distinct, "The *Cheepai*... they dance to-night!" The *cheepai*—I knew the word, the ghosts, the souls of the departed. His voice came again from the silence, "The *cheepai*—do not whistle for if you do, and you draw them right down into the canoe!"

We paddled on in silence; for all the scientific curiosity in the world I would not have whistled.

In the latitudes embraced by Reindeer Lake and Windy, from fifty-eight to sixty-one, the aurora attains its maximum brilliance. As one goes farther north into the extreme Arctic they appear to be more to the south and diminish in their vividness and clarity.

While we were having breakfast the next morning, Charles came in and reported deer near the house. As the Indians and Eskimos had taken all the meat, it was necessary that we attend to the matter of our meals to come. Charles and I went out and saw two deer that were feeding on the farther side of the wide muskeg stretch in back of the house. It was impossible to get to them without crossing the intervening bog. Then we saw a lone bull that seemed to be more accessible. We approached him warily, dodging behind large protecting boulders until he was within range. Charles fired twice with his long-barreled Winchester. The animal looked up from his feeding with a bewildered and uncertain vagueness. He searched about for the cause of the noise but made no effort to run off. Through my binoculars I could see that he was bleeding at the leg. Charles fired again with no success and handed the gun over to me. I killed the unfortunate creature with a shot through the heart and lungs. With the death of the caribou there was the consoling thought that at least we would now have meat and I could devote myself exclusively henceforth to photography. He was very splotchy. The fine, dark chocolate color of the full summer coat had not been completely developed and patches of white winter hair were still clinging to him giving him an odd piebald appearance.

I was cheered by the shot, for my own, had previously not been good. However, they had all been under poor light conditions, and even under the most favorable circumstances one's estimate of distance in the Barrens is very erratic. The big, old-fashioned, open buckhorn style sights on Charles's Winchester seemed much more effective than the very fine notch on my Mannlicher. This latter gun John now had; he had promised to leave it at Brochet when he arrived there.

If one was forced to hunt in the Barrens, the openness of the country and the frequent long ranges would make a telescopic sight a very useful thing providing one could keep the black flies from the lenses. Winter shooting in this country is very difficult. The endless whiteness and the lack of objects to establish relative distance and parallax within the eye make estimate of range almost impossible. Few caribou are killed at any real range before a shot or two, sometimes the whole magazine, have, by the snow, which they have kicked up, established something comparative and definite as to distance.

An old man who used to live at Reindeer Lake told this story: "One day in the winter," he said, "I was going along the big part of the lake where there are no islands. It was all just white and flat as far as you could see. I needed meat for the dogs and myself. Stopping and looking over the snow, I saw two little black things away out on the lake. They were walking back and forth very slowly. I fired my rifle at one of them, and then I fired again. I did not hit either of them, for they kept right on walking back and forth, quite undisturbed. I could not understand why my shooting was so poor. Then I fired twice more. By golly! You know when I put my gun down and wiped my eyes, I found that those two caribou were a couple of lice walking back and forth on my eyebrows!"

Though the stories of this particular old gentleman are North—famous for their Munchausenian detail, this one illustrates admirably the difficulty and strange illusions, the complete blankness of the open country in winter. In this connection very little game in the North is ever killed at the ranges that one is accustomed to hear about in sporting periodicals. For here shooting is not sport, it is a matter of life and death and a dead animal is more valuable than a heroic distance. I hazard that in the bush or tree country very little game is killed at more than fifty yards. As a general thing, the natives are not particularly expert shots at long ranges but they make up for this with their stalking ability and the certainty of results in their closer approach.

Later in the morning, I saw a big buck racing along a stony ridge directly in back of the house not more than sixty yards away. He charged up and down at a great pace, and of course I did not have the camera at hand. The flies and mosquitoes seem to bother these animals quite as much as they do human beings. Added to these pests, the caribou are hosts to a parasitic fly called the warble whose larva penetrate the hide in great numbers. Often the inside of the throat of a caribou is a mass of wiggling, nasty grubs. The Chipewyans sometimes gouge them out and eat them.

The next day was again bright and cool. Charles and I went west of the post to two high sandy hills called "Hudson's Bay Hills." From this vantage point, we began to see caribou in all directions. They were very restless and kept crashing through the bush and willows to escape the flies. Occasionally we would see one or more of them swinging across the open meadows and muskeg at a tremendous rate. There did not seem to be any fixed destination or purpose in their movements, just a constant and restless change of position. They might break out into the open and trot down to the river willows only to reappear and go over the same course again. Almost all of them were bucks and some were very large, with here and there an old grandfather still almost entirely white. No sooner would we spot one than another one would come into view.

To the west of us was a bare, sandy esker, and many of them seemed to prefer this natural highway. It suggested to me interesting speculation on how important the great esker chains may be in the North as a determining factor in the migration of these fascinating and variable animals.

We began to see an occasional doe. Though they, like the males, also carry huge antlers, the horns were not in the same stage of development and advancement as those of the bulls. All were in velvet, the soft dark covering of fuzz, which covers the growing horn, but the female horns had not really begun to form beyond the sprouting stage. Also the females did not appear to have as much winter hair, and the ones we saw had almost completely cast the dirty white patches and were approaching the full glossy brown coats of summer. It is the late August hide which both the Idthen-eldeli and the Eskimos favor for the making of their winter clothing. It is not so heavy and bulky and the hair does not so easily break off and pull out.

One very large bull crossed below us. We heard him thrashing about and coughing down in the thick willows close to the river. With grunting sighs of relief he at last plunged into the water and swam across to the other side. Caribou are remarkably strong, fine swimmers. They are more adapted to swimming than any other members of the deer family. Their hollow hair is buoyant, and they ride very high in the water. Their broad, flat hoofs coupled with great flexibility of ankle make them excellent aquatic animals. It is a fortunate adaptation in a land so replete with water. Rapids seem to have a peculiar and sometimes fatal attraction for them. Many times they will cross a river just above rapids though there are innumerable less hazardous crossings. It is not unusual for them to swim across the big lakes, from island to island and across open stretches of five or six miles. They are accustomed to string out in long single lines, which at a distance look like a spaced chain of small trees silently crossing the lake.

While on this sandy hill we heard a snuffing and snorting below us. Then a doe walked straight up the hill to us and posed very nicely for her picture some thirty feet away. Our mutual surprise over, she turned and in no great haste went down the hill again.

A few minutes later a yearling buck did exactly the same thing approaching from the opposite direction. He was so disturbed by the flies that he was quite oblivious to our presence until he was only a few feet away. For some time we watched him. He moved rapidly along, snuffing, snorting, and coughing, rubbing his face against the low bushes. He was very mottled, with an extremely incomplete change of coat, and unusually lean. I did not realize until I saw his photograph how effective his splotchy appearance was as a protective camouflage to color-blind animals.

We could not have chosen a more fortunate spot. What caribou there were in our immediate vicinity seemed to make directly for the hill, probably to take advantage of its open, wind-swept height to escape the flies, just as we were doing.

Seton, after his observations of the caribou east of Great Slave Lake in 1907, estimated: "This, then, is my summary of the Barren Ground Caribou between the Mackenzie River and Hudson's Bay. They number over *30,000,000 and may be double that.*"* (The italics are my own.) Seton's is perhaps the maximum figure of any competent observer. However, it must be borne in mind that Seton's acquaintance with the Barren Lands as such was in a very restricted area and on an exceptionally fine caribou range.

Further, the method by which he deduced this enormous figure has no real justification in fact. It was also his belief that, despite modern firearms, due to the decimation of Northern hunters by disease and the abandonment of the practice of spearing, contrary to the popular fancy, they were on the increase.

The fact of the matter is that there are many and some very large areas in the Barrens, which because of the charac-

* *The Arctic Prairies*, by Ernest Thompson Seton: New York, Scribner's, 1917.

ter of their soil, rock exposures, drainage, or sand do not bear growth sufficient to support large bands of caribou at all. Another factor is that the sphagnum moss and similar fodder of the caribou grows so slowly in the extreme cold of the far North that it cannot be annually grazed over. Thus, every year must find tremendous areas, which do not support caribou. Again, the caribou do not spread out uniformly over the Barrens but, particularly in migration, condense into bands and herds, which leave vast sections entirely denuded of them. Consequently, any estimate of the numbers of the caribou based upon the available square miles and the number of caribou that these might support is bound to be badly in error.

Seton and many other commentators in making their general estimates were inclined to base much of their data upon the annual slaughter of these animals by the particular natives with whom they were associated. For instance, the annual kill-estimate for the Indians with Seton who resort to Fort Resolution was put by him at ten to fifteen head. This may be very true of natives like these who live a great distance from the caribou range, or at least consume a great deal of potential killing time and opportunity in traveling to and from caribou country to a spot so distant as Resolution. When one considers the case of the Idthen-eldeli, who pass the entire winter literally among the caribou, and further, not only the winter but the spring and fall when the latter are bunched up in herds, when one further realizes that they feed not only themselves but their dogs almost exclusively on caribou, the average kill rises much higher and approaches figures in the neighborhood of hundreds per man and family.

It is almost impossible to obtain from the people themselves a reliable accounting or estimate. None of them can count that high; they have no interest in keeping any tally, and if they could or did, they would not reveal the true number, anyway. To them the caribou are exclusively their own and the white man has no business even asking about the matter. Almost the only time that the slightest flicker of other than dumb docility was aroused at "Treaty" time at Brochet was when an incautious reference was made about caribou conservation. The government Indian agent, quite unknown to himself, became the subject of the most bitter denunciation and abuse. As old Kasmere cried out to his people: "Who is this white man who presumes to talk about what is ours. The next thing we know we will be told how to treat our wives and children. The caribou are ours; they have been given our fore-fathers and to us forever. Who is this king that will send a man to talk like this? How dare this creature even use the word idthen in his mouth?"

The white trappers, of whom there are a number who rely on caribou, do not give out any figures on their own kill. But, considering that the ordinary white trapper in caribou coun-try each year outfits himself with at least a case of shells (1,000) for his "deer gun," it is obvious that not all the car-tridges are wasted.

When Indians or Eskimos get among a number of caribou only one thing stops or limits their killing, lack of ammunition.

My own estimate of the annual kill in such a comparative-ly small district as the country hunted over north of Brochet, exclusive of the Eskimo deer hunters farther north, would be placed at about twenty-two thousand. This estimation is based on a sober examination of a number of indices, which it would not be possible or politic to develop here.

Whether these magnificent animals are on the increase, holding their own, or decreasing is a matter over which one can stir up a rabid argument anywhere in the North and par-ticularly with anyone who is connected with game conserva-tion. Government officials, and especially those people hold-ing positions endowing them with any controlling duties over the caribou kill, are all unanimously and vociferously con-vinced that the caribou are on the verge of extinction.

Out of the maze of contradictory evidence and theory, the fact stands clear that unquestionably the caribou in many parts of the western borders of the Barrens have radically changed their customary migration routes. This change in itself, of course, indicates absolutely nothing about their num-bers. However, many people seem to think it does, and at least this is no doubt the most effective promulgator of the idea that they are disappearing and being killed out. The reason for the change in this region is not ipso facto the lessening in numbers but the increase in habitation of the white man in this section. In the last few years, great mines have sprung up in the very woods country to which these migrating bands formerly resorted. These mean not only the presence of the white man, attendant noise, and greater numbers of the caribou's potential enemies, but also with prospecting, an enlargement of the country which either by accident or design is burned off and the feeding grounds destroyed. Further, and of more importance than has been realized, this region has become a network of constant airplane transportation and activity. Caribou, particularly when on migration and bunched in vast herds, are singularly unconscious of or at least undisturbed by man or animals, but curiously they are terrified by the noise of planes. Any northern pilots who have flown over bands of caribou have witnessed this, and many of them have used it as an amusing and sporting diversion. It is no wonder that many of the hereditary routes have changed.

The fact also remains that far fewer hunters are killing caribou than were even a few years ago. The death rate among the northern hunters has been far greater than among the agricultural and sedentary Indians to the south. The decrease among the Idthen-eldeli, the thirty-year drop to within one-third of their number, is but one of numerous examples. Excellent but belated government control has also checked any appreciable new influx or increase in hunters. Some groups of hunters who were particularly assiduous in their year-round extermination of caribou have almost entirely died out, as has been the case with some of the small bands, which used to come into the Snowdrift River region of Great Slave Lake.

Of particular importance, many northern Indians, like the Idthen-eldeli at Brochet who have been for centuries primarily and almost exclusively caribou hunters, have been turned more and more to fur gathering. The long treks into the Barrens to follow and live on the caribou in the main have been abandoned for trap lines and campsites more accessible to the trading posts. Where the sustenance was once exclusively meat, trade goods are now used. This is particularly true of the western area, which has the greater population.

Added to this, the younger generation of men who have been sent away to schools return with an education utterly useless to the life of a hunter and they are increasingly less adapted, less artful, and less enthusiastic in the deer killing of their forefathers.

Another and not unimportant factor operates in favor of the caribou which was not in such wide existence when they were reported to be more numerous than they are today. Until a comparatively recent time, most of the Athapaskan peoples who are most associated with migrating caribou, refused to kill wolves. This wolf-killing taboo had existed from time immemorial, and from sources deeply entrenched in mythological backgrounds. The combination of the bounty, the missionary, the pinch of less fur, and the increased price of this fur from American markets, has broken down this ancient observance. Every wolf killed in the North, particularly anywhere near the tree line, guarantees a tremendous number of saved caribou. In the Barrens, during migration and the winter, wolves prey almost exclusively on caribou. Think, for instance, what a saving in caribou the catch of a single white trapper of my acquaintance amounted to four years ago. His bag of wolves numbered one hundred and ten, all of them taken in caribou country!

Except by the little handful of Inland Eskimos, caribou are no longer speared in the calculated and planned fashion, which was once so common. Actually, far more caribou can be slaughtered in this fashion than with the most high-powered modern rifle. For the noise causes the caribou to turn back and change their course.

Old inhabitants of the North who are in a position to judge the relative abundance of caribou down through the years are divided on the question. Few of them have had sufficiently widespread experience in parts of the North to form conclusions relevant to other than their immediate residence.

Despite nearly two hundred years of knowledge of them by white observers, despite centuries of watching their movements by the people who preyed upon them, little more is known about the caribou today than has ever been known. They are the living symbol of the North itself. What their routes may be, just when they will appear, how many there will be, only the next year will tell. There may be a certain crossing, which they have used as long as the oldest native can remember. Inexplicably not an animal may appear there the next year. One region may be utterly barren of them one year and overflowing with them the next. Wherever you are in the North, you cannot positively count on caribou. You can only believe that they are there when you yourself see them. What determines their direction and choice of routes is a mystery. Some claim the winds are a decisive factor that the caribou always move upwind. This may be so when they are feeding, but it is not so when they once decide, from some unknown and mysterious cause, to move. The theories about all these matters are endless. None of them stand up against a truly critical analysis.

It was not my fate, here at Windy to see the caribou in the great hordes in which they are known to travel. That, though I did not know it at the time, was a gift and privilege of the North for which another year; more portages, more rapids and labor must first be paid. But it is, when the North grants it, one of the most thrilling and moving sights left on the North American continent.[3]

After our experience with the last of the obliging caribou, we thought for a moment that we heard, far away and very faint, the distant hum of a plane. We listened intently, holding our breath and straining for the least suggestion of sound. For just a fleeting instant it seemed as if we heard it again. The sound, if it was that, was so slight and so distant that it was lost before either of us could judge whether we had really heard it or not. In any event, we returned to the post highly satisfied and gleeful over our anticipated results in the photographing of caribou.

We found Charles's father in a state of great excitement. He was sure that he had heard the plane. We all agreed that the sound had come from the east and northeast. What a plane could be doing over the northeast part of Nueltin Lake without coming in here to the post we could not imagine. The noon meal was prepared and eaten in an atmosphere of much expectancy. After the dishes were put away, Fred paced about talking to himself, asking questions and answering them with the most uncontrolled abandon. Then we all heard the sound again. We rushed out of doors. The sound was far away and to the east. As it had the first time, it died away. Fred was as if stung by a thousand gadflies of torture. He raced about on his long spindly legs searching the horizon with one hand cupped over his ear. It was now several hours since we had heard the first sound. To all of us this meant but one thing. The plane was either lost or it had been unable to locate the post and had turned back. We had heard the sound fading farther and farther away until once again it was gone.

Fred in his rage and disappointment would not yet give up. He dispatched Charles to a little patch of spruce some distance from the post. He was given a precious gallon of gasoline with which to start a fire and build a smudge. Then Fred and I went up to the hill by the flagpole.

We searched the horizon ceaselessly. Charles was hacking down stunted spruce and piling them up. But the rolling grim hills of the Barrens stretched before our eyes, the gray sky held no speck of bird or plane. Though our wishes fairly shrieked for the plane to reappear, there was nothing but silence to answer them. I do not know how long we watched and prayed, but at last even Fred gave up the fruitless vigil and we all turned back to the post. As we were about to enter the house, louder and plainer than ever we heard the drone of a plane and without saying a word we all rushed back.

This time the sound increased rapidly. Suddenly I spotted it with my binoculars. It was flying very high and as I watched, it turned to the northeast away from us. The tiny speck seemed to be circling in a great arc. It turned and wheeled about. It approached us and the sound became more audible, and then it turned again and I saw it fading, fading away. Fred kept shouting at me: "Where is it now? Where is it going? What in hell is he doing?"

After it had completed its swing and disappeared entirely from sight and hearing, it reappeared and seemed to be swinging in an even greater circle. After what seemed an infinity of time, it at last began to veer toward us though with no certain purposefulness. Absorbed watching it, I was vaguely conscious of Fred roaring at Charles to start the fire, and then I could hear his deafening shrieks of: "Put on more brush! For God's sake, put on more brush!"

The speck at last began to take form. Swiftly it became a plane with silver wings and fuselage. It was winging toward us, still very high and still on a curving course. Fred redoubled his roars as if to draw it to us by the command of his voice. In back of us I could hear the crackle of the burning spruce and smell the acrid smoke.

As it soared on, it seemed to me the smooth curve of its flight was momentarily broken. It veered and dipped a little; then with a roar it swept high above us and turned down Windy River. Losing altitude rapidly, it sank out of sight.

With mad haste we all ran down to the shore and got into the canoe. Planes are unable to land in front of the post in summer as the river is too narrow and shoal. It is their custom to come down on Simons Lake and taxi in to the southwest shore of that small river expansion. As we no longer heard the motor, we were sure that it had come down there. Fred in the agony of his impatience sat as far in the bow of the canoe as he was able and alternately craned his neck forward and turned and made savage gestures at Charles to speed up the outboard. Looking back at the latter I saw him unconcernedly and impassively staring at the riverbanks as we rushed along. In a few minutes we rounded the last bend and saw drawn up on the beach a gleaming Canadian Airways plane and two figures moving about it.

After greetings, they identified themselves as the pilot Dave, and the other man, a big strapping chap named Jim, a Hudson's Bay Company man who had come to relieve Fred and take over the post.' Fred was to go out on furlough and be transferred eventually to some other post.

After a cigarette, which in this case was literally heaven-sent, the mailbag was the first consideration. Fred and the new man, Jim, went back to the post, and I stayed down with the pilot and helped him transfer to the plane sixty gallons of gasoline which had been cached in the old Simons buildings. As we lugged and rolled the metal drums down to the shore the pilot gave me a fragmentary account of their almost fruitless search to find the post. The full narrative was to come later. The sixty reserve gallons were proving a great satisfaction to him, for without them he said that he would have been unable to consider flying back to Churchill at all. After we had transferred the gasoline, Charles appeared with the canoe and we all went up river to the post.

In the meantime, Jim had taken the opportunity to look over his new home. He was very glum. When I asked him, with cheery and malicious humor, how he liked it, he turned upon me the most reproachful of stares and said very bitterly: "Not for me! Either I get someone here with me or I quit!"

Fred had buried himself in the mail. Among other things, he found that in the seven months' silence his house and home in Winnipeg had burned down though fortunately his wife and children had escaped unharmed.

After the conventional meal the details of the nearly unsuccessful flight were supplied by Dave and Jim. The flight from Churchill, Manitoba, a seaport and end of the railroad on Hudson Bay, had been without event until they had reached Nueltin Lake. Their map, as all maps do, showed Windy River as coming in from the northwest. Even in flying across the lake they had some doubts as to whether this was Nueltin for they could see a very large lake still to the west. They managed to find a bay coming in from the northwest and also, as they circled over it, a small river which tallied with the map. They flew over this river for a long distance but they could find no trace of anything resembling a building or trading post. They then circled about the country in a wide arc and still saw nothing to suggest the habitation of a human being. In despair, they came down and landed in a protecting bay of the main lake to discuss the situation. It now appeared to them that they may not have reached Nueltin Lake at all and that the large lake to the west, which they previously had seen, might be it. Due to the fact that Nueltin is charted on the most recent maps almost a degree (nearly thirty-five miles) too far east, they had already a miscalculation of the required gas for the trip. Added to this, the reconnaissance flying they had been doing had so reduced their supply that it seemed doubtful that they could now even make a return to Churchill.

They decided in the face of a dubious return to make one more wide, swinging flight and to circle over toward the large lake to the west. This lake, which was of course Windy, has never been shown on maps with any degree of accuracy as to size or position. As they flew on, it seemed to them this was to be a repetition of previous air attempts to reach Nueltin Lake Post. The elusive and secretive Nueltin was once again not to be found from the air. Fortunately, they reflected, they had a two-way radio with which they could summon a relief plane with gas, but it would be almost impossible to give directions as to just where they were.

It was in this last desperate and nearly hopeless flight that, circling far back from Nueltin and looking over a terrain in which they had not the slightest expectation of finding the post, they had seen a thin ribbon of smoke against the dark background of a minute clump of spruce. Charles's frantic efforts had saved the day for everyone. Even when they flew toward the blue thread of smoke they did not see the buildings until they were directly over them and they had swung away from the smudge.

The visibility from the air of even a small column of smoke is extraordinary. This is particularly true if the smoke has a background of trees. The smudge Charles made had seemed to me at the time insignificant and futile.

They also brought the intelligence that the Hudson's Bay Company Arctic supply ship, the *Nascopie*, was in at Churchill as well as the schooner the Fort Severn. No one intended to go out in the plane the next day except Dave the pilot.

Immediately new plans began to swarm through my head. First, I should be able to get out in time to see many former acquaintances on the *Nascopie*. I had sailed in her twice to the Arctic.[5] A sudden urgent surge of desire swept over me to see my friends on her again. Further, I might have a chance to go up along the coast in the Fort Severn and in to Baker Lake. This latter possibility was particularly intriguing as it would mean the observation of much country with which I was previously only sketchily acquainted and would afford opportunity to make an examination of glacial evidence in almost the same longitude but north of my work here. Also there would be the chance to find out more, as the schooner touched along the coast, concerning the movements of the caribou. The plane trip would afford a tremendous saving in time, a saving for which I had not made allowance previously, and would leave me a full month for further work.

Fred and Charles intended to come out on a later flight of the plane. There were still several thousand pounds of freight to be flown into the post and at least two more trips were being contemplated. Fred seemed to be quite happy at the prospect of going "outside" and in the general excitement and enthusiasm I did not realize just how it might affect Charles.

The new man, Jim, seemed to sink into deeper despondency as the hours went by. We pointed out to him with great detail all the advantages which this possessed over other posts, the delightful seclusion, the lack of begging Indians, the caribou which he would have to kill for himself, the great abundance of fish which he would have to net and hang himself, the pleasures of an untroubled, unhampered survival by his own effort. It was, we admitted, somewhat annoying that it was impossible to get either an Indian or Eskimo to stay and do any work such as hauling wood, but even then there was the compensation that he would not have to fuss with their direction. He was far from an inexperienced man, but somehow the prospect did not seem inviting to him.

The morning of August 6 brought fine flying weather. Everything was bustle and hurry. We prepared to go down to the plane to take off the rest of the freight, and then Dave and I would be off. Various last minute matters were hastily attended to and then it was time to depart.

I had noticed that when we were scurrying about engaged in the last small details of leave-taking, Charles was absent. Since the news of Fred's transfer had been digested, I had thought more than once about him and how he would take the change. Though to his father, a veteran of thirty years in the North, a shift to some other post might be merely a temporary inconvenience; to Charles it meant a total disruption of his life. This was particularly true if his father should decide, as he had considered, staying "outside" in Winnipeg.

Life there, as Charles well knew, was far different from this existence he loved on the edge of the Barrens. It meant, among other things, leaving what was dearest to him above all else in the world, his dogs.

Fred decided to take Dave and me to the plane in the canoe. We placed it in the water and Jim came down to wish Dave good luck and me good-bye. He looked like a man about to be executed. Looking back at the little log house, I felt quite honestly that if fate were to offer me this, I would not be unhappy. Charles was not with him. Missing him, I searched about with my eyes and at first I could not find him. At last I saw him. He was back from the bank sitting among his dogs. His back was to us and his arms were around his big white leader.

Very quickly, too quickly, a bend in the river hid the forlorn little gray buildings. Their weather-beaten roofs with the big stones on them melted into the ground.

Fred was standing in the canoe and shouting and smiling. Last handshakes—faintly I heard Fred's roars of "Good luck …good luck,"—a whirring and a grinding, a roaring and a sputtering, we were moving.

Far below us I saw Fred, a tiny puppet, waving from a miniature canoe. Forever and forever a world of rock and tundra, and the eastern sun was in my face.[6]

CHAPTER 11

South Flight

Once in the air, the world below us again became a bewildering maze of lakes and ridges. But here there was no green sea of spruce; here all was water and the gray, wrinkled skeleton of the earth itself, smoothed, tired, solid rock.

From my seat next to Dave in the forward cockpit I could only see out the right side of the metal Junkers. I did, however, get a glimpse of Windy River and the bay into which it flows. It was like looking down upon the world in its first stage of creation, a gelid world where life had not yet begun to cloak the raw, awful shell.

The hills, which had seemed so high from the river, mysteriously flattened out into tortuously twisted masses of gray rock, here and there rent and gashed as if in a last dumb agony it could no longer stand the strain.

Windy Bay opened out in a great V to the southeast. For a fleeting moment I saw that it was marked by three small but striking islands. The north side of the bay looked like a tattered fragment of brown cloth trailing off into the gray, steely, wrinkled immensity of Nueltin Lake.

From here the great lake stretched away to the northeast as far as the eye could see and lost itself on a horizon indistinguishable from the water. To the south, the lake was seen to maintain a defined entity for many miles and then it merged with a mass of interlocking islands. So complex were the shores that it was impossible at our speed either to approximate a sketch or tell where the lake really ended.

Most surprising of all, this section of the lake was quite free of islands. There was an enormous expanse of open water. Those who maintained that the entire lake was choked with islands had obviously never been this far north on it.

Of all the lake, that section which is least known was the very part which was beyond our view to the extreme north. No Indians ever visit this area; it is too near the Eskimo country and they say that it is always covered with a mist in which bad creatures live. Even at our great height we could see no ending, no beginning to this mighty sea.

It was even impossible to tell just when we had reached the eastern shore for the islands became numerous, and bays and inlets baffled all description in their profusion and labyrinthine entanglement. When we judged we had reached the eastern side, we turned more south. There was a stiff southeast wind for which we were now compensating.

With the roaring of the engine no conversation was possible. I looked at Dave, a small and cherubic gargoyle in his helmet and glasses. He was studying the instruments with deep interest and a studied frown. I looked at the sun; we had swung more to the south and must be flying down the east side of the lake.

After some time we found ourselves passing over what seemed to be a large and very intricate lake. But studying it with the binoculars, I could see that in reality it was not a separate lake but a great bay connected with the main lake by a narrow island-infested channel. It suddenly came to me that this was the bay Hearne had entered and across which he had traveled when he made his estimate of the width of Nueltin. After one hundred and sixty-eight years that stanch traveler was vindicated and his judgment upheld at least in the mind of one lone fellow traveler.

As we began to fly away from the lake and gain more altitude, we could see eskers of great length wiggling over the land in a south and southwesterly direction. They were very striking and intricate. Being of sand, and their embankment tops in many cases being exposed by the worn caribou trails, they stood out white and gleaming against the somber background of dark rock. These tremendous sand chains dominated the entire country. They were very complex. They sometimes dissolved into delta-like fans and then recommenced again. Though they were serpentine, they had a definite and pronounced trend. From the south and southwest they gradually began to swing more to the east and after an hour and a half of flight they were uniformly wiggling over the shell of the earth in an east-southeast direction. Some of them contained tiny lakelets completely enclosed within them. In one case I saw two little lakes on the top of a broad esker, which were completely dry. Here and there the sand bulged out from the main ridge into lobate tongues.

All the country was barren, but the deeper ravines began to support dark bands of trees. This growth of somber green marked out in splendid detail the structure of the world below us. It was like the crenulated markings on the back of a giant tortoise. With all the confusion and masking splatter of innumerable lakes it was apparent that there was a certain complex relationship, an interlocking system of great joints and rifts. The stresses and strains of millions of years had cracked and shattered the whole country into hundreds of splintering breaks. These were the valleys, and, occupied by a more luxuriant growth of dwarf trees and bush, to us so far above them they had the appearance of a great mosaic. At first the complexity was so staggering and vast, the scale so great that there seemed to be no rhyme or reason to it all. But as I became more accustomed to the stupendous panorama passing below, gradually a certain linear organization and trend emerged. The structure and "grain" of the rock revealed itself by the shape of the islands and the direction of the bays and points. In the country we were now passing over I could see that the trend was northeast southwest. The points and bays were like the two ends of a broken stick, splinters in parallel alignment; the gap occupied by water. As we flew on, all the lakes had something of this character; long narrow bays and points, jagged, but subtly organized. We passed over some very large lakes, and though they were narrow and often trough-like they were inclined to stretch for great distances and split up into a multitude of extended, shining fingers.

By the second hour, a gradual change had begun to assert itself. The long narrow lakes began to disappear. The curious joint and fracture topography, the breaks, or "faults" died out and the lakes, though not decreasing in number, lost their irregularity and magnitude. Here they became a flock of small lakes shaped like drawn-out tears. They lay in a pattern roughly northwest southeast, but their southern ends were rounded and almost globular and they thinned out like a cone to the north.

After this we passed over a strikingly different section. The hills, the wrinkled relief, died out completely. The rocky knolls no longer appeared; the jigsaw lakes vanished. All the world seemed to be speckled and spotted with myriads of small round lakes. They glittered up at us like thousands of drops of water. Even the larger of them—some of them must have been ten miles across—were oval or round. They had few if any islands. In some places it looked as if some gigantic celestial bomb had sprayed the earth with round balls of shrapnel. It was just prior to this fantastic pock marked land that, as if in a farewell, we had passed over a very long straight-sided lake, which the Indians call, I believe, Duck Lake. And of all these thousands of lakes, our map carried not one.

Throughout the flight I was particularly alert to see where the transition from the Barrens proper to the tree line might take place. There was no fixed demarcation and indeed it was impossible to determine where it might be for the change was so insidious and gradual. The trees for a long time hugged only the deeper ravines and breaks along the water, but gradually and unobtrusively they began to creep up and capture higher slopes. One could only judge that some spots seemed less barren than others. It was only after a long time that the trees really had sufficiently established themselves to cloak the tops of the knolls and then the whole world slipped quietly under the obscuring mat of the dark forest.

No caribou were visible, though I watched very intently with the binoculars. Caribou, when they occur in numbers, and the land is not too heavily forested, are very noticeable from a plane. Possibly our altitude may have been too great, but in any event I saw no sign of them. In this respect, fortunately or unfortunately, depending upon whether your sympathies are with man or the animals, northern pilots are always questioned today by natives and white men alike as to the movements of game, which they can so easily spot from their planes.

It seemed to me that we had been flying for a very long time, and it also seemed that we were not getting anywhere. For a long while I had harbored an illogical but nonetheless powerful suspicion that we had been flying too much south of east. The wind for which we had originally been compensating had now shifted. We began to notice a low impenetrable blanket of smoke rapidly rolling up toward us from the south, shutting out the horizon from us. We could see no fires, but the smoke was so dense and so all-covering that it must have been from innumerable bush fires to the south, the summer conflagrations which rage every year throughout the North. Before long it became more than an annoyance for as it swirled below us the land and water began to fade and dissolve into a gray impenetrable haze.

I looked over at Dave. His hunched figure had begun to twitch and squirm about as he peered first this way and then that. He looked at the ground, which now could only be dimly seen. He searched the horizon, which could not be seen at all. He studied the instruments and then the big white blank on the map. We had been flying for well over two hours, and I knew that we should be in the vicinity of Churchill or at least near enough to see Hudson Bay and the landmark of the grain elevator. Over everything was a dense gray fog.

Once he had shouted at me to see if I could spot Caribou Post, a trading post at which we had intended to make a stop.[1] I searched for a long time but saw nothing resembling a building. At last he handed the map over to me. We began to drop down through the smoke. Once more the lakes flashed up at us. I studied the map and I heard his voice shrieking through the roaring of the engine:

"Do you see anything down there that looks like the map?"

I examined the nightmare below us for some time. The only resemblance was in the whiteness of the lakes and the blank of the map. I shook my head. There was nothing that jibed at all. He jammed the map into his coat and peered about him again. Then he leaned over to me and cried:

"I guess we better come down. We've only got five minutes of gas left!"

The thundering, great metal bird began to cease its hoarse roaring. Gently we began to slide and swoop down through the swirling smoke. The wind whistled and hummed. I saw a large lake a little to the south of us and I nudged Dave's elbow and pointed to it. The plane glided on with great powerful circling. I studied the lake with my binoculars but I could see nothing on its shores. Soon we were swooshing over the toy spruces. The water lay under us like wrinkled, silver cardboard. Gently we settled upon it and the engine began to thunder, the spray plumes rose about us and we taxied in toward a sandy beach. It was at this instant that we unexpectedly saw a small cabin on the shore.

We had landed well out in the lake. It was blowing very hard from the south and we made our approach to the shore slowly and with caution because of possible rocks and reefs. We could now see two little Indian children in front of the cabin, watching us and surrounded by a number of big dogs.

As we approached we discussed in staccato terms the problem of where we might be. Just before we landed we both had caught a glimpse of a stream flowing north from the lake and a single island in the lake itself. From these two observations and a hurried and rough picture of the general contour of the lake, we both felt that there might be a chance that we were down on one of the very few lakes plotted on the map. It was called South Knife Lake but was so far out of position from our intended and assumed course that it seemed impossible.

Coming nearer to the shore, we saw an Indian woman come out of the cabin and push off in a canoe. Though we were still some distance from the beach, the pontoons began to grind against the sand. Dave cut the engine. We flung back the roof of the cockpit. Both our minds were bursting with the all-important question: "Where are we?" I rummaged through my head to recall how to say it in Chipewyan and then, if that did not work, in Cree.

We stood up on the seat. The woman in the canoe also stood up. Before either of us could shout our question, she cried out in a high shrill voice:

"Hey, you fella, up there in the air, you seen my son-of-a-bitch husband?"

Startled and disconcerted by the woman's direct address and her command of the English idiom, Dave and I stared at each other for a moment. Then we turned to her and allowed that we had not. In our turn we asked where we might be. Amidst a renewed tirade of vituperation against her missing spouse the words "South Knife Lake" was somewhere negligently intermingled. Our guess, made *after* we had landed, was correct!

The plane was taxied the rest of the way into the shore. We scrambled out and tied it securely. Then we went up to the house followed by the children and a long procession of dogs. The Indian woman was already setting out a meal on the table.

During the meal, which was an excellent one, we learned that she was a Chipewyan married to a white trapper. Her husband had left over a month before and she had had no word from him. She assumed that he was at Churchill, but meanwhile she was left with the care of her four children and fifteen dogs.

She spoke clear though quaint English. Her name was Mary and she maintained her full house in excellent style and cleanliness. As we alternately ate and talked to her, I think we both were silently thanking our fortune that out of all the thousands and thousands of possible lakes we had, under the guidance of some unknown providence, happened to have dropped down on this one.

After lunch, Dave went back to the plane to see if he could work his radio and get in touch with his flying base at God's Lake, Manitoba. I turned my attention to Mary and the children. The latter were very bright and quiet little people ranging from a ten-year-old to a baby in arms. They were unusually neatly dressed, clean, and had watched us through-out the meal with the shining, black, sparkling eyes of shy and expectant wood mice. The two oldest were girls, Rita and Eva, the next in line was a fat little boy named Tommy, and the baby was called Wilfred. The mother was equally neat and clean and she was more angular and spare than most Indian women. Indicative of her total conversion to the white man's world was her bobbed black hair.[2]

While Dave was busy with the radio she and I went out to the nets. She was a very practical and practiced hand at extri-cating the fish, which were mostly jackfish and suckers. The nets were in poor shape and the duty is an unpleasant one at best. Sometimes the twine was so deeply imbedded in the gills that a liberal use of teeth as well as hands was necessary. The black flies and mosquitoes seemed to complicate the messy job further. Back on shore, the fish were cut up with an ax and fed to the dogs, which received them in a pandemonium of roaring welcome.

Dave had managed to get through to God's Lake, though his reception of their reply was not very clear. It looked as if we should be grounded several days at least. He was more than a little annoyed about the whole thing. Not only is it a blow to any pilot's pride to have to "sit down" on some lake far off the course, but it meant a further delay of the whole freighting process with the increasing uncertainty of flying weather as the season advanced.

For me, though it would mean losing both the *Nascopie* and the *Severn*, it was not at all unpleasant. I had seen a great deal of country which few people had or would ever see from either land or air; the experience of being lost in an airplane is one which only a limited number of beings undergo in this mechanical and perfect world of schedule and routine. The time element was not pressing in my case and I could afford to go out to Hudson Bay and Churchill by canoe if no rescue arrived. In a sense the whole thing was an unusual and inter-esting fillip to my summer.

Several factors had militated against our making a success-ful flight back to Churchill. One was certainly the utter inac-curacy of the map. This had of course been exaggerated when increasing trust had been put in it as the smoke obscured the ground and horizon. Another thing was the enormous change in compass variation between the point of departure and the proposed objective. At the former the compass needle is deflected about twenty-five degrees east of true north. At the latter it diminishes to about seven degrees. The rate of change between these two points is not at all constant. In a blind flight of two hundred and fifty miles or more this lack of knowledge can create a large margin of error particularly when all semblance of ground control has been lost. The last influence was the varying violence and direction of the wind. At the start, the wind had been a light northeast breeze. At higher altitudes and greater distance it had increased to a violent east, southeast, and then west wind. Though various compensations had been made for it, they were not made with any real knowledge of our fixed position at the moment.

After the details of fishing, splitting firewood, and the further mooring of the plane had all been completed, we returned to the cabin. Unlike most northern ones, this had been very artfully constructed with the logs standing upright rather than horizontal. The interior was very clean and nicely furnished. It seemed to hold more than just essentials and much to Dave's delight even a package of cards and a cribbage board were produced. This latter luxury initiated a series between Dave and myself, which was to go on for days and thoroughly cleansed my system of any desire to play the game again. While we were playing, Mary intoned a phrase that we were to hear at least four times an hour for the ensuing days of our enforced stay.

"Gee, I'm glad you fella show up."

The change in both the forest growth and the increased warmth of the air was very noticeable after Windy. We were well within "bush" country and the days seemed like real summer weather rather than the cold, chilling, damp ones of the Barrens. A good index of the type of river to be found in this area was afforded when Mary informed us that the canoe trip to Churchill might be made in about a week of fast travel with an engine. However, the return up the river from the same spot required almost a month. We were located on the edge of a widespread, fast-dropping dip to the bay, which is termed the "Hudson Bay Slope." If nothing else, our predicament illustrated the incalculable value of the two-way radio to the northern or bush flier.

The daily routine of our lives became very settled. We puttered about. We built a little wharf out to the plane. We chopped and split wood. I hunted about and visited the nets, wrote up my journal, and spent long hours enlarging my Chipewyan vocabulary. Dave worked his radio, but he did not have enough gasoline to run the engine very long and thus charge up his battery. His signals became weaker and he was soon unable to get through to Winnipeg at all. The God's Lake planes were all in operation, and it was necessary that one come all the way from Winnipeg, a distance of over six hundred miles.

Mary proved a tireless talker and an excellent cook. Her talents were many for also when the caribou had been very abundant the previous spring she herself had killed two with a hatchet and she had made some unusually fine coats for her husband and children. One was made entirely from the caribou leg skins. The hair of this part of the animal is very short, dense, and a rich brown. Though it is a task, which requires a great deal of sewing and arranging, the finished coat is the best wearing type one can secure. She cheerfully contracted to make me up a coat from some skins, which had been given me at Windy. Among all these duties and endless exertions as mother of a large wilderness family she had also delivered a friend of hers of a baby.

The whole family was a fine example of the traditional family struggle against a common adversary, the North. The children, despite their age, were wonderfully responsible. Eva, the oldest, belied her ten years in the volume of work she did, hauling wood, washing and drying dishes, assisting at the nets, and feeding the dogs were all part of her cheerful and uncomplaining daily lot. Rita, a year younger, assisted in these matters, and both of the little girls looked after Tommy and the five-months'-old Wilfred. They all spoke English and, of course, Chipewyan. With all these duties they seemed a cheerful and happy small brood, playing among themselves and finding a pleasure in their small home which so often seems denied to more sophisticated children.

Four evenings later we heard the distant hum of a plane. Dave scrambled up to the top of the roof and watched the skyline with my binoculars. For a long time we heard the noise and then we saw the plane coming up from the south, flying very high. As it approached us it began to lose altitude and at length, locating the cabin, it circled and swept down on the lake. As it taxied to the shore we saw it was a very small red Stinson.

Two men got out, Bill Catton of Winnipeg and Jock MacGeorge of God's Lake. There was a good deal of good-natured chafing as they came ashore. Fortunately, they had brought their own food supply. From the first interchange of news we gathered that they had come straight through from Winnipeg, a distance of six hundred and twenty miles, in a little over six hours. They had made a brief stop at God's Lake to pick up gasoline for us.

As it was now too late to start for Churchill, everyone decided to spend the night here and take off each for his respective destination the next morning. Catton had happened to bring along a big bag of oranges. The children were very curious about them and quite delighted when they were each given one. Tommy, the six-year-old, was particularly impressed. He held the fruit in his hands for a long time, his black eyes wide with wonder, and then pronounced solemnly: "Big berries!"

The evening was given over almost exclusively to aeronautical matters and from the discussion the facts emerged that we were about ninety miles west and south of Churchill, and one hundred and eighty miles north of Ilford, Manitoba. Once more the fortuitous circumstance of our happening to come down upon this lake out of the innumerable other possibilities was brought home to us all. Everyone accepted the whole matter as very much in the day's work, but Dave did not escape a number of shafts of humor.

The next morning we all got about the business of transferring the gasoline with no delay. It was a fine day for flying, clear, and the smoke pall seemed to have drifted off to the west. Soon our genial rescuers had lifted their small red plane up into the skies and were mere specks disappearing over the southern horizon. We made our adieus and thanks to our hostess and the children. As the engine of the Junkers began to growl and cough, Rita, Eva, and Tommy came down to the shore to watch us take off. The fifteen dogs began a wailing farewell. Mary, with Wilfred in her arms, came out and waved. My last glimpse was of the three little children standing hand in hand on the shore. With a final surge and rush we were up in the air and South Knife Lake was but one of a thousand other lakes below us.

The flight to Churchill was made with fine visibility. The country over which we passed did not exhibit any of the large, long, narrow lakes we had seen on our trip down from Windy. There were lakes without number but they were all of the pothole, sprinkled, bob-crater type. Twice we crossed over meandering rivers, which must have been the South and North Knife; though no maps indicate these rivers as being so far south. As we approached Hudson Bay the trees once more began to thin out and become increasingly sparse.

After some eighty miles of flying we could see the broad, silvery estuary of the Churchill River gleaming in the morning sun. Soon through a low, skittering bank of clouds, we saw the high cream-colored grain elevator of Churchill. Here the relief is so low that this great and lonely building stands forth very boldly. The broad curved sweep of Button Bay drew nearer. Far out in the blue waters of Hudson Bay a dim, white line of ice was glimpsed. Scarves of a broken, torn, low fog hurried in from the sea. We roared on. The gray ridges of volcanic diabase rock, which rise to the surface at Churchill, lay before us looking very wrinkled and ancient. As we circled over the wide mouth of the Churchill River I could see hundreds of white whales, beluga, diving and rolling below us. They seemed to be everywhere, and the thought flashed into both of our minds that they would be ugly things to run into when landing.

How different this toy town below us looked from the last time I had seen it, coming in from a month in the Arctic and from the other side of Hudson Bay! Then, the rusty waterfront mess, the tarpaper shacks, the barren and sterile shores, and all the dirt and relics of civilization and the white man's occupancy had seemed very repelling.

We circled far out over the bay. Above the flashing red roofs of the police barracks and the radio station we glided. Then, swinging back, the gray, grim ruins of old Fort Prince of Wales were momentarily below us. From that identical spot one hundred and sixty-nine years ago, Samuel Hearne himself had started out to the northwest and discovered Nueltin. From that spot he and the precious manuscript of his travels had been taken by the victorious French conqueror of the old fort, La Perouse. There in the sunlight the shabby, crumbling ruins lay almost as he had left them. In a long glide the plane swept down and then bumped on the waves of the river. The pontoons grounded against the rough, pebbly beach. A knot of men detached themselves from a small warehouse and came down to look at us.

I got out of the plane. The group of men, nondescript and huddled together, offered no comment or greeting. They just stared with vacuous curiosity. I was back in civilization. My ears began to register a number of sounds, unpleasant sounds, which I had not heard for a long time—the whistle of a train, the puffing of a tug, the bang and rumble of freight cars. I had an instantaneous flash of feeling. I wished very much that I were back at Windy. An indefinite sense of embarrassment swept over me as I gathered together my small outfit under the eyes of these unknown stolid white men. My first thought became; where could I camp, where do you camp in a town? For the first time, I felt inadequate. I stuck close to Dave and we carried our things up to a little tar-papered shack that he was temporarily occupying. Then I went up to the store to buy some things to send back with Dave to the children at South Knife.

Once inside the small general store, an enormous appetite for candy attacked me. This craving for sugar in some form is a very common reaction in coming out of the North. The story is told of one traveler who came into Churchill after more than a year in the far North. In that period he had reputedly undergone some very lean times. In any event, when he left Churchill on the train his first act was to get into his berth. He then bought all the candy, oranges, and such the train vendor possessed. These he piled in a great and enveloping heap about him as he lay in the berth. Supposedly he remained beneath this pile of sweets for two days devouring them. Regardless of the detailed truth of the story, the fact remains that this always seems one of the first delights and demands.

In an uncomfortable vacuum of purpose, in the timid estrangement with surroundings and people, which the first coming out of the North always brings, I idled about the store for some time. A few men came and went, making small purchases. Just before I went back to Dave's shack I heard snatches of conversation between some of them grouped in one corner of the store:

"...from Nueltin Lake... How in hell he get there?... Say... from the States! must be... prospector ...yes... always thought there's showin's in that country...gold, all right...." Their voices drifted into inaudible mumbles as I passed by. I was still in the North! Already fantastic rumor was about to spread its wings and enlarging in its flight travel over the moccasin telegraph.

That night we managed to get up a poker game. It was notable not for the stakes involved but the variety of the species indulged: straight, draw, stud (four-card flushes), jackpot, pee-in-the-ocean, topsy-turvy, baseball, and showdown. As the night went on and the game became more involved and the dealer's choices more esoteric, I became less interested for I could hear, now that the sun was down, the beating of drums.

There were some Chipewyans camped across the river over near the old Fort. Through the night came the booming of their drums: Boom! Boom!...Boom!... *Boom! Boom!* They were the opening and inviting beats of a gambling game thousands of years older than ours.

My thoughts and attention were so distracted that I withdrew from our game and went outside. The night was dark, but a pale aurora flickered across the northeastern sky. The measured beats were faster now. They must be passing out the little sticks and the players had perhaps already made the first gestures. The sound seemed to ebb and flow; sometimes it was far away and then it would approach like a living thing. Somewhere I heard a drunken white man singing, but as if overpowered the voice ceased. And still in the darkness the drums throbbed, but faster now. All the lights were out. Our own game had broken up and everyone had turned in. As I lay on the floor of the little shack in my sleeping bag the sound seemed to come up from the very ground itself: `Boom, boom, boom…boom, boom, boom….

Churchill or, as it was originally known, Fort Prince of Wales, seems to have been a spot in the North which the vagaries of fate particularly designated as a place where the white man should encroach upon the North in his most impressive style. The spot was originally discovered by a Danish sea captain, Jens Monk, in the year 1619. It was an incident in the age-long search for the fabled Northwest Passage. Later, in 1717 the Hudson's Bay Company arrived and established a trading post. In 1732 they commenced the building of a huge and massive stone fort, Fort Prince of Wales. The completion of this grim bastioned monument to the fur trade was carried on for a number of years and in fact it was still in the process of improvement when it capitulated to La Perouse in 1782. The solid stone walls of this structure facing out to the gray cold waters of Hudson Bay are in places as much as 37 feet thick.* Here Samuel Hearne had labored as trader and manager. Perhaps it was the tedium of the residence, which had much to do with his later great wanderings. Perhaps it was this too which prompted him to cut carefully in the face of a ledge at a spot called Sloop Cove his name, which can still be seen: "Sl. Hearne," and under it, "July ye 1 1767."

* The early history of Churchill with considerable quotation from original sources may be found in: *The Founding of Churchill*, edited by James F. Kennedy. J. M. Dent and Sons Ltd., Toronto, London, Vancouver, 1932.
If one wishes to probe still further into the past, a first-hand account of the building of Fort Prince of Wales and some observations on life in the area may be found in: A*n account of Six Years' Residence in Hudson's Bay, from 1733 to 1736, and 1744 to 1947*. By Joseph Robson. London, 1752.

As the years rolled on and the French hold on Canada was broken, the location once more came under the flag of the Hudson's Bay Company, but the old fort was not reoccupied and was allowed to crumble into disuse and decay. So Churchill might have remained, a bleak small trading post at the edge of the tree line infested by mosquitoes, a few wandering Chipewyans, and an occasional band of Eskimos. But the spirit that envisaged and created the mighty works of stone was to reassert itself almost two hundred years later. Clamoring for an outlet to the sea, the voice of the prairie provinces was at last answered. The railroad was pushed east from The Pas. Through the trackless forest, over the endless muskeg, lay on the frozen tundra came the two thin steel rails. They crossed the Nelson, headed for the mouth of that river, and then hesitating for some years finally ended here in latitude fifty-eight, on the bleak shores of Hudson Bay. Through five hundred miles of "bush" and muskeg the track was laid. And here across the river from the old stone fort a still mightier structure was erected, a great grain elevator. To be sure, some years next to no grain at all might be stored, the train might make the trip once a month in the winter, yet the great achievement, like the old fort, had been accomplished, what its true worth might be, time alone could tell.

Churchill for all its glowing promise has not yet fulfilled the dreams of its modern creation. Built on the flat foreshore of a prehistoric beach it supports not a tree or shrub. The original town site is indicated by a lonely cannon and a flagpole. Most of the activity of the town is centered around the north end near the grain elevator where a cluster of frame buildings and tarpaper shacks play host to various seasonal employees, and it is known as "The Department." The population fluctuates from sixty to sixteen. There are a few small stores, the inevitable Hudson's Bay Company post, police and signal stations, a Roman Catholic Mission, and a loose and heterogeneous scattering of shacks and shanties, some occupied by itinerant trappers and others who have some reason for being in the North. Here and there among the rocks and pebbles may be found a tent or two of Chipewyan or Cree.

In the summertime the train comes bumping and ambling

in twice a week. It is usually met by all the townsfolk, and the event rises to a great and annual occasion when in the second week of August a special train arrives with the "excursion." This notable event marks the highlight of the Churchill year for the train is loaded with curious adventurers from the "outside," some of them from the United States, who linger for a weekend and then disappear to the south. It is always climaxed by a dance in the freight shed that brings the Churchill social season to a deafening and enthusiastic apex.

There was quite a group of northern men scattered about "Moccasin Flats" and the town site. Since there were no decent campsites, I gravitated to the end of this settlement and was very hospitably received by two veterans' who maintained a small cabin that we called the "chateau." Life now took on an interest and human relationship, which on my first disembarking from the plane had not seemed likely. It was a happy refuge while my plans and aspirations for the next few weeks were given time to formulate.

In this gathering of northern white trappers down from their winter haunts, a subtle and not at first distinguishable gradation of aristocracy existed. This was not determined by the size of the annual catch, for the years and fortunes vary for each man. Rather it was based on longevity in the country and the distance from civilization which each called his base camp.

The trappers who still hunted in the Northwest Territories stood at the top for this indicated their uninterrupted pursuit of fur over a greater number of years than the others as government restriction has closed this vast area to newcomers. It also meant that these men must hunt to some degree out in the Barrens, a living proof of a toughness and immunity to hardship not demanded of those trapping in the "bush" country nearer at hand.

It was a veritable foreign legion of adventurers. Among the veteran northern men, Canadians in the sense of Canadian-born, are more of an exception than a rule. Here were Americans, Swedes, Germans, Norwegians, and Danes. In conversation one always noticed a difference drawn between themselves and all the rest of the world; other people were spoken of as Canadians or the "people outside." In the brief two months of summer they gathered here to trade in their fur, overhaul and prepare their outfits for the coming winter, visit about and exchange comment and prediction on next year's abundance of fur and the probabilities of price, and relax in whatever manner and with whatever aids they could command. By the middle of August a restlessness and foreboding of the coming season began to seize each one. Canoes were patched and repaired, engines overhauled, and then silently they slipped away north.

They asked little from the world, and if one was so fortunate as to be taken in by them even for a short while, they gave back much in friendship and observation on a world and life which is theirs and which the "outsider" can never know.

Theirs was an independent, free, roving life. It was a life with no tangible great reward, but an intangible recompense, which to them was worth all that they fiercely gave to gain it. Once in a while someone would mention going "outside" and one of them might say with a nervous abruptness, "Yes, outside, that would be nice, but you know, I don't think that I could stick there now, having someone always telling you what to do, when to get up, how to do it... no, I don't think I could stick it."

Though they shunned the world in actuality, they did not in thought or fancy. Several were omnivorous readers. Many times during the night I would be awakened as one of my hosts lit a small candle, seized a book, and read until nearly dawn. One of the brotherhood was a prolific and fecund poet. In discussions and arguments, particularly if enhanced by a case of beer or two, monologues and conversations soared to the most prolix and profound spirals of philosophic thought.

The weather turned particularly bad. Day after day the damp cold winds and fog rolled in off the waters of Hudson Bay, the gray, cold waters, which regardless of month bore floating, ice. The season seemed to be advancing rapidly. Already many of the shorebirds, which flock in myriads here and pursue their long-legged searching among the sloughs and mud flats through the summer, had begun to go south.

Pipits, Lapland longspurs, and snow buntings, first sentinels of winter began to appear. Happenings were few. A polar bear was shot in the harbor, white whales were captured and cut up for dog feed, a grain boat came in and discharged from her rusty hulk some barbed-wire, plate glass, and Scotch whisky.

One night above all the others stood out. It had been one of the very few warm days, and as the gray twilight gave way to night a black bank of thunderclouds arose out of Hudson Bay. It circled around the whole horizon like a dense wall. It became a giant dark bowl, its rim raised to the zenith. To the east the sullen wall was rent with long jagged cracks of lightning. The thunder was far away and grumbling. Then while the lightning flashed over the Bay a soft red glow began to stream down from the heavens directly above. It was as if great cones of luminous blood were pouring down from the zenith. It was an extraordinary and weird sight; the combination of lightning and the aurora was one I had never seen before.

Throughout all these days I could not but feel a restlessness and impatience. Somehow they did not seem to fit with the summer and Nueltin. And so too were the days to come: the refusal to take me on up to Repulse Bay, the jolly and agreeable American scientist and his wife, the conversations and friendship at the "chateau," these were all a summer distinct and dissociated from Nueltin. So too was my return to Pelican and the freighting by canoe between there and Flin Flon.

Only one last phase completes the great circle of two thousand miles. In the interim since my leaving Brochet, a two-way radio had been installed there. Pelican also had been re-equipped in this manner and there was a young man there to run it. By the time I returned to Pelican, John had long since been due. I had a message sent in to Brochet to ask him how he had found the return trip. The reply came back that no word had been heard from him.

All the anxiety of that last night before we had parted a month before flooded back over me. Where could he be? What had happened? Had my travel luck, which I felt had somewhat deserted me, also deserted him?

It was now too late, too near freeze-up, to attempt to make the long trip back by canoe and look for him. And yet, I was the only one who knew the exact route he must have traveled, and it was by my map that he was traveling. Our very first agreement, made that night before we left early in July, came back with a bitter mockery and was swept aside. Morally exonerating perhaps, it was of no comfort. I waited a few days. September had come. Again my message brought the same reply—no word.

The time had come for me to go back to my life and my profession. Once more I saw from the air Pelican and all it had always stood for: happiness, friendship, the stepping stone to freedom and adventure, the first portage to the North. I watched it fade away beneath me. Once again I saw the broad waters of Mirond Lake and the tortured, twisted channels and bays of Wildnest. But in that flight, the thought crystallized in my mind that I would go south, yes, to Winnipeg and there see what I could do about chartering a plane and going back to look for John. This year I would not be stepping into my classroom in September.

I was a little grim when I walked into the offices of the Hudson's Bay Company, those same offices I had so gaily walked into three months before. The preliminaries and the greetings over, I was interrupted in my first extended feelers to broach my plan. One of the men commented:

"Oh, by the way, I have a package for you!"

He left and as I waited, mystified and apprehensive, he returned with a long burlap-wrapped bundle. I opened it. It was the Mannlicher and my maps that I had loaned John. They had been sent down from Brochet. John had returned!

The summer was over. The search for the lake of the sleeping island was nothing more than a dream. Outside the newsboys were shouting headlines. There was martial music. The white man's world of civilization and culture, of a benign religion, had turned in its wisdom and logic to slaughter and war.

It was very hot in the broad streets. I felt desperately lonely. I began to wonder about Lop-i-zun and Zah-bah-deese and if the caribou were as thick as flies at Nueltin and… if the war would let me get back to the North just once more.

Notes to the Heron Dance Edition

Nearly every page of *Sleeping Island* invites one or more notes. To have fully identified every individual mentioned or to have elaborated on every intriguing detail or anecdote would have resulted in a companion volume. The notes that follow are those the editor regards as being especially pertinent or interesting.

Notes shown in quotation marks are Downes's own marginal comments from his personal copies of the American and the British editions of the book.

Chapter One

1. William Brooks Cabot, redoubtable Labrador traveler and author of *In Northern Labrador* (Boston: The Gorham Press, 1912). He began a trip to Brochet in 1918 but turned back at Pelican Narrows.
2. "This is the Eskimo name. It is called Yathkyed Lake in Chipewyan."
3. No more. In 1987 the Hudson's Bay Company sold off its northern posts—or "stores," as they had come to be—thereby jettisoning its inheritance, its traditions, and its soul.
4. R. A. Talbot. The aforementioned district manager was J. W. Anderson.

5. See "Floats: A Flying Episode off Eskimo Point, Hudson Bay," *The Beaver*, June 1933, p. 48: "From Churchill [in 1932], freight was carried in to Nueltin Lake... . Owing to the inaccuracy of the maps of this region, Nueltin was difficult to locate." Further evidence of Nueltin's obscure character can be seen in the Aeronautical Edition of the Nueltin Lake 8:1 Sheet, National Topographic Series, Department of Mines and Resources, 1946.

6. The misleading map had been drawn by one Syd Keighley, who served with the HBC in the Reindeer Lake country in the 1920s.

Chapter Two

1. Jeff Home-Hay, Royal Flying Corps veteran.

2. "Pete was named for me. They had seen my initials, P.G.D., and thought the 'P' stood for Peter."

3. W. W. Buxton was to remember Downes. "It is strange that I have never been able to relive those days in the Churchill River country without thinking of P. G. Downes...a great morale booster for me... . P.G. had a fine sense of humor, which extended even to himself, great powers of observation, an inquiring mind, a bulldog determination, and was capable of enduring extreme hardship. ...He carried only essentials, this included clothing. When he returned from his wild adventures he stank, and worse, he didn't know it. We made him burn some of his clothes and wash the hell out of the rest" (W.W. Buxton, letter to editor, 9 August 1982).

4. Father Nicholas Guilloux served as an Oblate missionary at Pelican from 1906 until the 1950s.

5. "An historical error. Though Frobisher was later to join the N.W. Co., it was not in existence at this time."

6. More about Downes's collecting of Cree myths can be found in his "Nine Indian Tales," *Northward Journal 32* (1984), pp. 4–27 and in the present writer's "Like Words of Fire': Lore of the Woodland Cree from the Journals of P.G. Downes," The Beaver, Winter 1984/85, pp. 37–45.

Chapter Three

1. The HBC outpost manager was Curry MacArthur; Jim Cumines was the provincial game guardian.

2. "This is rather an oblique statement. What he means is that

'hoping' is a passive state, and you must be physically and mentally active in this type of situation." Solomon Merasty, Downes's 1936 partner, is still alive at this writing.

3. A misprint. Tyrrell's exploration took place in 1894.

4. Padley Post, situated some seventy miles north of the mouth of the Kazan, was established in 1925 and shut down in 1960.

5. "My recording and drawings of these figures was sent to the National Museum, Ottawa. They are the most northerly pictographs that have been found in N. America."

6. "This paragraph was altered by the proofreader. Instead of the Cree, I mean anyone—you or me or an Indian."

7. This was the Swiss-born Lance Corporal Marcel Chappuis, with whom Downes traveled up Reindeer Lake in 1937. He was renowned for his far-reaching winter patrols. See R. Nemeth's "Chappie," The *RCMP Quarterly 1* (1985), pp. 28–34.

Chapter Four

1. The withdrawal occurred in 1931. The reasons can be found in the HBC's Annual Report (1930–31) Outfit 261, Saskatchewan District, Hudson's Bay Company Archives.

2. Shieffs Ltd.

3. "I should have said, really a very inadequate account."

4. "The cabin stood until Father Egenolf discovered that it was being used as a *maison d'amour* by the young bloods and tore it down."

5. The departed manager was Archie Hunter, the newcomer Alex Macintosh. For Hunter's recollections of his time at Brochet, see his *Northern Traders: Caribou Hair in the Stew* (Vancouver: Sono Nis Press, 1983), pp. 83–89.

6. "*Small*-scale map: a bad error."

7. John Albrecht. From Downes's journal: "As a mere boy he enlisted in von Kluck's Black Division—a crack all-Prussian division. Cut off at Ypres, he spent $2^{1}/_{2}$ years in a British prison camp and then eventually came to Canada and became a trapper—first out of Big River [Saskatchewan] and the Snake Lake-Souris country and then on to Wollaston Lake."

8. Father Joseph Egenolf, a German-born Oblate, had been posted to Brochet in 1905; he was never to leave, and died there in 1957.

9. "It is a point to note that a year later I discovered that all the Indians at Brochet...were very vociferous in their claims that, one, we would *never* reach Nueltin Lake and, two, very likely not get back."
10. The date was July 6.

Chapter Five

1. For confirmation of this paddling style, peculiar to northern Manitoba and Saskatchewan, see H. S. M. Kemp, *Northern Trader* (London: Jarrolds, 1957), p. 36 and L. Donovan dark, *Raisins in the Rice* (Renfrew, Ontario: Juniper, 1983), p. 42.
2. "He was. He had learned to pole a canoe as a boy in East Prussia. Not enough has been made in the book of John's extraordinary patience with me. Though I had learned to pole [in 1938] with George Murray, a Cree at He a la Crosse, I could not for a moment approach John's skill."
3. "This was my introduction to the profound pessimism of Alfred Peterson, of which I was to have a complete dose the following year." See R. H. Cockburn, "North of Reindeer," *The Beaver*, Spring 1983.
4. As the reader will by now have observed, Downes was fond of this indefinite, tantalizing, and quite romantic stylistic quirk. The "one year" referred to was in fact the previous year, 1938.
5. The cross, though decrepit, was still standing in the summer of 1987 (Alan W. Meadows, letter to editor, 17 July 1987). According to Downes's marginalia, when Kasmere, "76 years of known age," remarried that winter, "a big dance was held, and he was victim of being struck by a branch while riding in his cariole."
6. The following note of Downes's should be of interest to recent canoemen who, taking his route, have been puzzled by discrepancies between their experience and his account: "This was similar to observations elsewhere and by other travelers—unquestionably the water level has dropped throughout much of the North since 1894 [the year of Tyrrell's expedition]."
7. "I have pondered this evening. One of the [best things about] this trip was that neither of us was prone to being very introspective. Certainly there was plenty of silent introspection, but the doubts and fears that everyone has [on such a trip] did not occupy our time.

Also, John was not the swaggering, braggadocio sort, nor was he too humble. He was a truly tough guy. Many times since, I have wondered how fair I have been to John. Now I see it in a different light—but this book is almost 90% from the diaries and describes the way I felt then."

Chapter Six

1. "This is an interesting example of good luck due to timidity. If this had been later in the trip, we would have taken this portage unhesitatingly and gone on into a maze without beginning or ending, for it leads into a completely different lake series. However, it being the first dubious portage, I was ultra-conservative and careful. In reading these pages, one should remember that actually there were days when we never knew positively if we were on the correct track."

2. "The sketch maps in this book are not the finished product, which was redrawn to a polyconic projection and later published as the Nueltin Lake sheet of the Canadian Topo. series (Air) 1:506,000." In his letter of 15 February 1951 to George M. Douglas, Downes recalled a criticism of his *Sleeping Island* maps by Trevor Lloyd, who had reviewed the book for *The Geographical Review* in 1944: "… The book went to press in 1942. I was of course working for the air force and engineers on maps at the time. There was a real fear then (at least in the higher echelons) of a possible Nazi use of Hudson Straits and Bay for an air strike against Chicago (this seems incredible, but in that crazy period of 1942 it was very real). Therefore, when I reproduced my maps I quite deliberately left off coordinates and some other data, assuming that if anyone really wanted to use them they would go to the proper sources. As a then-professional cartographer, I was somewhat grieved by this, but then a lot of things seemed to be going on which were much more important."

3. "Your portages seem short, remembering some of ours," wrote a nostalgic W. B. Cabot, then eighty-six but still dwelling fondly on nightmarish sufferings in Labrador long ago: "A real one was 10 miles over a 1,000-ft. hill…"

4. "Named for my friend Windy Smith [see chap. 11, n. 3], who once had his base camp here. Of course, this name was discovered a year later."

Chapter Seven

1. Herbert H. Hall was the most skilled and venturesome Barren Lands traveler of his generation. In 1906 he established an HBC outpost at Ennadai Lake, on the Kazan River; it became known as "Eskimo Post" and lasted until 1929.

2. "This confusion was heightened by the Keighley map, which was absolutely wrong."

3. Fort Hall was erected by Herbert Hall in 1907 or 1908 on the site formerly occupied by a cabin belonging to a Chipewyan named Red Head. Records for this, as for most of the outposts operated seasonally by the HBC, are all but nonexistent. Downes's later inquiries, and the editor's, suggest that the 'fort' saw intermittent use as an outpost of Brochet into the 1920s. "Only one building, roof collapsed, was standing in 1987" (Allan Meadows, letter to editor, October 1987).

4. "One building, walls only, was standing in 1987" (Meadows, op. cit.). "Very interesting to learn that the walls of Kasmere Post are still standing," writes A. Wallace Laird, who was a Revillon trader from 1924 to 1931. "I stayed in it four times in the winter of 1928–29; it was snug and well built, and a welcome change from sleeping [on the trail]. There was an excellent model of an Eskimo kayak, about four feet long, on one wall" (A. Wallace Laird, letter to editor, 1 May 1988). The observations mentioned by Downes were those of the Dominion Observatory Magnetic Survey of 1922, led by R. Glenn Madill. That undertaking, which went as far north as Nueltin Narrows, had been preceded by the Carnegie Institution of Washington's Land Magnetic Observations Survey of 1908, led by J. P. Ault, which established "fixes" at Fort Hall and at "Canoe Limit," their northernmost site, on Putahow Lake. Downes had met Madill aboard the *Nascopie* in 1937.

5. "I think now that this was the case. John had no real stake in the venture; also he was drawn very thin. I know that after the trip was over and I went back to Pelican and helped to freight stuff [mainly gasoline drums] to Amisk Lake [and then back to Pelican], I had attacks of great physical and mental weakness on the portages."

6. The HBC had run an outpost on Putahow Lake, at what was known as Husky Portage or Canoe Limit; canoe freight bound for Ennadai was stored here to await winter and transport by dog team.

Keighley had served at Putahow in the late 1920s, just before the route was abandoned.

7. "Eskimo Charlie" Planinshek, a Yugoslav, was found at home by Downes the next summer, his gardens on Putahow protected from native depredations by Chipewyan and Eskimo skulls on stakes. Well-spoken and intelligent, he lived in squalor, his dogs his only company. Stories about him were legion. Before coming north, it was said, he had ridden with Pancho Villa, the Mexican revolutionist. When Downes met him, he was in his late fifties. Charlie expired in 1944 in his hovel, where his remains were found some eighteen months later by Lance Corporal Chappuis, during his winter patrol of 1945. See Cockburn, "North of Reindeer," (see chap. 5, n. 3), pp. 42–43.

8. Now Downes Lake.

Chapter Eight

1. Downes learned of Oberholtzer's remarkable journey only after he reached Churchill and spoke with Harris. Before 1939 was out, Downes was corresponding with his predecessor and fellow Harvard man, whom he would meet after the war. For an account of Oberholtzer's trip, see R. H. Cockburn, "Voyage to Nutheltin," *The Beaver*, January/February 1986.

2. "John was far more ready to quit here than the narrative suggests. At this point you have the comparison of the rational man (John) and the romantic man (me)."

3. "I was scared during all this. The narrative does not reveal the true character of this incident. The Indians were getting their revenge for lack of respect for them by John—they would not have anything at all to do with him after this incident."

4. The date was July 28.

Chapter Nine

1. Fred Schweder.

2. "This is the translation of Ennadai."

3. Downes is alluding to the American David Irwin, whose exploits had been represented by J. S. O'Brien in his *Alone Across the Top of the World* (Chicago: John C. Winston Co., 1935).

4. "This has always impressed me. They get into a bloodcraze."

5. Downes would come to think less favorably of "the last of the great pioneer roamers of the North," John Hornby, whose bizarre life and sorry death have been tellingly recreated by George Whalley in *The Legend of John Hornby* (Toronto: Macmillan of Canada, 1962/1977).

6. "Many years before": 1937.

7. Downes never saw John Albrecht again. Following his lone return voyage to Brochet, John disappeared into the wilderness; it was Downes's surmise that he feared being put behind barbed wire again. The once feverishly powerful Zah-bah-deese is still alive at this writing, at *Lac du Brochet*; he remembers Downes clearly.

Chapter Ten

1. Del Simons, a native of Ogdensburg, N.Y., traveled with Madill's 1922 expedition, during which he established the French Company's first trading post on Nueltin, at the mouth of the Putahow River. He also served as guide for Revillon Frères inspector Captain Thierry Mallet on their 1926 trip to the Kazan River and was the unacknowledged source of several of the tales told by Mallet in his second book, *Glimpses of the Barren Grounds* (New York: Revillon Frères, 1930).

2. Downes's comments on the killing frenzy that overcame Indians once they got among the caribou are not far-fetched: see, for example, Warburton Pike, *The Barren Ground of Northern Canada* (New York: E. P. Dutton & Co., 1917), pp. 51–52.

3. See Cockburn, "North of Reindeer," (see chap. 5, n. 3), pp. 38–41.

4. Dave Glenn and Jim Trafford.

5. The famed *Nascopie*, launched at Newcastle-upon-Tyne in 1911, served the HBC from 1912 until July 1947, when she was wrecked and lost off Cape Dorset.

6. "In my comments on Nueltin there is a serious omission. Freshwater seals [Harbor seals] are known to be found in Nueltin and in at least two of the lakes of its outlet. Big River [the Thiewiaza]." See Cockburn, "Voyage to Nutheltin," (see chap. 8, n.1), p. 16. Fred Schweder returned to the mouth of the Windy River in 1940 as a free trader. He and Charles received published praise from wildlife biologist Francis Harper for the assistance they

gave him during his Nueltin Lake Expedition of 1947. Fred and his children also figured, under disguised names, in Parley Mowat's book *People of the Deer* (1952). The HBC post at Windy was abandoned in 1941. Charles is still living.

Chapter 11

1. Caribou Post, situated approximately halfway inland between Churchill and Nueltin, was operated from 1930 until 1956.

2. Her name was Mary Fortin. Her children have done well for themselves; Wilfred now traps in the South Knife country.

3. I.H. "Windy" Smith and Jerry Kemp. For some years afterwards, Downes corresponded with Smith, who's articulate, richly detailed letters were usually written during the winter and gave "The Barrens" as their return address. Smith, a native of Johnstown, Pennsylvania, had prospected and trapped the Big River–Nueltin–Kasmere country since 1919. He was reputedly the "dirtiest bachelor trapper" working out of Churchill, was believed by many to be "a crook and con-man," and lived until 1964, thanks to "using a transplanted goat's stomach" (Bryan Clements, letter to editor, 19 January 1987).

Readers wishing to learn more about Downes's earlier travels may turn to the following of his journals, which have been edited by R. H. Cockburn and published in their entirety:

"Prentice G. Downes's Eastern Arctic Journal, 1936." *Arctic: Journal of the The Arctic Institute of North America* 36, no. 3 (September 1983), pp 232–250.

"To Reindeer's Far Waters: P.G. Downes's Journal of Travels in Northern Saskatchewan, 1936." *Fram: The Journal of Polar Studies 1*, no. 1 (Winter 1984), pp. 130–176.

"Distant Summer: P.G. Downes's 1937 Inland Journal." *Fram* 2, no. 1 (1985), pp. 31–119.

"To Great Slave and Great Bear: P. G. Downes's Journal of Travels North from Ile á la Crosse in 1938." *Arctic*, five parts; June 1985, pp. 324–335; March 1986, pp. 68–77; June 1986, pp. 164–171.

Descriptions and photographs of the Churchill–Reindeer– Nueltin countries can also be found in these articles by the editor:

"Revillon Man: The Northern Career of A. Wallace Laird," *The Beaver* (February/March 1990), pp.12–26.

"The Past in Colour: Northern Photographs of Prentice G. Downes," *The Beaver* (April/May 1993), pp. 4–11.

ABOUT THE EDITOR

Robert Cockburn is a professor Emeritus of English at The University of New Brunswick in Fredericton. His writings on the North have appeared in *Appalachia*, *Arctic*, *The Beaver*, *Fram*, and *Northward Journal*. He is the contributing editor of *Toward Magnetic North: The Oberholtzer-Magee 1912 Canoe Journey to Hudson Bay* (2000).

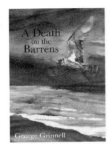

A Death on the Barrens by George Grinnell

Five young men canoe through Canada's arctic and must find their way home, after the death of their leader, Art Moffat, from hypothermia. Winter closes in, the group runs out of food. The book is both an account of a journey through then unmapped northern lakes and rivers, and a story of the spiritual awakening of the young men on the trip. A Death on the Barrens was first published in 1996, and quickly sold out. This second edition contains watercolors by Roderick MacIver. 182 pages.

#6075   A Death on the Barrens – $19.95

True North by Elliott Merrick
with an introduction by Lawrence Millman

In 1929, at the age of 24, Elliott Merrick left his position as an advertising executive in New Jersey and headed up to Labrador to work as an unpaid volunteer for the Grenfell Mission. In 1933 he wrote True North about his experiences in the northern wilderness, living and working with trappers, Indians and with the nurse he met and married in a remote community. The book describes the hard work and severe conditions, along with the joy and friendship he and his wife experienced. 320 pages

#6078   True North – $19.95

Forest Under My Fingernails
Reflections and Encounters on the Long Trail

Years ago we excerpted this book about Walt McLaughlin's wilderness trek. The book sold out, but has recently been reprinted. His reflections and encounters are beautifully told. We highly recommend it. 192 pages.

#6013   Forest Under My Fingernails – $15.95